T0370058

Tanks
& Military Vehicles

300 of the World's Greatest
Military Vehicles

Tanks

& Military Vehicles

300 of the World's Greatest
Military Vehicles

Philip Trewhitt

amber
BOOKS

Reprinted in 2018, 2021, 2023, 2024

Revised edition published in 2016

Published by
Amber Books Ltd
United House
North Road
London N7 9DP
United Kingdom
www.amberbooks.co.uk
Facebook: amberbooks
YouTube: amberbooksltd
Instagram: amberbooksltd
X(Twitter): @amberbooks

ISBN: 978-1-78274-706-2

Design: Wilson Design Associates

Printed in China

Picture Credits:
TRH Pictures

Artwork Credits:
All artworks © Aerospace Publishing except the following:
Bob Garwood: 77, 79, 83, 85, 88, 89, 90, 91, 92, 93, 94, 95, 96, 131, 275, 282

CONTENTS

Introduction

Despite the fact that, at the beginning of World War I, all the combatant armies relied heavily on horses (many continued to do so at the beginning of World War II, and many would continue to use horses for general transport duties), the benefits of using the relatively recent innovation of the combustion engine to provide mobility, firepower and protection were evident from the first days of the conflict. The British Admiralty was soon pressing commercial motor cars such as the Lanchester and Rolls-Royce into service, with the British Army taking over these armoured units by the beginning of 1915. Their well-made suspensions needed little reinforcing, and with a machine gun mounted on the top and some additional armour these vehicles proved versatile and useful, albeit for reconnaissance and not direct attacks against enemy positions. They were particularly valued in the desert campaigns of World War I, in Africa and in the Middle East, where they proved themselves in difficult terrain.

Above: The most powerful main battle tank in the world – the American Abrams.

But even armoured cars could not operate effectively against entrenched and well-defended positions, and it was the murderous stalemate of the Western Front which gave the impetus to serious development of armoured fighting vehicles. When the trench network began to spread to eventually form a continuous line between the English Channel and the Swiss frontier, it was realised that barbed wire and machine guns were spelling the end of the horse in a combat role, and a new form of mobile strike force was needed to cope with a new type of war. The 'tank',

Above: The crude Russian T-62, one of the tanks that made up the massed Warsaw Pact armoured force during the Cold War, and which was inferior to NATO rivals.

as it was codenamed for reasons of security, carried the hope that it might break the deadlock. Well armoured and bristling with weapons, the idea was to cross trenches with ease using the all-round tracks of the early vehicles (such as the Tank Mk V) and destroy enemy resistance with impunity.

The idea was sound enough, and when they first appeared at the Battle of the Somme in 1916 they proved effective in frightening German conscripts, if not in fulfilling their intended role. Early models were highly unreliable and the tactics employed – using them singly to support infantry attacks – did not make the most effective use of them. However, by the time of their first significant action at Cambrai in 1917, improvements had been made. German efforts to catch up with the Allies, in the shape of the Sturmpanzerwagen A7V, a truly monstrous vehicle, proved unsuccessful, and by the end of war tanks were being produced and used in considerable quantities by the Allies only. It would be inappropriate to suggest that the tank was in any way a war winner. German stormtrooper attacks during the offensives of March 1918 proved more effective in breaking the trench stalemate than tanks. However, it proved that the idea of armoured machines was workable.

If Germany lagged behind the Allies in armoured warfare at the end of World War I, it would labour under less of a disadvantage by the advent of the next global war. Despite the restrictions of the Treaty of Versailles, Germany developed an armoured force during the interwar period which was to have an impact on warfare the like of which had rarely been seen. It was not the quality of the armoured vehicles – the French Char B1 bis was superior to most German tanks in May 1940, for example – but the way in which they were used that proved the value of the armoured fighting vehicle. Whereas the French, and the British to some extent, used their armour in dribs and drabs in an infantry support role (as they had been used in World War I), the German Army believed in the value of massed armoured formations. They were right to do so. The early panzers, many based on Czech designs appropriated after the 1938 annexation of Czechoslovakia by Germany, proved too much for the Allies. It was at a price, though. The German panzer divisions suffered heavy casualties in the early campaigns, and all sides realised that the future of armoured warfare lay in bigger, better-armed and better-armoured vehicles. Any complacency felt by the German High Command over the early victories evaporated when the first T-34s appeared on the Russian Front.

HEAVIER AND MORE POWERFULLY ARMED TANKS

With the development of the superb Panzer V Panther, developed in response to the T-34's challenge, and then the Tiger and King Tiger tanks, the Germans maintained a slight armoured advantage throughout the war, despite the excellent qualities of Allied tanks such as the M4 Sherman. Evidence of this advantage can be found in the combat records for the Normandy campaign of 1944, where the exploits of Tiger aces such as Michael Wittmann speak for themselves. The Tiger proved an awesome vehicle on the battlefield, respected and feared by the Allies. However, no matter how powerful and how invulnerable a vehicle was, if it was not mechanically reliable and not available in numbers, then its value was limited. The brilliant German counterattack through the Ardennes forest in late 1944 was impeded through lack of fuel, which rendered the tank force impotent and immobile.

Increasing use of tanks led to development of specialist tank destroyers, which had the advantage of being much cheaper and easier to build as a rule than tanks themselves. The German Marder, for example, was a superb vehicle/weapon combination, so good in fact that it found itself being used more and more in a tank role and being attached to mobile panzer divisions, a job for which it was unsuited. The ensuing high attrition rate left the Marder a victim of its own success. The concept of mobile firepower continued with self-propelled artillery, with any useful artillery weapon being mounted on a mobile tracked chassis. The StuG III was perhaps the most famous of the type in World War II, though in terms of numbers employed the American M7 Priest would certainly rank first. Like the tank destroyer, the self-propelled gun was not designed for the all-purpose fighting vehicle role. Its job was to move to a spot, fire and then move again when required. Superficially similar to tanks, both self-propelled guns and tank destroyers were inferior to tanks in terms of mobility and armour protection, and thus suffered when called upon to fill the role of a tank.

VARIANTS OF THE MAIN BATTLE TANK

One of the more startling aspects of the development in armoured vehicles is the number of variants of the vehicles produced. Most main battle tanks since World War II have been adapted for a number of different roles, such as flamethrower and combat engineer tank. For example, the Centurion could be adapted to carry dozer blades, mine-clearing flails, demolition charges, cranes and fascine-laying equipment amongst other equipment. Most vehicles since World War II have been equipped with an amphibious capability, with widely varying levels of sophistication. The World War II Sherman BARV, for example, was designed as a recovery vehicle during amphibious landings, and thus needed to be able to operate in open water. This vehicle was fully sealed and equipped with periscopes and breathing apparatus for the crew. It came as a severe shock to the Germans when it made its debut, as they had been trying to perfect a similar vehicle for a considerable time. Other vehicles were given more rudimentary amphibious capability, in the form of flotation bags. Some had propellers or water jets fitted. Vehicles designed specifically for amphibious operations included the famous American-built DUKW, known universally as the 'Duck'. This vehicle operated well on land or in the water, and proved a magnificent transport carrier for the Americans and British.

Above: The right blend of armament, powerplant, design and armour produces an outstanding main battle tank, such as the British Centurion, in service for over 50 years.

For transporting personnel or equipment across difficult terrain, the halftrack, which was first used on a significant scale by the German Army in World War II but soon adopted by all armies, has proved an excellent and lasting innovation. The American M3 and the German SdKfz 251 were the forefathers of modern tracked personnel carriers such as the Bradley M2 Infantry Fighting Vehicle. Interestingly enough, modern developments in wheeled vehicles, such as effective tyre-pressure regulation systems, has cut the mobility deficit between the tracked and wheeled vehicle over rough terrain, and the greater speed and lower maintenance of the latter vehicle may well spell the end for tracked personnel carriers on the modern battlefield.

Most armoured fighting vehicles during the twentieth century have been hurried improvisations, labouring under all the deficiencies which such vehicles are prone to. However, some vehicles have seemed so dominant that they have become synonymous with their theatre of operations. The lumbering Mk V crashing over the barbed wire on the Western Front during World War I; the King Tiger during the Ardennes counterattack in 1944; and the Abrams chasing across the desert during Operation 'Desert Storm' in 1991. There have been few constants in armoured warfare. One has been that tactics can compensate for deficiencies in the quality or quantity of equipment (as shown by Germany in 1940 when routing the British and other Allied armies, and Israel during the 1960s and 1970s when fighting against superior numbers of Arab tanks), but only so far. With the complexities of modern tanks, such as the Leclerc, the M1 Abrams and the Challenger, crews must be ever more expert and ever more specialist. The dangers of throwing inadequately trained crews in inferior equipment into battle against such specialists in the best vehicles available was fully illustrated in the 1991 Gulf War. The Iraqi armoured divisions were decimated by the Coalition forces with practically no loss to the latter. The second constant is that no matter how big, how devastating its firepower and how invulnerable an armoured vehicle may seem, within a short space of time the opposition will have come up with its match and probably its successor. Experiences on the Eastern Front during World War II show this,

Above: The Bradley infantry fighting vehicle, designed to transport infantry close to the enemy. Fast and reliable, it is designed to operate with Abrams tanks.

with both sides battling for advantage and constantly increasing armour and armament.

Fighting vehicles cannot operate independently. The most formidable tank will fail if the trucks are not there to provide logistical support; if armoured personnel carriers (APCs) cannot get troops to the area to support and consolidate the breakthroughs. In turn APCs cannot operate if protection is not provided for them and if reconnaissance vehicles have not surveyed the terrain. Advances will falter if bridgelayers and combat engineer vehicles are not there to provide support. The concept of mutual protection is vital for the success of an armoured battle group.

THE ALL-ARMS BATTLEFIELD

Armoured warfare has made war faster and seemingly more destructive. The same problems encountered in the early days of armoured warfare remain, though. The first tanks were only effective when used in significant numbers, over open terrain, with secure and efficient logistical support. The rules are the same in modern times. The vast resources of the Soviet Army were unable to defeat small numbers of *Mujahideen* guerrillas in Afghanistan. The terrain and conditions prevented effective use of armoured resources.The same applied during the Vietnam War. Fighting vehicles are useful but not all-powerful. However, they have done what the first tank was intended to do: make attritional trench warfare impractical and perhaps, perversely, saved a few lives in the process.

The vehicles included in this book are the most influential and important fighting machines to have taken part in land warfare since World War I. Trucks have been included because they have played, and continue to play, an essential role in armoured warfare. Though most are not tracked and do not carry a main gun, they transport ammunition and troops to and from the battlefield; they are the lifeblood of mechanised armies. Similarly, light vehicles are also included because they too are essential to the success of mechanised armies. In addition, many of these light vehicles are armed and armoured to take part in hit-and-run operations (such as the converted British Special Air Service Jeeps that operated behind Axis lines in North Africa in World War II). The modern American M998 'Hummer', for example, can be armed with numerous weapons ranging from machine guns to anti-tank missiles. In this way it becomes a fighting vehicle, one that can knock out many tanks currently in service around the world.

Medium Tank Mk A

The World War I Medium Tank Mk A light tank was designed not so much for crossing obstacles as for exploiting breakthroughs brought about by heavier tanks. The emphasis was thus on speed and mobility. Designed by William Tritton, the Mk A was soon nicknamed 'Whippet'. The prototype was powered by London bus engines and was ready in February 1917, but it was not until late 1917 that the first production models appeared. The Whippet first saw combat in March 1918, being used initially to plug gaps in the line. Its worth was proved in counterattacks, making deep forays behind the lines and creating havoc in the German rear areas. After the war, the Mk A saw service in Ireland and a number were exported to Japan in the 1920s.

Country of origin:	UK
Crew:	3 or 4
Weight:	14,300kg (31,460lb)
Dimensions:	length 6.10m (20ft); width 2.62m (8ft 7in); height 2.74m (9ft)
Range:	257km (160 miles)
Armour:	5-14mm (0.2-0.55in)
Armament:	two Hotchkiss machine guns
Powerplant:	two 45hp (33.6kW) Tylor four-cylinder petrol engines
Performance:	maximum road speed 13.4km/h (8.3mph)

Tank Mk V

The Tank Mk V was the last of the lozenge-shaped tanks to see service in any number. It was designed to take part in the massive armoured thrusts envisaged for 1919. Improvements on earlier models included a Wilson epicyclic gearbox which allowed the tank to be driven by one man as opposed to two in earlier models. There was a cupola for the commander. Semaphore arms were mounted to give effective communication for the first time. The Tank Mk V* variant had a new 1.83m (6ft) section introduced into the hull to improve trench-crossing capability and provide extra internal space. From mid-1918, the tank saw action with the British and Americans. Post-war variants included bridge-laying and mine-clearing versions, and it remained in service with the Canadians until the early 1930s.

Country of origin:	UK
Crew:	8
Weight:	29,600kg (65,120lb)
Dimensions:	length 8.05m (26ft 5in); width over sponsons 4.11m (13ft 6in); height 2.64m (8ft 8in)
Range:	72km (45 miles)
Armour:	6-14mm (0.24-0.55in)
Armament:	two 6-pounder guns, four Hotchkiss machine guns
Powerplant:	one 150hp (112kW) Ricardo petrol engine
Performance:	maximum road speed 7.4km/h (4.6mph)

Char d'Assaut Schneider

The Char d'Assaut Schneider was developed as an armoured tractor for towing armoured troop sledges across to the German trenches on the Western Front. Based on the American Holt agricultural tractor, the first were available in the middle of 1917. The petrol tanks were very vulnerable to enemy fire and burned easily. Used mainly for infantry support rather than as personnel carriers, they were restricted by poor cross-country mobility, mainly due to their short tracks and long body which hindered the vehicle when crossing obstacles. The gun version ceased production in May 1917, to be replaced by the Char de Ravitaillement variant, used for carrying stores. Attrition and poor reliability led to less than 100 being in service at the end of the war.

Country of origin:	France
Crew:	7
Weight:	14,800kg (32,560lb)
Dimensions:	length 6.0m (19ft 8in); width 2.0m (6ft 6.66in); height 2.39m (7ft 10in)
Range:	48km (30 miles)
Armour:	11.5mm (0.45in)
Armament:	one 75mm gun, two additional machine guns
Powerplant:	one 55hp (41kW) Schneider four-cylinder petrol engine
Performance:	maximum road speed 6km/h (3.7mph)

Char d'Assaut St Chamond

The St Chamond was the French Army's own development. The first prototype appeared in 1916 and the vehicle entered service a year later. Like the Schneider, the St Chamond was based on the Holt tractor. An unusual petrol engine-driven electric transmission added an extra 5.1 tonnes (five tons) to the design weight. The hull extended both forward and rear of the track which, when combined with the weight, caused the St Chamond to become stuck on rough ground or over trenches. Its poor cross-country performance restricted its use in action, its last major action being a counterattack near Reims in July 1918. Many were converted into Char de Ravitaillement supply carriers. By the end of the war, only 72 out of 400 produced were still in service.

Country of origin:	France
Crew:	9
Weight:	23,400kg (51,480lb)
Dimensions:	length with gun 8.83m (28ft 11.75in); length of hull 7.91m (25ft 11.5in); width 2.67m (8ft 9in); height 2.34m (7ft 5.66in)
Range:	59km (36.7 miles)
Armour:	17mm (0.67in)
Armament:	one Modèle 1897 75mm gun; up to four machine guns
Powerplant:	one 90hp (67kW) Panhard four-cylinder petrol engine powering a Crochat-Collardeau electric transmission
Performance:	maximum road speed 8.5km/h (5.3mph)

Renault FT 17

The FT 17 was one of the most successful of all World War I tanks. It was the first of the classic tank design with features mounted directly onto the hull and a turret with a 360-degree traverse. They were ordered in large numbers (over 3000 during World War I) and needed to be, for they had been designed with little thought for maintenance and repair and as a result were often out of action. A self-propelled gun version and a radio-equipped version were among variants produced. In action, they were used *en masse*. For example, 480 being used in a counterattack near Soissons in July 1918 alone. They remained in service right up until 1944, when the Germans used captured FT 17s for street-fighting in Paris. By this time, of course, they were hopelessly out of date.

Country of origin:	France
Crew:	2
Weight:	6600kg (14,520lb)
Dimensions:	length with tail 5.0m (16ft 5in); width 1.71m (5ft 7.33in); height 2.133m (7ft in)
Range:	35.4km (22 miles)
Armour:	16mm (0.63in)
Armament:	one 37mm gun or one machine gun
Powerplant:	one 35hp (26kW) Renault four-cylinder petrol engine
Performance:	maximum road speed 7.7km/h (4.8mph)

Sturmpanzerwagen A7V

The Sturmpanzerwagen A7V was an enormous vehicle, hurriedly designed following the appearance of British tanks in 1916. Ground clearance was only 40mm (1.57in) and the length of track on the ground was too short for a vehicle of its size. The result was an unstable vehicle with poor cross-country performance. 100 A7Vs were ordered in December 1917, but the German war machine was already stretched and only about 20 were ever produced. Their shortcomings over rough ground were manifested in March 1918 when they first saw action, and they often lagged behind the infantry they were designed to support. Variants included the Uberlandwagen, an open-topped, unarmoured supply version, and the A7V/U with 'all-round' tracks. Post-war, they were used by the Polish Army for some years.

Country of origin:	Germany
Crew:	18
Weight:	33,500kg (73,700lb)
Dimensions:	length 8.0m (26ft 3in); width 3.06m (10ft 0.5in); height 3.30m (10ft 10in)
Range:	40km (25 miles)
Armour:	10-30mm (0.39-1.18in)
Armament:	one 57mm gun; six machine guns
Powerplant:	two 100hp (74.6kW) Daimler petrol engines
Performance:	maximum road speed 12.9km/h (8mph)

Tanks

PzKpfw 38(t)

The Panzerkampfwagen (PzKpfw) – armoured fighting vehicle – 38(t) began life as the Czech-designed LT vz 38, although none had entered service with the Czech Army prior to the German occupation of Czechoslovakia in 1938. More than 1400 were built for the Axis forces between 1939-42. When it became outclassed as a light tank, the type was used widely as a reconnaissance vehicle and the chassis was used as the basis for a large number of vehicles, including the Marder tank destroyer, several self-propelled anti-aircraft guns, a weapons carrier and the Hetzer tank destroyer, which continued in service with the Swiss Army until the late 1960s. During its combat career its armour thickness was steadily increase. For example, the Ausf E version onwards had armour 50mm (2in) thick.

Country of origin:	Germany
Crew:	4
Weight:	9700kg (21,340lb)
Dimensions:	length 4.546m (14ft 11in); width 2.133m (7ft); height 2.311m (7ft 7in)
Range:	200km (125miles)
Armour:	10-25mm (0.4-1in); later increased from Ausf E version onwards to 50mm (2in)
Armament:	one 37.2mm Skoda A7 gun; two 7.92mm machine-guns
Powerplant:	one Praga EPA six-cylinder water-cooled inline petrol engine developing 150hp (112kW)
Performance:	maximum road speed 42km/h (26mph); fording 0.9m (3ft); vertical obstacle 0.787m (2ft 7in); trench 1.879m (6ft 2in)

Panzer I

The Panzer I was the first German tank to go into mass production, with nearly 600 having being ordered by July 1934. Three separate companies were engaged to build the tank (deliberately to spread experience of tank manufacture as widely as possible) and over 800 had been produced by June 1936, when production ceased. To avoid being seen to break the Treaty of Versailles, which prohibited the Germans from building tanks, the design was disguised as an 'agricultural tractor'. The Panzer I Ausf A was found in varying numbers in all panzer units and served extensively during the early campaigns of World War II. However, its limitations in armour and armament were soon evident, and it had been withdrawn from frontline service by 1941.

Country of origin:	Germany
Crew:	2
Weight:	5500kg (12,100lb)
Dimensions:	length 4.02m (13.2ft); width 2.06m (6ft 7in); height 1.72m (5ft 7in)
Range:	145km (81 miles)
Armour:	6-13mm (0.2-0.5in)
Armament:	two 7.92mm MG13 machine guns
Powerplant:	one Krupp M305 petrol engine developing 60hp (45kW)
Performance:	maximum road speed 37 km/h (21mph); fording 0.85m (2ft 10in); vertical obstacle 0.42m (1ft 5in); trench 1.75m (5ft 9in)

Panzer II Light Tank

The first production model PzKpfw II Ausf A appeared in 1935, having been designated as a tractor since German rearmament was hindered by the restrictions of the Treaty of Versailles. The initial tanks were a collaboration between the firms of MAN and Daimler-Benz. The Ausf B, C, D, E, and F versions were built during the years up to 1941, the main improvements being in the thickness of the armour. The tank formed the backbone of the invasions of Poland and France, with around 1000 seeing service. By the time of the invasion of the USSR in 1941, the tank was obsolete but was used as the basis for the Luchs reconnaissance tank. Other variants included an amphibious version designed for the invasion of Britain and the Flammpanzer II flame-throwing tank.

Country of origin:	Germany
Crew:	3
Weight:	10,000 kg (22,046lb)
Dimensions:	length 4.64m (15ft 3in); width 2.30m (7ft 6.5in); height 2.02m (6ft 7.5in)
Range:	200km (125miles)
Armour:	(Ausf F version) 20-35mm (0.8-1.38in)
Armament:	one 20mm cannon; one 7.92mm machine gun
Powerplant:	one Maybach six-cylinder petrol engine developing 140hp (104kW)
Performance:	maximum road speed 55km/h (34mph); fording 0.85m (2ft 10in); vertical obstacle 0.42m (1ft 5in); trench 1.75m (5ft 9in)

Panzer III Medium Tank

Following a 1935 German Army requirement for a light medium tank design, Daimler-Benz began mass production of the Pzkpfw III in September 1939. The early Ausf A, B and C models saw action in Poland, and in 1940 the Ausf F entered production, with heavier armour and an uprated engine. By the time the final version, the Ausf N, ceased production in August 1943, when the army was fighting in Russia, the tank carried twice as big a gun and weighed twice as much as the original prototype. Variants included an amphibious version, a command vehicle, an armoured recovery vehicle, an observation vehicle and one adapted for desert warfare. In addition, the chassis was used for a number of self-propelled guns right to the end of World War II in 1945.

Country of origin:	Germany
Crew:	5
Weight:	22,300kg (49,060lb)
Dimensions:	length 6.41m (21ft); width 2.95m (9ft 8in); height 2.50m (8ft 2.5in)
Range:	175km (110 miles)
Armour:	30mm (1.18in)
Armament:	(Ausf M version) one 75mm L/24 gun; one 7.92mm machine gun
Powerplant:	one Maybach HL 120 TRM 12-cylinder petrol engine developing 300hp (224kW)
Performance:	maximum road speed 40km/h (25mph); fording 0.8m (2ft 8in); vertical obstacle 0.6m (2ft); trench 2.59m (8ft 6in)

Panzer IV Medium Tank

The PzKpfw IV was built under a 1934 requirement from the German Army Weapons Department and was later to become the backbone of the Wehrmacht's panzer arm. The tank was in production right throughout the war, with the final version, the Ausf J, appearing in March 1944. In total, nearly 9000 vehicles were built by Krupp, with the basic chassis remaining the same in all models, but with heavier armour and armament being added as requirements changed. Despite the extra weight, the PzKpfw IV retained a good power-to-weight ratio throughout its production life and thus had good mobility. Like the Panzer III, the chassis was used as the basis for various self-propelled guns as well as armoured recovery vehicles and bridge-layers and the Jagdpanzer IV tank destroyer.

Country of origin:	Germany
Crew:	5
Weight:	25,000kg (55,000lb)
Dimensions:	length 7.02m (23ft); width 3.29m (10ft 9.5in); height 2.68m (8ft 9.5in)
Range:	200km (125miles)
Armour:	50-60mm (1.97-2.4in)
Armament:	(Ausf H version) one 75mm gun; two 7.92mm MG 34 machine guns
Powerplant:	one Maybach HL 120 TRM 12-cylinder petrol engine developing 300hp (224kW)
Performance:	maximum road speed 38km/h (24mph); fording 1.0m (3ft 3in); vertical obstacle 0.6m (2ft); trench 2.20m (7ft 3in)

Panzer V Panther

The Panther is widely considered to be one of the best tanks of World War II. Designed to combat the Soviet T-34 tanks which were outclassing the PzKpfw IV on the Eastern Front in early 1942, the Panther fulfilled the requirement for a tank with a powerful gun, good mobility and good protection. MAN completed the first production models in September 1942. The early versions suffered from mechanical problems, particularly at the Battle of Kursk in July 1943, borne from a lack of proper testing. However, once the problems were ironed out, the Panther saw action in all theatres and proved to be very effective. Over 4500 were built up to early 1945, and they continued to see service with the French Army in the immediate post-war period.

Country of origin:	Germany
Crew:	4
Weight:	45,500kg (100,100lb)
Dimensions:	length 8.86m (29ft 0.75in); width 3.43m (11ft 3in); height 3.10m (10ft 2in)
Range:	177km (110miles)
Armour:	30-110mm (1.2-4.3in)
Armament:	one 75mm gun; three 7.92mm MG34 machine guns (one coaxial, one anti-aircraft, one on hull front)
Powerplant:	one Maybach HL 230 12-cylinder diesel developing 700hp (522kW)
Performance:	maximum road speed 46km/h (29mph); fording 1.70m (5ft 7in); vertical obstacle 0.91m (3ft 0in); trench 1.91m (6ft 3in)

Panzer VI Tiger

The Tiger heavy tank was produced by Henschel based on a 1941 design and entered production in August 1942. A total of 1350 were built before production ceased in August 1944 and the type was replaced by the King Tiger. There were three main variants: a command tank, a recovery vehicle fitted with a winch and the Sturmtiger, which was fitted with a rocket launcher. The Tiger was an excellent tank, but complicated and therefore difficult to produce in large numbers and maintain. The overlapping wheel suspension had a tendency to clog with mud and stones which, if it froze in cold conditions such as during the Russian winter, could immobilise the vehicle. It first saw action against the British in Tunisia in 1942 and thereafter appeared on all fronts.

Country of origin:	Germany
Crew:	5
Weight:	55,000kg (121,000lb)
Dimensions:	length 8.24m (27ft); width 3.73m (12ft 3in); height 2.86m (9ft 3.25in)
Range:	100km (62miles)
Armour:	25-100mm (1-3.94in)
Armament:	one 88mm KwK 36 gun; one 7.92 coaxial MG 34 machine gun
Powerplant:	one Maybach HL 230 P45 12-cylinder petrol engine developing 700hp (522kW)
Performance:	maximum road speed 38km/h (24mph); fording 1.20m (3ft 11in); vertical obstacle 0.79m (2ft 7in); trench 1.8m (5ft 11in)

Panzer VI Tiger II

The Henschel design for the Tiger II (King Tiger) was completed in October 1943. Early production models carried a turret designed by Porsche, but after the first 50 models had been built, the tanks were wholly produced by Henschel. The tank was similar to the Panther and used the same engine, although its heavier armour, impenetrable to most Allied weapons, resulted in a lower power-to-weight ratio and consequent loss of speed and mobility. The main problem with the Tiger II was unreliability. Many were abandoned by their crews when they broke down or ran out of fuel, as their bulk made them difficult to move or conceal. The Tiger II first saw combat on the Eastern Front in May 1944 and in the battles in Normandy in the autumn of that year.

Country of origin:	Germany
Crew:	5
Weight:	69,700kg (153,340lb)
Dimensions:	length 10.26m (33ft 8in); width 3.75m (12ft 3.5in); height 3.09m (10ft 1.5in)
Range:	110km (68miles)
Armour:	100-150mm (3.94-5.9in)
Armament:	one 88mm KwK 43 gun; two 7.92 MG34 machine guns (one coaxial, one on hull front)
Powerplant:	one Maybach HL 230 P30 12-cylinder petrol developing 700hp (522kW)
Performance:	maximum road speed 38km/h (24mph); fording 1.60m (5ft 3in); vertical obstacle 0.85m (2ft 10in); trench 2.5m (8ft 2in)

Fiat L6/40 Light Tank

The Fiat L6/40 arose from a 1930s design based on the British Carden-Loyd Mark VI tankette. Intended primarily for export, the first production models arrived in 1939 and a total of 283 were built. At the time of its introduction, the L6/40 was roughly equivalent to the German PzKpfw II, but was never really suitable for frontline service. However, it saw service with reconnaissance and cavalry units in Italy, North Africa and Russia. Variants included a flame-thrower version and a command tank, the latter having extra communications equipment and an open-topped turret. In addition, a number of L6/40s were converted into Semovente L40 self-propelled anti-tank guns. Like most Italian tanks in World War II, it was hopelessly outclassed when it came up against Allied armour.

Country of origin:	Italy
Crew:	2
Weight:	6800kg (14,960lb)
Dimensions:	length 3.78m (12ft 5in); width 1.92m (6ft 4in); height 2.03m (6ft 8in)
Range:	200km (124miles)
Armour:	6-40mm (0.23-1.57in)
Armament:	one Breda Model 35 20mm cannon; one coaxial Breda Model 38 8mm machinegun
Powerplant:	one SPA 18D four-cylinder petrol engine developing 70hp (52kW)
Performance:	maximum road speed 42km/h (26mph); fording 0.8m (2ft 8in); vertical obstacle 0.7m (2ft 4in); trench 1.7m (5ft 7in)

Fiat M 13/40 Medium Tank

The M 13/40 was based on an earlier design, the M 11/39, which was not produced in numbers as it was considered already obsolete by the time of its introduction. The M 13/40 used the same chassis but had a redesigned hull with better armour. Nearly 800 were produced in total and the tank was widely used in North Africa during Italian attempts to drive British and Commonwealth forces out of the region. In combat the M 13/40's shortcomings became very apparent: it was cramped, unreliable and caught fire easily when hit by anti-tank rounds. Many abandoned and captured M 13/40s were pressed into service by the British and Australian forces and used to fill a serious shortage of Allied tanks in early 1941. They did not remain in Allied service for long.

Country of origin:	Italy
Crew:	4
Weight:	14,000kg (30,800lb)
Dimensions:	length 4.92m (16ft 2in); width 2.2m (7ft 3in); height 2.38m (7ft 10in)
Range:	200km (125miles)
Armour:	6-42mm (0.24-1.65in)
Armament:	one 47mm gun; two Modello 38 8mm machine guns (one coaxial, one anti-aircraft)
Powerplant:	one SPA TM40 eight-cylinder diesel engine developing 125hp (93kW)
Performance:	maximum road speed 32km/h (20mph); fording 1.0m (3ft 3in); vertical obstacle 0.8m (2ft 8in); trench 2.1m (6ft 11in)

Tanks

Type 95 Light Tank

The Type 95, known as the KE-GO, was developed in the early 1930s to meet the requirements of the Japanese Army at that time. When production ceased in 1943, over 1100 had been built. The major drawback of the vehicle was that the commander had to operate the gun in addition to his normal duties, which impeded combat effectiveness. While this was acceptable when faced with infantry in Manchuria, it proved disastrous when up against American armour in the later years of the war. Despite later upgunning, the tank's poor armour and lack of firepower ensured that it was wholly inadequate. The Type 95 also served as the basis for the Type 2 KA-MI amphibious tank which was widely used in the early Pacific campaigns of World War II.

Country of origin:	Japan
Crew:	4
Weight:	7400kg (16,280lb)
Dimensions:	length 4.38m (14ft 4in); width 2.057m (6ft 9in); height 2.184m (7ft 2in)
Range:	250km (156miles)
Armour:	6-14mm (0.25-0.6in)
Armament:	one 37mm gun; two 7.7mm machine guns
Powerplant:	one Mitsubishi NVD 6120 six-cylinder air-cooled diesel engine developing 120hp (89kW)
Performance:	maximum road speed 45km/h (28mph); fording 1.0m (3ft 3in); vertical obstacle 0.812m (2ft 8in); trench 2.0m (6ft 7in)

Light Tank M3

Having followed the battles of 1940 on the European mainland closely, the American military realised that its main light tank, the M2, was obsolete, and that a more heavily armoured version was required. The result was the M3 which entered full-scale production in 1941, and nearly 6000 were built. Many were passed to the Soviet Red Army and to British forces where they were known as Stuarts. Their reliability and mobility were impressive and they were popular with crews, being used in all theatres of the war. Obsolete as a combat tank by 1944, many were converted to command and reconnaissance vehicles with the turrets removed and extra machine guns added instead. Variants included mine-clearing, flame-throwing and anti-aircraft versions.

Country of origin:	USA
Crew:	4
Weight:	12,927kg (28,440lb)
Dimensions:	length 4.54m (14ft 10.75in); width 2.24m (7ft 4in); height 2.30m (7ft 6.5in)
Range:	112.6km (70 miles)
Armour:	15-43mm (0.59-1.69in)
Armament:	one 37mm gun; two 7.7mm machine guns
Powerplant:	one Continental W-970-9A six-cylinder radial petrol engine developing 250hp (186.5kW)
Performance:	maximum road speed 58km/h (36mph); fording 0.91m (3ft 0in); vertical obstacle 0.61m (2ft); trench 1.83m (6ft 0in)

Light Tank M24 Chaffee

By 1942 it was evident that the 37mm gun was inadequate for the needs of America's light tanks, and indeed as a main armament of any tank. Attempts to install larger weapons in M5 tanks failed and so a new tank was designed by Cadillac, the first being ready by late 1943. Known as the Chaffee, the M24 entered full service with the US Army in late 1944, too late in the war to make a big impression. It was in Korea that the M24 realised its full combat value, with the agility for reconnaissance, but well-armed for battle. Its biggest contribution was in its concept. It was designed to be part of a combat family of vehicles, all using the same chassis, including self-propelled guns and anti-aircraft tanks. The tank continues to see service with some nations to this day.

Country of origin:	USA
Crew:	5
Weight:	18,370kg (40,414lb)
Dimensions:	length 5.49m (18ft); width 2.95m (9ft 8in); height 2.48m (8ft 1.5in)
Range:	161km (100 miles)
Armour:	12-38mm (0.47-1.5in)
Armament:	one 75mm gun; two 7.62mm machine guns; one 12.7mm gun on turret; one 51mm smoke mortar
Powerplant:	two Cadillac Model 44T24 V-8 petrol engines developing 110hp (82kW) each
Performance:	maximum road speed 56km/h (35mph); fording 1.02m (3ft 4in); vertical obstacle 0.91m (3ft); trench 2.44m (8ft)

Medium Tank M3

The M3 was developed by the Americans following the realisation, based on observation of the armoured battles in France in 1940, that a more powerful armament would be required than that mounted on the M2 in development at the time. The M3 was shipped to British forces with minor modifications and was known as the General Grant. The Grant proved highly effective against the *Afrika Korps* in North Africa in its first actions in May 1942, and was popular with the tank crews of hard-pressed British forces. The original version retained by US forces was known as the General Lee. Reliable and hard-wearing, its only drawback was the limited traverse of the hull-mounted main gun. The M3 saw action on all fronts and was widely exported after the war.

Country of origin:	USA
Crew:	6
Weight:	27,240kg (59,928lb)
Dimensions:	length 5.64m (18ft 6in); width 2.72m (8ft 11in); height 3.12m (10ft 3in)
Range:	193km (120 miles)
Armour:	12-38mm (0.47-1.5in)
Armament:	one 75mm hull-mounted gun; one 35mm gun on turret; four 7.62mm machine guns
Powerplant:	one Continental R-975-EC2 radial petrol engine developing 340hp (253.5kW)
Performance:	maximum road speed 42km/h (26mph); fording 1.02m (3ft 4in); vertical obstacle 0.61m (2ft); trench 1.91m (6ft 3in)

Medium Tank M4A2

The M4 Sherman used the same basic hull and suspension as the M3, but mounted the main armament on the gun turret rather than the hull. Easy to build and an excellent fighting platform, it proved to be a war-winner for the Allies. By the time production ceased in 1945, over 40,000 had been built. There were many variants, including engineer tanks, assault tanks, rocket launchers, recovery vehicles and mine-clearers. The British employed the Sherman extensively, notably at El Alamein in 1942. Though outgunned by German tanks and with insufficient armour to compete in the later stages of the war, the sheer numbers produced overwhelmed enemy armoured forces. Its hardiness kept it in service with some South American countries until very recently.

Country of origin:	USA
Crew:	5
Weight:	31,360kg (69,000lb)
Dimensions:	length 5.9m (19ft 4in); width 2.6m (8ft 7in); height 2.74m (9ft)
Range:	161km (100 miles)
Armour:	15-76mm (0.59-2.99in)
Armament:	one 75mm gun; one coaxial 7.62mm machine gun; 12.7mm anti-aircraft gun on turret
Powerplant:	twin General Motors 6-71 diesel engines developing 500hp (373kW)
Performance:	maximum road speed 46.4km/h (29mph); fording 0.9m (3ft); vertical obstacle 0.61m (2ft); trench 2.26m (7ft 5in)

Medium Tank M4A3

The M4A3 was one of the most developed of all the Sherman variants used during World War II. It differed from the M4A2 mainly in the design of its turret and suspension (using a more effective horizontal volute spring system) and in its armament, employing the larger and more powerful 76mm gun as well as having thicker armour. This particular model was the production type most favoured by the US Army. Ford built 1690 A3s between June 1942 and September 1943, before ceasing tank production. Manufacture was then taken over by Grand Blanc from February 1944. Improved features included a vision cupola for the commander, a loader's hatch and so-called 'wet stowage' for the ammunition. In addition, its petrol engine was specifically developed for the vehicle.

Country of origin:	USA
Crew:	5
Weight:	32,284kg (71,024lb)
Dimensions:	length, with gun 7.52m (24ft 8in), and over hull 6.27m (20ft 7in); width 2.68m (8ft 9.5in); height 3.43m (11ft 2.875in)
Range:	161km (100 miles)
Armour:	15-100mm (0.59-3.94in)
Armament:	one 76mm gun; one 7.62mm coaxial machine gun
Powerplant:	one Ford GAA V-8 petrol engine developing 400 or 500hp (335.6 or 373kW)
Performance:	maximum road speed 47km/h (29mph); fording 0.91m (3ft); vertical obstacle 0.61m (2ft); trench 2.26m (7ft 5in)

Tanks

T-70

The Soviet military had spent a great deal of time and effort in the development of a series of light tanks during the 1930s. The T-70 was the culmination of this effort at the time of the German invasion of Russia in June 1941. Reasonably armoured, the T-70's armament was of limited use against heavier tanks, especially as the commander of the tank had to operate the gun single-handed, thus reducing his combat effectiveness. Its service record was unremarkable, mainly being used for reconnaissance and close infantry support. Over 8000 were produced up to 1943, but despite the numbers, the T-70 was at best only an adequate combat tank. It was certainly better than the tank it superseded, the T-60, but was outgunned by the German panzers in 1941-42.

Country of origin:	USSR
Crew:	2
Weight:	9367kg (20,608lb)
Dimensions:	length 4.29m (14ft 0.9in); width 2.32m (7ft 7.3in); height 2.04m (6ft 8.3in)
Range:	360km (223.7 miles)
Armour:	10-60mm (0.39-2.36in)
Armament:	one 45mm gun; one 7.62mm machine gun
Powerplant:	two GAZ-202 petrol engines delivering a total of 140hp (104kW)
Performance:	maximum road speed 45km/h (28mph); fording not known; vertical obstacle 0.70m (2ft 3.6in); trench 3.12m (10ft 2.8in)

T-28

Inspired by British and German tank designs, the T-28 medium tank had a centrally mounted main turret and two auxiliary machine-gun turrets in front. The vehicle's suspension was directly copied from the British Vickers vehicle, and though the prototype was armed with a 45mm main gun, production models were equipped with the more powerful 76.2mm low-velocity gun. There were a number of different models and variants, some of which were produced as a result of combat experience. The T-28C, for example, was given additional armour on the hull front and turret as a result of the Red Army's unhappy time in the Russo-Finnish War. An interesting variant was the T-28(V), a commander's tank fitted with a radio which had a frame aerial round the turret.

Country of origin:	USSR
Crew:	6
Weight:	28,509kg (62,720lb)
Dimensions:	length 7.44m (24ft 4.8in); width 2.81m (9ft 2.75in); height 2.82m (9ft 3in)
Range:	220km (136.7 miles)
Armour:	10-80mm (0.39-3.15in)
Armament:	one 76.2mm gun; three 7.62mm machine guns
Powerplant:	one M-17 V-12 petrol engine developing 500hp (373kW)
Performance:	maximum road speed 37km/h (23mph); fording not known; vertical obstacle 1.04m (3ft 5in); trench 2.90m (9ft 6in)

Tanks

T-34/76A

The T-34 was an advanced tank for its era, produced in vast numbers to an excellent design, a design borne from two decades of Soviet experimentation and a readiness to embrace the best of foreign ideas. Mass production began in 1940 and its powerful gun and thick armour came as a nasty surprise to the Germans in 1941-42. Finesse was sacrificed for speed of production, but their rough and ready appearance belied their effectiveness. The T-34 was used in every role from recovery vehicle to personnel carrier and reconnaissance, and distinguished itself at every turn forcing the Germans back on the defensive. It is no exaggeration to say that the T-34 was the most decisive tank of World War II. The upgunned T-34/85 tank introduced in 1944 is still in use with many armies today.

Country of origin:	USSR
Crew:	4
Weight:	26,000kg (57,200lb)
Dimensions:	length 5.92m (19ft 5.1in); width 3.0m (9ft 10in); height 2.44m (8ft)
Range:	186km (115 miles)
Armour:	18-60mm (0.71-2.36in)
Armament:	one 76.2mm gun; two 7.62mm machine guns
Powerplant:	one V-2-34 V-12 diesel engine developing 500hp (373kW)
Performance:	maximum road speed 55km/h (34mph); fording 1.37m (4ft 6in); vertical obstacle 0.71m (2ft 4in); trench 2.95m (9ft 8in)

KV-1 Heavy Tank

Design on the KV-1 began in 1938, with the intention that it should be the successor to the T-35 heavy tank. The first models were field-tested during the Red Army's disastrous 1940 campaign in Finland. Nevertheless, the KV-1 set the standard for Soviet tank design for several years to come and proved to be a formidable vehicle, being used as an assault tank or to spearhead breakthroughs. However, the tank was not particularly mobile and suffered from automotive problems. In addition, it was uparmoured progressively without any increase in power being allotted, which resulted in poor power-to-weight ratio and performance. The importance of the KV-1 is that it paved the way for later generations of Russian heavy tanks, such as the Josef Stalin.

Country of origin:	USSR
Crew:	5
Weight:	43,000kg (94,600lb)
Dimensions:	length 6.68m (21ft 11in); width 3.32m (10ft 10.7in); height 2.71m (8ft 10.7in)
Range:	150km (93.2 miles)
Armour:	100mm (3.94in)
Armament:	one 76.2mm gun; four 7.62mm machine guns
Powerplant:	one V-2K V-12 diesel engine developing 600hp (448kW)
Performance:	maximum (rarely achieved) road speed 35km/h (21.75mph); fording not known; vertical obstacle 1.20m (3ft 8in); trench 2.59m (8ft 6in)

IS-2 Heavy Tank

The IS-2 (Josef Stalin) was a development of the earlier KV series of Russian tanks. It was a lighter tank than the KVs with improved transmission and suspension and a redesigned hull and turret. The first examples appeared in 1944, helping to exploit the strategic initiative which the Red Army had achieved by that stage of World War II on the Eastern Front. A massive vehicle, the tank was well-armed and armoured, the only drawback of the early versions was a slow rate of fire using separate charges and shells. This was remedied by the time the IS-3 entered production. Symbolically, Josef Stalin tanks were at the head of the advance to Berlin in 1945 and remained in production after the war being the world's most powerful tank for well over a decade.

Country of origin:	USSR
Crew:	4
Weight:	46,000kg (101,200lb)
Dimensions:	length 9.9m (32ft 5.8in); width 3.09m (10ft 1.6in); height 2.73m (8ft 11.5in)
Range:	240km (149 miles)
Armour:	132mm (5.2in)
Armament:	one 122mm gun; one 12.7mm machine gun; one 7.62mm machine gun
Powerplant:	one V-2-IS (V-2K) V-12 diesel developing 600hp (447kW)
Performance:	maximum road speed 37km/h (23mph); fording not known; vertical obstacle 1.0m (3ft 3in); trench 2.49m (8ft 2in)

Hotchkiss H-39

The Hotchkiss H-39 first appeared in 1939, intended for use by French cavalry formations. Despite production problems common to all French tanks in the period before World War II, about 1000 were built. The tank gave a good account of itself in combat during the German invasion of France in 1940, but had too little firepower to compete with enemy armour. In addition, French tactics at the time envisaged tanks being used as infantry support rather than in mass formations, diminishing its effectiveness. After the surrender, the Germans employed the H-39 for occupation duties. Some saw action with the Free French and Vichy French forces in the Middle East, where they were later used by the Israelis, remaining in service until 1956.

Country of origin:	France
Crew:	2
Weight:	12,100kg (26,620lb)
Dimensions:	length 4.22m (13ft 10in); width 1.95m (6ft 4.8in); height 2.15m (7ft 0.6in)
Range:	120km (74.5 miles)
Armour:	40mm (1.57in)
Armament:	one 37mm gun; one coaxial 7.5mm machine gun
Powerplant:	one Hotchkiss six-cylinder petrol engine developing 120hp (89.5kW)
Performance:	maximum road speed 36km/h (22.3mph); fording 0.85m (2ft 10in); vertical obstacle 0.50m (1ft 8in); trench 1.80m (5ft 11in)

Renault R-35

The Renault R-35 was designed in the mid-1930s to replace the ageing World War I-vintage Renault FT 17. By 1940, some 1600 had been built and it was the most numerous French tank in service, even though it never managed to fulfil its role as the FT 17's replacement. An adequate vehicle, it was no match for German panzers, particularly as it was deployed piecemeal against their massed formations. The gun was unable to penetrate even light German armour and many were abandoned during the French retreat in May 1940. The Germans used the R-35 as a garrison and training tank and adapted many for use as artillery tractors, ammunition carriers and self-propelled artillery carriages. For the latter, the turrets were removed and used for coastal defences.

Country of origin:	France
Crew:	2
Weight:	10,000kg (22,046lb)
Dimensions:	length 4.20m (13ft 9.25in); width 1.85m (6ft 0.75in); height 2.37m (7ft 9.25in)
Range:	140km (87 miles)
Armour:	40mm (1.57in)
Armament:	one 37mm gun; one coaxial 7.5mm machine gun
Powerplant:	one Renault four-cylinder petrol engine developing 82hp (61kW)
Performance:	maximum road speed 20km/h (12.4mph); fording 0.80m (2ft 7in); vertical obstacle 0.50m (1ft 7.7in); trench 1.60m (5ft 3in)

SOMUA S-35 Medium Tank

The SOMUA S-35 was one of the first tanks used to mechanise the French cavalry in the mid-1930s. It was a very advanced vehicle for its time and many of its features were to become standard for future tank designs, such as cast, rather than rivetted, armour. A radio was fitted as standard and the tank was supplied with a sufficiently powerful main armament to be still in service in German hands on D-Day in June 1944. Production was slow and there were only around 250 in frontline service by the time the Germans invaded in 1940. The major drawback was that the commander was required to operate the gun and the radio as well as his normal duties. Despite this reduced effectiveness, the S-35 was still the best Allied tank in service in 1940 (which says a lot about Allied armoured strength).

Country of origin:	France
Crew:	3
Weight:	19,500kg (42,900lb)
Dimensions:	length 5.38m (17ft 7.8in); width 2.12m (6ft 11.5in); height 2.62m (8ft 7in)
Range:	230km (143 miles)
Armour:	20-55mm (0.8-2.2in)
Armament:	one 47mm gun; one coaxial 7.5mm machine gun
Powerplant:	one SOMUA V-8 petrol engine developing 190hp (141.7kW)
Performance:	maximum road speed 40km/h (24.85mph); fording 1.0m (3ft 3in); vertical obstacle 0.76m (2ft 6in); trench 2.13m (7ft)

Char B1 Heavy Tank

The first B1s appeared in 1937. Despite its appearance, which was reminiscent of World War I tanks, the Char B1 was a powerful tank for the time and carried a range of advanced design features such as self-sealing fuel tanks. The crew were seated some way from each other, however, which made internal communication difficult. These crews needed to be highly trained to operate the B1 to full advantage, and such crews were rare in 1940. In addition, the tank's complexities made maintenance difficult and many broke down in combat. Those that entered the fray were really too cumbersome for their powerful armament to have much effect. The Germans later employed captured Char B1s as training tanks or self-propelled artillery carriages.

Country of origin:	France
Crew:	4
Weight:	31,500kg (69,300lb)
Dimensions:	length 6.37m (20ft 10.8in); width 2.50m (8ft 2.4in); height 2.79m (9ft 1.8in)
Range:	180km (112 miles)
Armour:	14-65mm (0.6-2.6in)
Armament:	one 75mm gun; one 45mm gun
Powerplant:	one Renault six-cylinder petrol engine developing 307hp (229kW)
Performance:	maximum road speed 28km/h (17.4mph); fording not known; vertical obstacle 0.93m (3ft 1in); trench 2.74m (9ft)

Vickers Light Tank

Originally based on the Carden-Loyd tankette of the 1920s, the Vickers light tanks were developed in the 1930s. Mobile and fast across country, the Vickers was widely used in the 1930s for policing the British Empire and in the early years of World War II. However, World War II combat experience proved them to be virtually useless. Their thin armour was easily pierced and their machine-gun armament was utterly inadequate on the battlefield. Lack of equipment forced the British to use them in combat rather than for reconnaissance, as they were designed to be used, and the consequences were disastrous. Attempts to convert them into anti-aircraft tanks failed, although the Germans managed to employ some captured vehicles as anti-tank gun carriers.

Country of origin:	UK
Crew:	3
Weight:	4877kg (10,729lb)
Dimensions:	length 3.96m (13ft); width 2.08m (6ft 10in); height 2.235m (7ft 6in)
Range:	range 201km (215 miles)
Armour:	10-15mm (0.4-0.6in)
Armament:	one 7.7mm/12.7mm machine gun
Powerplant:	one Meadows ESTL six-cylinder petrol engine developing 88hp (66kW)
Performance:	maximum road speed 51.5km/h (32mph); fording 0.6m (2ft); vertical obstacle – ; trench –

Light Tank Mk VII Tetrarch

When the prototype of the Tetrarch, known at the time as the Purdah, appeared in 1938, it was received without enthusiasm as it had no outstanding attributes. Like other light tanks, it fared badly in combat in the early years of the war, being poorly armed and armoured and lacking a specified purpose. It was withdrawn quickly, although some were passed on to the Soviet Union (where it was greeted with a similar lack of enthusiasm). However, it was given new life as an airborne tank and the Hamilcar glider was specifically designed to carry it. Fitted with a more powerful armament, the tank landed with British airborne forces on D-Day, but proved no match for enemy armour and its role was later assumed by the American M22 Locust.

Country of origin:	UK
Crew:	3
Weight:	7620kg (16,764lb)
Dimensions:	length overall 4.305m (14ft 1.5in); length of hull 4.115m (13ft 6in); width 2.31m (7ft 7in); height 2.121m (6ft 11.5in)
Range:	224km (140 miles)
Armour:	4-16mm (0.16-0.63in)
Armament:	one 2-pounder gun; one coaxial 7.92mm machine gun
Powerplant:	one Meadows 12-cylinder petrol engine developing 165hp (123kW)
Performance:	maximum road speed 64km/h (40mph); maximum cross-country speed 45km/h (28mph); fording 0.914m (3ft 0in); trench 1.524m (5ft)

Cruiser Tank Mk VI Crusader

The Crusader's attractive design belied the fact that by the time it first appeared in 1941 it was already outdated. Fast and mobile (their suspension was so tough that theoretical maximum speed was often exceeded), they were thinly armoured and lacked firepower, being no match for their German counterparts. Reliability was also a problem. Even with gradual improvements, the Crusader failed to prove itself in the North African campaigns and was replaced as quickly as possible by the M4 Sherman. Once withdrawn from frontline combat duties, the Crusader was adapted for a variety of roles, such as anti-aircraft tank, recovery vehicle and combat engineer tank with a dozer blade. Many saw service in the last years of the war as artillery tractors, pulling the 17-pounder gun.

Country of origin:	UK
Crew:	3
Weight:	20,067kg (44,147lb)
Dimensions:	length 5.994m (19ft 8in); width 2.64m (8ft 8in); height 2.235m (7ft 4in)
Range:	204km (127 miles)
Armour:	40mm (1.57in)
Armament:	one 2-pounder gun; one coaxial 7.62mm machine gun
Powerplant:	one Nuffield Liberty Mk III petrol engine developing 340hp (254kW)
Performance:	maximum road speed 43.4km/h (27mph); maximum cross-country speed 24km/h (15mph); fording 0.99m (3ft 3in); vertical obstacle 0.686m (2ft 3in); trench 2.59 (8ft 6in)

Cruiser Tank Mk VIII Cromwell

The Cromwell was produced in response to a requirement for a more heavily armed and armoured tank to replace the Crusader. The first Cromwells appeared in 1943 armed with a 6-pounder gun. However, it was realised that this would be inadequate and the tanks were soon being equipped with heavier weaponry, which gave some parity with contemporary German tanks. That said, most units were equipped with the M4 Sherman, but the Cromwell gave valuable service as a training tank in the run-up to D-Day and was used for many other roles, such as mobile observation posts and armoured recovery vehicles. Although not quite equal to German tanks, the Cromwell was at least better than previous British efforts and fared reasonably well in combat.

Country of origin:	UK
Crew:	5
Weight:	27,942kg (61,472lb)
Dimensions:	length 6.42m (21ft 0.75in); width 3.048m (10ft); height 2.51m (8ft 3in)
Range:	278km (173 miles)
Armour:	8-76mm (0.3-3in)
Armament:	one 75mm gun; one coaxial 7.62mm machine gun
Powerplant:	one Rolls-Royce Meteor V-12 petrol engine developing 570hp (425kW)
Performance:	maximum speed 61km/h (38mph); fording 1.219m (4ft); vertical obstacle 0.914m (3ft); trench 2.286 (7ft 6in)

Infantry Tank Matilda

The Mk I Matilda was developed in response to a 1934 requirement for an infantry tank. Well armoured for its day, it was a small, simple tank. However, despite being sturdy enough to withstand hits from most German tank guns in the early stages of World War II, it was too poorly armed to be of much use as the war progressed. The Mk II had improved armament and this helped the Matilda to fare reasonably well in combat, particularly in North Africa where it was widely used in the run-up to El Alamein in 1942. Following its replacement in frontline service, the Matilda was used for a variety of specialised roles, such as mine-clearing (the Baron); as a flame-thrower tank (the Frog); and as the basis of a Canal Defence Light for illuminating night operations.

Country of origin:	UK
Crew:	4
Weight:	26,926kg (59,237lb)
Dimensions:	length 5.613m (18ft 5in); width 2.59m (8ft 6in); height 2.51m (8ft 3in)
Range:	257km (160 miles)
Armour:	20mm - 78mm (0.8in - 3.1in)
Armament:	one 2-pounder gun; one 7.92mm Besa machine gun
Powerplant:	two Leyland 6-cylinder petrol engines each developing 95hp (71kW) or two AEC diesels each developing 87hp (65kW)
Performance:	maximum speed 24km/h (15mph); maximum cross-country speed 12.9km/h (8mph); fording 0.914m (3ft 0in); vertical obstacle 0.609m (2ft); trench 2.133 (7ft)

Infantry Tank Mk III Valentine

In 1938 Vickers was asked to produce an infantry tank based upon their A10 Cruiser tank. There were initial doubts about the new Valentine's two-man turret, which would limit the possibility of increased armament at a later date, but as war was imminent necessity overcame this caution. Mass production began in 1940 and the Valentine soon proved to be a sturdy, reliable vehicle, if a little slow. Armament was gradually improved as the war progressed, and the Valentine saw service in all theatres. Variants included a mobile bridge, a flame-thrower tank, a mine-clearing tank and a self-propelled gun. Over 8000 Valentines were built before production ceased in 1944, thus making the Valentine one of the most important British tanks in numbers if nothing else.

Country of origin:	UK
Crew:	3
Weight:	17,690kg (38,918lb)
Dimensions:	length 5.41m (17ft 9in); width 2.629m (8ft 7.5in); height 2.273m (7ft 5.5in)
Range:	145km (90 miles)
Armour:	8-65mm (0.3-2.6in)
Armament:	one 2-pounder gun; one 7.62mm machine gun
Powerplant:	one AEC diesel developing 131hp (98kW) in Mk III or GMC diesel developing 138hp (103kW) in Mk IV
Performance:	maximum speed 24km/h (15mph); fording 0.914m (3ft); vertical obstacle 0.838m (2ft 9in); trench 2.286 (7ft 6in)

Infantry Tank Mk IV Churchill

The Churchill began life as a 1939 requirement which envisaged a return to trench-warfare, and was thus slow and heavily armoured. The final prototype, however, was a much lighter vehicle than had first been thought of, not unlike a World War I tank in appearance. Rushed into production at a time when invasion seemed imminent, it suffered early reliability problems and was not fully introduced until 1943. Early combat experience during the Dieppe raid in 1942 was disappointing, but the Cromwell proved mobile over rough terrain in North Africa. The tank excelled in its specialised variants, such as the AVRE, the Crocodile flame-thrower tank, the bridgelayer and many more. The tank gave excellent service and the final Churchill was not retired until the 1960s.

Country of origin:	UK
Crew:	5
Weight:	40,642kg (89,412lb)
Dimensions:	length 7.442m (24ft 5in); width 2.438m (8ft); height 3.454m (11ft 4in)
Range:	144.8km (90 miles)
Armour:	16-102mm (0.6-4in)
Armament:	one 6-pounder gun; one coaxial 7.62mm machine gun
Powerplant:	one Bedford twin-six petrol engine developing 350hp (261kW)
Performance:	maximum speed 20km/h (12.5mph); maximum cross-country speed about 12.8km/h (8mph); fording 1.016m (3ft 4in); vertical obstacle 0.76m (2ft 6in); trench 3.048m (10ft)

Cruiser Tank Ram Mk I

At the start of World War II, Canada had no tank units. With no possibility of obtaining tanks from a desperate Britain, the Canadians were forced to build their own. The decision was taken to use the basic components of the American M3, but swap the sponson-mounted main gun for a turret mounting the readily available 40mm gun, with the option of upgunning later. Production began at the end of 1941, but the tank never saw action as by the time it arrived in Europe, the M4 Sherman was being produced in numbers and it was decided to adopt this as the standard for Canadian units. Many Rams had their turrets removed and were used as armoured personnel carriers. The Ram's greatest contribution to the Allied victory was as the basis for the Sexton self-propelled gun.

Country of origin:	Canada
Crew:	5
Weight:	29,484kg (64,864lb)
Dimensions:	length 5.79m (19ft); width 2.895m (9ft 6in); height 2.667m (8ft 9in)
Range:	232km (144 miles)
Armour:	25-89mm (1-3.5in)
Armament:	one 2-pounder gun; two coaxial 7.62mm machine guns
Powerplant:	one Continental R-975 radial petrol engine developing 400hp (298kW)
Performance:	maximum road speed 40.2km/h (25mph); vertical obstacle 0.61m (2ft); trench 2.26m (7ft 5in)

Sherman Crab Mine-Clearing Flail

Invented by a South African, the concept of using flails to clear mines was developed in the UK culminating in the development of the Crab, usually fitted to Sherman tanks. Some 43 chains were mounted on a revolving drum powered by the main tank engine. Further developments included the addition of barbed wire-cutting disks and a contour-following device to allow the flails to operate effectively over rough ground. The Crab carried the standard Sherman armament and could thus be used in a combat role if the need arose. The drive for the rotor was taken by roller chain from the tank propeller shaft, through an aperture in the hull off-side armour, to a carden shaft. The drive from this shaft was taken by another carden shaft to a spiral bevel double reduction gear on the off-side end of the rotor.

Country of origin:	UK
Crew:	5
Weight:	31,818kg (70,000lb)
Dimensions:	length 8.23m (27ft); width 3.5m (11ft 6in); height 2.7m (9ft)
Range:	62km (100 miles)
Armour:	15-76mm (0.59-2.99in)
Armament:	one 75mm gun; one 7.62mm machine gun
Powerplant:	one Ford GAA V-8 petrol engine developing 500hp (373kW)
Performance:	maximum road speed 46km/h (28.75mph); fording 0.9m (3ft); vertical obstacle 0.6m (2ft); trench 2.26m (7ft 5in).

SdKfz 265 kleiner Panzerbefehlswagen

The concept of the Command Tank came about following the realisation that the leaders of massed panzer formations would not only have to travel in tanks themselves, but the vehicles would have to carry extra equipment and personnel to assist the commander in his duties. In 1938, the PzKpfw I training tank was converted. The rotating hull was changed to a box superstructure to give more space and allow room for map boards and paperwork (though even then the space was not voluminous). More powerful radios were installed and a signaller added to the crew. Around 200 conversions were made, and the tank first saw action in the Polish Campaign in September 1939, later being used in France and North Africa, before being replaced by conversions of larger tanks.

Country of origin:	Germany
Crew:	3
Weight:	5800kg (12,768lb)
Dimensions:	length 4.445m (14ft 7in); width 2.08m (6ft 9.9in); height 1.72m (5ft 7.7in)
Range:	290km (180 miles)
Armour:	6-13mm (0.24-0.5in)
Armament:	one 7.92mm machine gun
Powerplant:	one Maybach NL38TR petrol engine developing 100hp (74.6kW)
Performance:	maximum road speed 40km/h (25mph); fording 0.85m (2ft 10in); vertical obstacle 0.42m (1ft 5in); trench 1.75m (5ft 9in)

M48 A3

When the Korean War began, the US military had no medium tanks in production. The M47 appeared as an interim measure but work immediately began on the M48. The first 'Pattons' were completed in July 1952. The speed of development resulted in numerous teething troubles for the early Pattons, including poor reliability and a short operating range. The A3 was a highly modified version designed to rectify these failings, and the M48 served successfully in Vietnam, India and with the Israelis in the Middle East. The M48 has been used as the basis for flame-thrower tanks, recovery vehicles and an AVLB. The A5 was an upgraded version produced in the mid-1970s which extended the M48's shelf-life considerably, and it is still being used in many countries today.

Country of origin:	USA
Crew:	4
Weight:	47,040kg (103,488lb)
Dimensions:	length 8.6m (28ft 6in); width 3.6m (11ft 11in); height 3.2m (10ft 3in)
Range:	463km (288 miles)
Armour:	12.7-120mm (0.5-4.72in)
Armament:	one 90mm gun; one 7.62mm coaxial machine gun; one 12.7mm machine gun in commander's cupola
Powerplant:	one Continental AVDS-1790-2A 12-cylinder diesel engine developing 750hp (560kW)
Performance:	maximum road speed 48.2km/h (30mph); fording 1.219m (4ft); vertical obstacle 0.915m (3ft); trench 2.59m (8ft 6in)

M103 Heavy Tank

The advent of the Cold War saw the Americans begin work on a new tank designed for direct assault and long-range anti-tank support for medium tanks against Soviet armour. Early prototypes of what was to become the M103 showed deficiencies in both the turret and gun control equipment. Despite modifications, the 200 built by Chrysler for deployment in Europe were found to be difficult to employ because of their size (which made concealment difficult), weight and small range, as well as poor reliability. They were phased out during the 1960s. Their bulk required a specialised recovery vehicle, built on the M103's chassis and named the M51. Nevertheless, the M103 was part of a trend for bigger and more heavily armed tanks on NATO's frontline.

Country of origin:	USA
Crew:	5
Weight:	56,610kg (124,544lb)
Dimensions:	length 11.3m (37ft 1.5in); width 3.8m (12ft 4in); height 2.9m (9ft 5.3in)
Range:	130km (80 miles)
Armour:	12.7-178mm (0.5-7in)
Armament:	one 120mm rifled gun; one 7.62mm coaxial machine gun; one 12.7mm anti-aircraft machine gun
Powerplant:	one Continental AV-1790-5B or 7C V-12 petrol engine developing 810hp (604kW)
Performance:	maximum road speed 34km/h (21mph); vertical obstacle 0.91m (3ft); trench 2.29m (7ft 6in)

M-51 Isherman

A joint development by French and Israeli engineers, the M-51 Isherman incorporated the superb French 105mm (4.1in) CN 105 F1 gun into the original turret of the M4A1 Sherman tank, which had originally mounted a 75mm (2.9in) cannon. The tank also had installed a US-made Cummins diesel engine and wide-track HVSS suspension. First displayed in 1965, the tank was known in Israel as the Sherman M-51, but the moniker elsewhere became Isherman, from 'Israeli Sherman'. Seeing service in the Six Day War in 1967 and the Yom Kippur War in 1973, it was capable of knocking out the T-34 variants and T-55 MBTs employed by Syria and Egypt. It was noted for being an obsolete tank, the Sherman, that was successfully upgraded and its service history lengthened.

Country of origin:	Israel
Crew:	5
Weight:	39,000kg (85,980lb)
Dimentions:	length 5.84m (19ft 2in); width and height unknown
Range:	270km (168 miles)
Armour:	unknown
Armament:	one 105mm (4.1in) CN 105 F1 gun, two 7.62mm (0.3in) machine guns (1 coaxial and one hull-mounted)
Powerplant:	338kW (460hp) Cummins V8 diesel
Performance:	unknown

Tanks

Conqueror

The FV214 Conqueror was the result of a requirement for a post-war heavy tank for the British Army for the expected massed armoured clash with the tanks of the Warsaw Pact on the central European plain. The British were determined that the experience of 1940, when their tanks had been out-gunned by the German panzers, would not happen again. Based on the Centurion, nearly 200 Conquerors were built between 1955 and 1958, mostly deployed in support of Centurion squadrons in the British Army of the Rhine. Unfortunately the Conqueror proved too cumbersome and difficult to maintain. Its advantage over the Centurion was limited to a longer-range gun, and when the Centurion was upgunned there was no longer a role for the Conqueror. The type was phased out during the 1960s.

Country of origin:	UK
Crew:	4
Weight:	64,858kg (142,688lb)
Dimensions:	length (gun forwards) 11.58m (38ft 0in); length (hull) 7.72m (25ft 4in); width 3.99m (13ft 1in); height 3.35m (11ft 0in)
Range:	155km (95 miles)
Armour:	17-178mm (0.66-7in)
Armament:	one 120mm rifled gun; one 7.62mm coaxial machine gun
Powerplant:	one 12-cylinder petrol engine developing 810hp (604kW)
Performance:	maximum road speed 34km/h (21.3mph); vertical obstacle 0.91m (3ft); trench 3.35m (11ft 0in)

Centurion

The Centurion Main Battle Tank had its origins in World War II, when it was developed as a cruiser tank. The first prototype appeared in 1945 and the tank entered production shortly after. The Centurion saw action in Korea, Vietnam, Pakistan and the Middle East. Nearly 4500 were built before production ceased in 1962 and it was replaced by the Chieftain. However, its excellent capacity for upgrading ensured that it has remained in service beyond the 1960s with foreign armies. Among the many variants are an armoured recovery vehicle (as well as an amphibious recovery vehicle which was used in the Falklands conflict in 1982), a bridge-layer and an AVRE. It is considered one of the most successful tank designs in the history of warfare.

Country of origin:	UK
Crew:	4
Weight:	51,723kg (113,792lb)
Dimensions:	length 9.854m (32ft 4in); width 3.39m (11ft 1.5in); height 3.009m (9ft 10.5in)
Range:	205km (127 miles)
Armour:	51-152mm (2-6in)
Armament:	one 105mm gun; two 7.62mm machine guns; one 12.7mm machine gun
Powerplant:	Rolls-Royce Meteor Mk IVB V-12 petrol, developing 650hp (485kW)
Performance:	maximum road speed 43km/h (27mph); fording 1.45m (4ft 9in); vertical obstacle 0.91m (3ft); trench 3.352m (11ft)

Tanks

T-10 Heavy Tank

The T-10 was developed in the USSR after the end of World War II to fulfil the perceived need for a heavy tank, shared by both the USA and UK. At least 2500 were built up to the late 1950s. It was kept purely for the domestic market and was designed to provide long-range fire-support for the T-54/55s, and act as a spearhead for thrusts through heavily defended areas. Its cramped confines required the use of separate-loading ammunition as there was insufficient room for complete shells. After leaving frontline service it was, like all Soviet tanks, kept in reserve for many years. The decrease in speed compared to the earlier T-34 was surprising given the Red Army's emphasis on speed and mass during and after World War II. The Soviets certainly possessed mass, but vehicles such as the T-10 reduced overall speed.

Country of origin:	USSR
Crew:	4
Weight:	49,890kg (109,760lb)
Dimensions:	length (including gun) 9.875m (32ft 4.75in); length (hull) 7.04m (23ft 1in); width 3.566m (11ft 8.5in); height 2.25m (7ft 4.5in)
Range:	250km (155 miles)
Armour:	20-250mm (0.79-9.84in)
Armament:	one 122mm gun; two 12.7mm machine guns (one coaxial, one anti-aircraft)
Powerplant:	one V-12 diesel engine developing 700hp (522kW)
Performance:	maximum road speed 42km/h (26mph); vertical obstacle 0.9m (35.5in); trench 3.0m (9ft 10in)

T-54

The prototype of the T-54 was completed in 1946 and production began some years later. The T-54 and its variants were produced in larger numbers than any other Soviet tank after World War II (around 50,000), also being produced in Czechoslovakia, Poland and China. The T-54 was continually updated prior to the arrival of the T-55, with gun-stabilisers and an infrared capability being added. Variants included flame-throwers, dozers, bridge-layers, mine-clearers, recovery vehicles and a combat engineer vehicle. The tank saw extensive combat in Angola, North Africa, the Far East and in particular the Middle East, where it suffered by comparison to Israeli Centurion and M48 tanks during the Arab-Israeli wars. The T-54 was archetypal Soviet tank: it was simple and produced in mass numbers.

Country of origin:	USSR
Crew:	4
Weight:	35,909kg (79,000lb)
Dimensions:	length 9m (29ft 6.3in); width 3.27m (10ft 8.75in); height 2.4m (7ft 10.5in)
Range:	400km (249 miles)
Armour:	20-250mm (0.79-9.84in)
Armament:	one 100mm gun; two 7.62mm machine guns (one coaxial, one in bow); one 12.7mm anti-aircraft machine gun
Powerplant:	one V-12 diesel engine developing 520hp (388kW)
Performance:	maximum road speed 48km/h (30mph); fording 1.4m (4ft 7in); vertical obstacle 0.8m (2ft 7.5in); trench 2.7m (8ft 10.25in)

Tanks
Stridsvagn 103 (S-tank)

Immediately after World War II, Sweden's armoured forces consisted mainly of light tanks. To fill this gap, work began on an indigenous heavy tank with the gun fixed to the chassis rather than a turret, with aiming being achieved by turning the vehicle and raising or lowering the suspension – an entirely new concept in tank design. Its only real drawback was that it was unable to fire on the move, but as Sweden was only likely to be engaged in defensive actions, this was not too problematic. Bofors began production in 1966, and 300 were completed by the time they ceased in 1971. The tank included a dozer blade and a flotation screen for amphibious capability. The radical Swedish S-tank generated considerable foreign interest, but few export orders.

Country of origin:	Sweden
Crew:	3
Weight:	38,894kg (85,568lb)
Dimensions:	length (with gun) 8.99m (29ft 6in); length (hull) 7.04m (23ft 1in); width 3.26m (10ft 8.3in); height (overall) 2.5m (8ft 2.5in)
Range:	390km (242 miles)
Armour:	90-100mm (3.54-3.94in)
Armament:	one 105mm gun; three 7.62mm machine guns
Powerplant:	one diesel engine developing 240hp (119kW) and a Boeing 553 gas turbine, developing 490hp (366kW)
Performance:	maximum road speed 50km/h (31mph); fording 1.5m (4ft 11in); vertical obstacle 0.9m (2ft 11.5in); trench 2.3m (7ft 6.5in)

AMX-30

Until the mid-1950s, both France and Germany relied on American M47s for their armour, though France also had a number of the excellent German Panther tanks. A requirement was drawn up for a new main battle tank, lighter and more powerfully armed than the M47, to supply both countries. However, typically, each adopted their own design. The French produced the AMX-30, the first production tanks appearing in 1966, half of which were destined for export. The AMX-30 chassis has been used for a number of other vehicles including the Pluton tactical nuclear missile launcher, as well as a self-propelled anti-aircraft gun, a recovery vehicle, bridge-layer and engineer vehicles. The tank has seen service with the Iraqi, Saudi Arabian and Spanish Armies in addition to the French.

Country of origin:	France
Crew:	4
Weight:	35,941kg (79,072lb)s
Dimensions:	length (with gun forward) 9.48m (31ft 1in); length (hull) 6.59m (21ft 7in); width 3.1m (10ft 2in); height (overall) 2.86m (9ft 4in)
Range:	600km (373 miles)
Armour:	15-80mm (0.6-3.1in)
Armament:	one 105mm gun; one coaxial 20mm cannon; one 7.62mm machine gun
Powerplant:	one Hispano-Suiza 12-cylinder diesel, developing 720hp (537kW)
Performance:	maximum road speed 65km/h (40mph); vertical obstacle 0.93m (3ft 0.6in); trench 2.9m (9ft 6in)

Chieftain Mk 5

The Chieftain was designed in the late 1950s as a successor to the Centurion, with production beginning in 1963. Over 900 entered service with the British Army, with considerable numbers being sold to Kuwait and Iran (they saw service in the Iran-Iraq War). Until the Leopard 2 entered German service in 1980, the Chieftain was the best armed and armoured main battle tank in the world, and remained the mainstay of British armoured forces on NATO's frontline in Germany, with frequent technological additions such as laser-rangefinders and thermal-imaging devices until being slowly replaced by the Challenger in the late 1980s. It included a bridge-layer, engineer tank and recovery vehicle amongst its variants. The Chieftains in British Army service are now in reserve.

Country of origin:	UK
Crew:	4
Weight:	54,880kg (120,736lb)
Dimensions:	length (with gun forward) 10.795m (35ft 5in); length (hull) 7.518m (24ft 8in); width 3.657m (11ft 8.5in); height (overall) 2.895m (9ft 6in)
Range:	500km (310 miles)
Armour:	classified
Armament:	one 120mm rifled gun; one 7.62mm coaxial machine gun; six smoke dischargers
Powerplant:	one Leyland six-cylinder multi-fuel engine developing 750hp (560kW)
Performance:	maximum road speed 48km/h (30mph); fording 1.066m (3ft 6in); vertical obstacle 0.914m (3ft); trench 3.149m (10ft 4in)

Leopard 1

Germany's design for the intended 1960s Franco-German joint venture was the Leopard 1 and it was this vehicle that the Germans eventually adopted independently of the French. Built by Krauss-Maffei, the first production vehicles appeared in 1965 and production continued until 1979, a total of 2237 being built for the German Army and many more for export. There were four basic versions, differing in armour, turret-type and fire-control systems. The tank formed the basis of a complete family of vehicles designed to support the vehicle on the battlefield. Optional equipment for the tank included a snorkel for deep-wading and a hydraulic blade to be attached to the front. The Leopard 1 is undoubtedly one of the best tanks designs to have come out of Europe.

Country of origin:	West Germany
Crew:	4
Weight:	39,912kg (87,808lb)
Dimensions:	length (with gun forward) 9.543m (31ft 4in); length (hull) 7.09m (23ft 3in); width 3.25m (10ft 8in); height (overall) 2.613m (8ft 7in)
Range:	600km (373 miles)
Armour:	classified
Armament:	one 105mm gun; one coaxial 7.62mm machine gun; 7.62mm anti-aircraft machine gun; four smoke dischargers
Powerplant:	one MTU 10-cylinder diesel engine developing 830hp (619kW)
Performance:	maximum road speed 65km/h (40.4mph); fording 2.25m (7ft 4in); vertical obstacle 1.15m (3ft 9.25in); trench 3m (9ft 10in)

Leopard 2

The Leopard 2 was an offshoot of a cancelled joint development between the USA and West Germany in the late 1960s, the project being the MBT-70. The West Germans continued the project, however, first production vehicles were delivered in 1977 and exports were soon equipping the Dutch Army. The Leopard 2 is equipped with laser-rangefinder, thermal-imaging, a nuclear, biological and chemical (NBC) defence system and amphibious capability. Its fire-system is unusual in that the cartridge cases are combustible. When the shell is fired, all that remains is the base of the cartridge, which frees up extra space. It has a 30 percent better power-to-weight ratio than the Leopard 1, which results in increased cross-country mobility and thus survivability.

Country of origin:	West Germany
Crew:	4
Weight:	54,981kg (120,960lb)
Dimentions:	length (with gun forward) 9.668m (31ft 8.7in); length (hull) 7.772m (25ft 6in); width 3.7m (12ft 1.7in); height (overall) 2.79m (9ft 1.75in)
Range:	550km (342 miles)
Armour:	classified
Armament:	one 120mm gun; one coaxial 7.62mm machine gun; one 7.62mm anti-aircraft machine gun; eight smoke dischargers
Powerplant:	one MTU 12-cylinder multi-fuel, developing 1,500hp (1119kW)
Performance:	maximum road speed 72km/h (45mph); fording 1m (3ft 3in); vertical obstacle 1.1m (3ft 7.25in); trench 3m (9ft 10in)

M60A3

The development of the American M60 series of tanks began in 1956 following a decision to create an improved version of the M48. Built by General Dynamics, the M60 entered service in 1960, but was quickly superseded by the A1 to A3 versions. The A3 is notable for its laser fire-control system and thermal sights amongst various other modifications. The two main variants are an AVLB and a Combat Engineer Vehicle, armed with a demolition charge and dozer blade. The M60A3 has been widely exported to Austria, Italy (where it was built under licence), North Africa and many Middle East countries. It is still in frontline service in Africa and the Middle East, particularly in Egypt and Israel, while in the United States it is in National Guard use.

Country of origin:	USA
Crew:	4
Weight:	48,872kg (107,520lb)
Dimensions:	length 9.436m (30ft 11.5in); width 3.631m (11ft 11in); height 3.27m (10ft 8.25in)
Range:	500km (310 miles)
Armour:	25-127mm (0.98-5in)
Armament:	one 105mm gun; one 12.7mm machine gun; one 7.62mm coaxial machine gun
Powerplant:	one Continental 12-cylinder diesel engine developing 750hp (560kW)
Performance:	maximum road speed 48.28km/h (30mph); fording 1.219m (4ft); vertical obstacle 0.914m (3ft); trench 2.59m (8ft 6in)

M1 Abrams

The M1 Abrams was the next stage in American tank development after the M60. Chrysler completed the prototypes in 1978 and the first production vehicles appeared in 1980 with 30 tanks a month being built in following years. Its advanced Chobham armour makes the M1 the best protected US main battle tank yet. Its gas turbine engine is smaller and easier to service than a diesel engine, but the extra fuel requirement negates the space saved, which is perhaps why the idea was rejected for the Leopard 2. Thermal sights, laser rangefinder and gun stabilisation system give the M1 excellent firepower on the move, be it day or night. In the 1991 Gulf War, the Abrams proved itself the best tank in the world, knocking out Iraqi T-72s with impunity – no Abrams were destroyed by enemy fire.

Country of origin:	USA
Crew:	4
Weight:	54,269kg (119,392lb)
Dimensions:	length 9.766m (32ft 0.5in); width 3.655m (12ft); height 2.895m (9ft 6in)
Range:	450km (280 miles)
Armour:	classified
Armament:	one 105mm gun; two 7.62mm machine guns (one coaxial, one on loader's hatch); one 12.7mm machine gun
Powerplant:	Avco Lycoming AGT-1500 gas turbine, developing 1,500hp (1119kW)
Performance:	maximum road speed 72.5km/h (45mph); fording 1.219m (4ft); vertical obstacle 1.244m (4ft 1in); trench 2.743m (9ft)

Merkava

Prior to the Six-Day War in 1967, Israel had relied on Sherman and Centurion tanks for its armoured forces. However, doubts as to future supplies and also concerns that these tanks did not fully meet Israeli requirements prompted development of an indigenous tank. The first production Merkavas appeared in 1980 and saw action for the first time against Syrian forces in Lebanon in 1982. Compared to other modern main battle tanks, the Merkava is slow and has a poor power-to-weight ratio. However, it is designed for specific tactical requirements, which differ from those of most other tank producers. The emphasis is on crew survivability, which explains the Merkava's small cross-section which makes it less of a target, and well-sloped armour for greatest protection.

Country of origin:	Israel
Crew:	4
Weight:	55,898kg (122,976lb)
Dimensions:	length 8.36m (27ft 5.25in); width 3.72m (12ft 2.5in); height 2.64m (8ft 8in)
Range:	500 miles (310 miles)
Armour:	classified
Armament:	one 105mm rifled gun; one 7.62mm machine gun
Powerplant:	one Teledyne Continental AVDS-1790-6A V-12 diesel engine developing 900hp (671kW)
Performance:	maximum road speed 46km/h (28.6mph); vertical obstacle 1m (3ft 3.3in); trench 3m (9ft 10in)

Tanks

T-62

The Russian T-62 was a development of the T-54/55 series of tanks, but due to the cost of each tank never managed to replace its predecessor which in fact outlived it in production. Produced from 1961 until the early 1970s, the T-62 had an unusual integral shell case ejection system. The recoil of the gun ejected the case out of a trapdoor in the turret, thus saving space but reducing the overall rate of fire. Capable of deep-fording by means of a snorkel over the loader's hatch, the tank was fitted with infrared night-vision equipment, turret-ventilation system, nuclear, biological and chemical (NBC) protection and the ability to create an instant smoke screen by injecting diesel into the exhaust. The tank was first used operationally in the Middle East during the Arab-Israeli wars.

Country of origin:	USSR
Crew:	4
Weight:	39,912kg (87,808lb)
Dimensions:	length 9.34m (28ft 6in); width 3.3m (10ft 1in); height: 2.4m (7ft 5in)
Range:	650km (406 miles)
Armour:	15-242mm (0.59-9.52in)
Armament:	one 115mm U-5TS gun; one 7.62mm coaxial machine gun
Powerplant:	one V-55-5 V-12 liquid-cooled diesel, developing 580hp (432kW)
Performance:	maximum road speed: 60km/h (37.5mph); fording 1.4m (4ft 7in); vertical obstacle 0.8m (2ft 7.5in); trench 2.7m (8ft 10.25in)

T-72

The T-72 came into production in 1971. Smaller and faster than such tanks as the Chieftain, the T-72 was poorly armoured with less versatility and effective firepower than its competitors. This became brutally clear in 1982 when Syrian T-72s proved no match for Israeli Merkava tanks and were knocked out in droves. The T-72 was designed for a conscript army and thus is easy to operate and maintain. This accounts for its export success, being transferred to 14 other countries. It is quite versatile, though, and can be equipped for deep-fording, unlike most other tanks, within a matter of minutes, as well as being fully nuclear, biological and chemical (NBC) protected. Variants include a command vehicle, an anti-tank Cobra missile launcher and an armoured recovery vehicle.

Country of origin:	USSR
Crew:	3
Weight:	38,894kg (85,568lb)
Dimensions:	length 9.24m (30ft 4in); width 4.75m (15ft 7in); height 2.37m (7ft 9in)
Range:	550km (434 miles)
Armour:	classified
Armament:	one 125mm gun; one 12.7mm anti-aircraft machine gun; one 7.62mm coaxial machine gun
Powerplant:	one V-46 V-12 diesel engine developing 840hp (626kW)
Performance:	maximum road speed 80km/h (50mph); fording 1.4m (4ft 7in); vertical obstacle 0.85m (2ft 9in); trench 2.8m (9ft 2in)

Tanks

T-80

The T-80 entered service with the Soviet Red Army in the mid-1980s. A development of the T-72 main battle tank. Like the T-72, the tank had an automatic loader for the main gun, thus allowing the crew to be kept to a minimum of three. The main gun was a standard fully stabilised 125mm weapon as fitted in the T-72, but was capable of firing a much greater range of ammunition, including depleted uranium rounds for extra armour-piercing capability. A laser rangefinder led to an improved fire-control system. Like all Soviet tanks, the T-80 was capable of making its own smoke screen and carried four dischargers on the hull for launching chaff or decoys to distract enemy missiles. Adjustable ground clearance provided extra cross-country mobility.

Country of origin:	USSR
Crew:	3
Weight:	48,363kg (106,400lb)
Dimensions:	length 9.9m (32ft 6in); width 3.4m (11ft 2in); height 2.2m (7ft 3in)
Range:	450km (281 miles)
Armour:	classified
Armament:	one 125mm gun; one coaxial 7.62mm machine gun; one 12.7mm anti-aircraft machine gun
Powerplant:	one multi-fuel gas turbine, developing 1000hp (745kW)
Performance:	maximum road speed 70km/h (43.75mph); fording 5m (16ft 5in); vertical obstacle 1m (3ft 4in); trench 2.85m (9ft 4in)

Arjun Mk 1

The Arjun is India's first indigenous main battle tank design. The Indian Army's Combat Vehicle Research and Development Establishment encountered numerous problems with the project, resulting in significant delays which held up the in-service date until 1994. One of the main problems was the lack of an indigenous powerplant, which forced the Indians to use a German MTU diesel. The Arjun's main armament is a locally designed stabilised 120mm rifled gun capable of firing a variety of ammunition types, such as high explosive, high explosive anti-tank and high explosive squash head. The tank has an advanced fire-control system integrated with a combined day/night thermal imaging gunner's assembly with built-in laser rangefinder. In addition, there is a full weather sensor package.

Country of origin:	India
Crew:	4
Weight:	58,000kg (127,600lb)
Dimensions:	length 9.8m (32ft 2in); width 3.17m (10ft 5in); height 2.44m (8ft)
Range:	400km (250 miles)
Armour:	classified
Armament:	one 120mm gun; one 7.62mm machine gun
Powerplant:	one MTU MB 838 Ka 501 water-cooled diesel developing 1400hp (1044kW)
Performance:	maximum road speed 72km/h (45mph); fording 1m (3ft 3in); vertical gradient 1.1m (3ft 7in); trench 3m (9ft 10in)

ENGESA EE-T1 Osorio

Designed to meet both home and export markets, the first prototype Osorio was completed in 1985. The layout is conventional with laser rangefinder, stabilisers to allow firing whilst on the move and thermal-imaging cameras, as well as a full nuclear, biological and chemical (NBC) defence system. The tank can be fitted with two different sizes of main gun. Variants include a bridgelayer, armoured recovery vehicle and an anti-aircraft gun vehicle. There is little innovation in the design of the Osorio compared to the latest designs being produced in Europe and the United States. However, it is attractive for smaller countries which lack the capacity to manufacture their own main battle tank, and for whom the European and American tanks are too expensive and complicated.

Country of origin:	Brazil
Crew:	4
Weight:	39,000kg (85,800lb)
Dimensions:	length 9.995m (32ft 9.5in); width 3.26m (10ft 8.3in); height 2.371m (7ft 9.3in)
Range:	550km (342 miles)
Armour:	classified
Armament:	one British 105mm/French 120mm gun; one 7.62mm machine gun
Powerplant:	one 12-cylinder diesel engine developing 1000hp (745kW)
Performance:	maximum road speed 70km/h (43.5mph); fording 1.20m (3ft 11in); vertical obstacle 1.15m (3ft 4in); trench 3.0m (9ft 10in)

AMX-40

Designed in the early 1980s, primarily for export, the GIAT-built AMX-40 was a significant improvement on its predecessor, the AMX-30, in the key areas of armour, mobility and firepower. The tank has a laser rangefinder, gun stabilisation equipment and a low-light television for night-fighting. One interesting feature is the ammunition stowage. Carried in the turret and surrounded by bulkheads, the ammunition compartment is designed so that if it is hit, the ammunition will explode upwards, away from the crew below. As it was intended for export, the French Army was forced to rely on the AMX-30 until the advent of the Leclerc. The AMX-40 carries the traditional number of crew for a main battle tank: four (commander, gunner, radio operator and driver).

Country of origin:	France
Crew:	4
Weight:	43,000kg (94,600lb)
Dimensions:	length 10.04m (32ft 11.3in); width 3.36m (11ft 0.3in); height 3.08m (10ft 1.3in)
Range:	600km (373 miles)
Armour:	classified
Armament:	one 120mm gun; one 20mm cannon in cupola; one 7.62mm machine gun
Powerplant:	one Poyaud 12-cylinder diesel engine developing 1100hp (820kW)
Performance:	maximum road speed 70km/h (44mph); fording 1.30m (4ft 3in); vertical obstacle 1.0m (6ft 7in); trench 3.20m (10ft 6in)

Leclerc

The Leclerc was designed to replace the French Army's fleet of AMX-30 tanks. Development began in 1983, and the first production Leclercs appeared in 1991. The Leclerc is an excellent vehicle. An automatic loading system for the main armament and remote-control machine guns allow the crew to be cut down to three. The tank can be fitted with extra fuel tanks to increase operational range, and standard equipment includes a fire-detection/suppression system, thermal-imaging and laser rangefinder for the main gun, and a land navigation system. The on-board electronic systems are fully integrated to allow automatic reconfiguration in case of battlefield failure or damage. As well as in French service, around 390 Leclercs have been exported to the United Arab Emirates.

Country of origin:	France
Crew:	3
Weight:	53,500kg (117,700lb)
Dimensions:	length 9.87m (30ft); width 3.71m (11ft 4in); height 2.46m (7ft 6in)
Range:	550km (345 miles)
Armour:	classified
Armament:	one 120mm gun, one 12.7mm machine gun, one 7.62mm machine gun, 3 x 9 smoke dischargers
Powerplant:	one SAEM UDU V8X 1500 T9 Hyperbar eight-cylinder diesel engine developing 1500hp; SESM ESM500 automatic transmission
Performance:	maximum road speed: 73km/h (45.6mph); fording 1m (3ft 3in); vertical obstacle 1.25m (4ft 1in); trench 3m (9ft 10in)

Close Combat Vehicle – Light

The CCV-L was designed as a private venture by the FNC Corporation, manufacturer of the M113 and Bradley Armoured Fighting Vehicles, and was destined for the US Army's Light Divisions. When the prototype appeared in 1985, it created interest because it only required a three-man crew, allowed for by an automatic loading system for the main armament. This gave a rate of fire of 12 round per minute. The CCV-L borrowed parts from various other vehicles, such as the M113 Armoured Personnel Carrier, in order to reduce development time. The CCV-L has a hull of all-welded aluminium construction with bolt-on steel to enhance ballistic protection. Additional armour can be applied to the outside of the tank if required, including explosive reactive armour.

Country of origin:	USA
Crew:	3
Weight:	19,414kg (42,710lb)
Dimensions:	length 9.37m (30ft 9in); width 2.69m (8ft 10in); height 2.36m (7ft 9in)
Range:	483km (300 miles)
Armour:	classified
Armament:	one 105mm gun
Powerplant:	one Detroit Diesel Model 6V-92 TA 6-cylinder diesel engine developing 552hp (412kW)
Performance:	maximum road speed 70km/h (43.5mph); fording 1.32m (4ft 4in); vertical obstacle 0.76m (2ft 6in); trench 2.13m (7ft)

TAM

For many years the Argentinian Army relied on World War II Sherman tanks to form the basis of its armoured forces. By the early 1970s, these were becoming difficult to maintain. Most foreign tanks of the period were too heavy for domestic conditions and thus a new tank was ordered from Thyssen Henschel of West Germany. Once developed, production moved to Buenos Aires and production began towards the end of the 1970s. The hull of the TAM was based on that of the MICV in use with the West German Army. The armour is comparatively poor against that of other main battle tanks, such as the Leopard 1 and the AMX-30, but is well-sloped to give as much protection as possible. The tank was not produced in time to have any impact on the 1982 Falklands conflict.

Country of origin:	Argentina
Crew:	4
Weight:	30,500kg (67,100lb)
Dimensions:	length, gun forward 8.23m (25ft 2in); width 3.12m (9ft 6in); height 2.42m (7ft 5in)
Range:	900km (560 miles)
Armour:	classified
Armament:	one 105mm gun; one coaxial 7.62mm machine gun; one 7.62mm anti-aircraft machine gun
Powerplant:	one V-6 turbo-charged diesel engine developing 720hp (537kW)
Performance:	maximum road speed: 75km/h (46.9mph); fording 1.5m (4ft 11in); vertical obstacle 1m (3ft 3in); trench 2.5m (8ft 2in)

Challenger 1

The Challenger 1 was introduced in 1982 as a replacement for the Chieftain. It reflected British thinking on tank design, being heavily armed and armoured. It was slower than contemporary Warsaw Pact vehicles, but made up for it with its composite Chobham armour, which was virtually impenetrable to enemy rounds, and the greater accuracy of its armament. In any case, NATO thinking regarding the war in central Europe with the forces of the Soviet Union and her allies, always placed the emphasis on defence and holding enemy forces until reinforcements arrived. Its armour and nimbleness, despite its lack of speed, allow for good survivability. As tanks become more complicated, this is important as the tanks are often easier to replace than their crews.

Country of origin:	UK
Crew:	4
Weight:	62,000kg (136,400lb)
Dimensions:	length, gun forward: 11.56m (35ft 4in); width 3.52m (10ft 8in); height 2.5m (7ft 5in)
Range:	400km (250 miles)
Armour:	classified
Armament:	one 120mm gun; two 7.62mm machine guns; two smoke dischargers
Powerplant:	one liquid-cooled diesel engine developing 1200hp (895kW)
Performance:	maximum road speed: 55km/h (35mph); fording 1m (3ft 4in); vertical obstacle 0.9m (2ft 10in); trench 2.8m (9ft 2in)

Challenger 2

The Challenger 2 is the current main battle tank of the British Army. The hull is similar to that of the Challenger 1, as is the powerpack, but the turret has been redesigned to fit updated armament, and the tank is in many ways a completely new tank. The first production versions appeared in mid-1994, boasting a carbon dioxide laser rangefinder, thermal-imaging and fully computerised fire-control systems, giving a high first-round hit probability. In addition, turret traverse is all electric and the gun is fully stabilised. It also has the capacity to be fitted with the Battlefield Information Control System in future years, to give even greater combat capability. A dozer can be fitted to the front of the hull. Nearly 400 were ordered by the British Army, with 18 being exported to Oman.

Country of origin:	UK
Crew:	4
Weight:	62,500kg (137,500lb)
Dimensions:	length 11.55m (35ft 4in); width 3.52m (10ft 8in); height 2.49m (7ft 5in)
Range:	400km (250 miles)
Armour:	classified
Armament:	one 120mm gun; two 7.62mm machine guns; two smoke rocket dischargers
Powerplant:	one liquid-cooled diesel engine developing 1200hp (895kW)
Performance:	maximum road speed: 57km/h (35.6mph); fording 1m (3ft 4in); vertical obstacle 0.9m (2ft 10in); trench 2.8m (9ft 2in)

Type 59

The Type 59 was a Chinese version of the T-54 which had been supplied in numbers by the USSR in the early 1950s. Early models were very basic, with no gun stabilisation or infrared night vision equipment, though the latter was supplied to later models by the British company MEL. A laser rangefinder was also added later, but unusually this was mounted on the front of the turret, where it was vulnerable to shell splinters and small-arms fire. The tank can generate its own smoke screen by injecting diesel fuel into the exhaust pipe, and extra fuel can be mounted in drums on the rear hull. The Type 59 was exported in some quantity to Albania, the Congo, North Korea, Pakistan, Sudan and Vietnam, the latter proving an unwise choice given the war between China and Vietnam in 1979.

Country of origin:	China
Crew:	4
Weight:	36,000kg (79,200lb)
Dimensions:	length 9m (27ft 6in); width 3.27m (10ft); height 2.59m (7ft 8in)
Range:	600km (375 miles)
Armour:	39-203mm (1.5-8in)
Armament:	one 100mm gun; two 7.62mm machine guns; one 12.7mm machine gun
Powerplant:	one Model 12150L V-12 diesel engine developing 520hp (388kW)
Performance:	maximum road speed: 50km/h (31.3mph); fording 1.4m (4ft 7in); vertical obstacle 0.79m (2ft 7in); trench 2.7m (8ft 10in)

Type 69

The Type 69 was the replacement for the Type 59. First seen in public in 1982, during a parade in Beijing, the tank was very similar in appearance to the Type 59, but was fitted with a new 105/106mm gun, probably based on that of the Soviet T-62, examples of which were captured by the Chinese during border clashes with the USSR. There are a number of variants, including a self-propelled anti-aircraft gun, armoured bridgelayer and armoured recovery vehicle. The latter has a Type 69 chassis but the turret removed and replaced by a superstructure; there is also a dozer blade at the front and crane at the rear. Large quantities of the Type 69 were exported to Iraq in the early 1980s, with Saudi Arabia acting as intermediary, to make up for losses experienced during the war with Iraq.

Country of origin:	China
Crew:	4
Weight:	36,500kg (80,300lb)
Dimensions:	length 8.68m (26ft 6in); width 3.3m (10ft 1in); height 2.87m (8ft 10in)
Range:	375km (250 miles)
Armour:	100mm (3.94in)
Armament:	one 100mm gun; one 12.7mm machine gun; two 7.62mm machine guns; two smoke rocket dischargers
Powerplant:	one V-12 liquid-cooled diesel engine developing 580hp (432kW)
Performance:	maximum road speed: 50km/h (31.3mph); fording 1.4m (4ft 7in); vertical obstacle 0.8m (2ft 7in); trench 2.7m (8ft 10in)

Type 80

The Chinese Type 80 main battle tank was a development of the T-69 series. It differs in design by having a brand new hull, as well as a larger main armament and a more modern computerised fire-control system, which includes a laser rangefinder, mounted either over the gunner's sights, or over the 105mm gun itself, depending on the version. The vehicle carries a snorkel which can be fitted to allow for deep fording. It has an in-built fire-detection/ suppression system and the capability of being easily uparmoured (by the addition of composite armour plates) to give increased battlefield survivability. Crew configuration is as follows: the driver sits at the front left with some of the ammunition, while the loader, commander and gunner sit in the turret.

Country of origin:	China
Crew:	4
Weight:	38,000kg (83,600lb)
Dimensions:	length 9.33m (28ft 6in); width 3.37m (10ft 4in); height 2.3m (7ft)
Range:	570km (356 miles)
Armour:	classified
Armament:	one 105mm gun; one 7.62mm coaxial machine gun; one 12.7mm coaxial machine gun
Powerplant:	one V-12 diesel engine developing 730hp (544kW); manual transmission
Performance:	maximum road speed: 60km/h (37.5mph); fording 1.4m (4ft 7in); vertical obstacle 0.8m (2ft 7in); trench 2.7m (8ft 10in)

Type 85

The Type 85 main battle tank entered production on a small scale in the late 1980s. The tank was based on the chassis of the Type 80, but, in something of an innovation for Chinese tanks, it was given an all-welded turret instead of the usual cast steel type, armour being increased all round. It also carried improved communications equipment. The increased main armament (125mm as opposed to the 105mm of the Type 80) is fed by an automatic loader, which allows the crew to be reduced to a minimum. However, space inside is reduced by the ammunition being made up of separate projectile and charge. The Type 85 is still in production and has been exported to Pakistan, where it is known as the Type 85-IIM. It is still inferior to American and European tanks.

Country of origin:	China
Crew:	3
Weight:	41,000kg (90,200lb)
Dimensions:	length 10.28m (31ft 5in); width: 3.45m (10ft 6in); height: 2.3m (7ft)
Range:	500km (312 miles)
Armour:	classified
Armament:	one 125mm gun; one 7.62mm coaxial machine gun; one 12.7mm anti-aircraft machine gun; two smoke grenade launchers
Powerplant:	one V-12 supercharged diesel engine developing 730hp (544kW)
Performance:	maximum road speed: 57.25km/h (35.8mph); fording 1.4m (4ft 7in); vertical obstacle 0.8m (2ft 7in); trench 2.7m (8ft 10in)

Type 74

The Type 74 main battle tank, a successor to the Type 61, entered production on a small scale in the late 1975, with the production rate never increasing above around 50 vehicles per year which meant a very high unit cost. The tank carries a laser rangefinder, computerised fire-control and nuclear, biological and chemical (NBC) defence system as standard. However, the Type 74 has an unusual cross-linked hydro-pneumatic suspension system, which allows it to raise or lower different parts of the chassis in order to cross difficult terrain or to engage targets outside of the gun's normal elevation/depression range. Internal layout is conventional, with a centre turret and rear powerplant. The Type 74 forms the basis of the Type 87 35mm self-propelled anti-aircraft gun tank.

Country of origin:	Japan
Crew:	3
Weight:	38,000kg (83,600lb)
Dimensions:	length 9.42m (28ft 8in); width 3.2m (9ft 10in); height 2.48m (7ft 7in)
Range:	300km (188 miles)
Armour:	classified
Armament:	one 105mm gun; one 7.62mm coaxial machine gun; one 12.7mm anti-aircraft machine gun; two smoke dischargers
Powerplant:	one 10ZF V-10 liquid-cooled diesel, developing 720hp (536kW)
Performance:	maximum road speed: 55km/h (34.4mph); fording; 1m (3ft 4in); vertical obstacle 1m (3ft 4in); trench 2.7m (8ft 10in)

Type 90

The Type 90 main battle tank was placed in development in the mid-1970s to meet the needs of the Japanese Ground Self-Defence Force. It entered production on a small scale in the 1992. Its slow production rate makes this the most expensive unit cost tank produced by any nation in the world. The vehicle carries a laser rangefinder, computerised fire control and NBC system as standard, as well as thermal imaging and night-driving capability. Like the Type 74, the vehicle has a cross-linked hydro-pneumatic suspension system, which allows it to raise or lower different parts of the chassis in order to cross difficult terrain or to engage targets outside of the gun's normal elevation/depression range. Variants include the Type 90 ARV with dozer blade and winch and the Type 91 AVLB bridgelayer.

Country of origin:	Japan
Crew:	3
Weight:	50,000kg (110,000lb)
Dimensions:	length 9.76m (29ft 10in); width: 3.4m (10ft 5in); height 2.34m (7ft 1in)
Range:	350km (219 miles)
Armour:	classified
Armament:	one 120mm gun; one 7.62mm coaxial machine gun; one 12.7mm anti-aircraft machine gun; two smoke dischargers
Powerplant:	one 10ZG V-10 fuel-injection diesel, developing 1500hp (1118kW)
Performance:	maximum road speed: 70km/h (43.8mph); fording 2m (6ft 6in); vertical obstacle 1m (3ft 4in); trench 2.7m (8ft 10in)

C1 Ariete

The C1 Ariete main battle tank was developed in response to a 1982 specification of the Italian Army for a replacement for its obsolete M47 Pattons. It has the typical slab-sided appearance of modern main battle tanks due to its special composite armour. The Ariete is conventional in layout, with the driver at the front right, a power-operated turret in the centre, gunner on the right, loader on the left and the powerplant at the rear of the vehicle. The main smoothbore armament has a thermal sleeve and fume extractor and uses the latest Galileo computerised fire-control system, the thermal vision night sight and laser rangefinder giving high single-shot kill probability, whether moving or stationary. An armoured recovery vehicle and AVLB based on the C1 chassis are expected to follow.

Country of origin:	Italy
Crew:	4
Weight:	54,000kg (118,800lb)
Dimensions:	length 9.67m (29ft 6in); width 3.6m (11ft); height: 2.5m (7ft 7in
Range:	600km (375 miles)
Armour:	classified
Armament:	one 120mm gun; one 7.62mm coaxial machine gun; one 7.62mm anti-aircraft machine gun; 2 x 4 smoke dischargers
Powerplant:	one IVECO FIAT MTCA V-12 turbocharged diesel engine developing 1250hp (932kW)
Performance:	maximum road speed: 66km/h (41.3mph); fording 1.2m (3ft 11in); vertical obstacle 2.1m (6ft 11in); trench 3m (9ft 10in)

Type 88

Also known as the K1, the Type 88 was developed by General Dynamics in the early 1980s in response to a South Korean requirement for a main battle tank which could be locally built. The main smoothbore armament has a thermal sleeve and fume extractor and uses a computerised fire-control system based on the M1 ballistic computer and an environmental sensor package. The vehicle has a nuclear, biological and chemical (NBC) system designed to give individual crew protection. Its successor, the K1A1, is already in development, armed with a larger gun and improved fire control system. An AVLB variant, based on the K1 chassis has been designed in the UK and 56 have already been ordered by the South Koreans. A new version of the Type 88 is under development, mounting a 120mm smoothbore gun.

Country of origin:	South Korea
Crew:	4
Weight:	52,000kg (114,400lb)
Dimensions:	length 9.67m (29ft 6in); width: 3.59m (10ft 11in); height: 2.25m (6ft 10in)
Range:	500km (313 miles)
Armour:	classified
Armament:	one 105mm gun; one 7.62mm coaxial machine gun; one 12.7mm anti-aircraft machine gun; 2 x 6 smoke dischargers
Powerplant:	one liquid-cooled turbocharged diesel, developing 1200hp (895kW)
Performance:	maximum road speed: 65km/h (40.6mph); fording 1.2m (3ft 11in); vertical obstacle 1m (3ft 4in)

Olifant Mk 1A

Like the Israelis with their Sho't programme, the South Africans took a basic Centurion tank and upgraded it to produce an indigenous main battle tank specifically suited to their needs, with improved firepower and mobility. The fire control system of the Olifant ('Elephant') remained that of the original Centurion, but the tank was fitted with a hand-held laser rangefinder for the commander and image-intensifier for the gunner. The Mk 1B version of the Olifant is much different, with a lengthened hull, new engine and transmission, and updated armour, as well as enhanced fire control systems. Variants include an armoured recovery vehicle and repair vehicle. The Olifant is undoubtedly the best indigenous tank design on the African continent.

Country of origin:	South Africa
Crew:	4
Weight:	56,000kg (123,200lb)
Dimensions:	length 9.83m (30ft); width: 3.38m (10ft 4in); height: 2.94m (8ft 11in)
Range:	500km (313 miles)
Armour:	17-118mm (0.66-4.6in)
Armament:	one 105mm gun; one 7.62mm coaxial machine gun; one 7.62mm anti-aircraft machine gun; 2 x 4 smoke dischargers
Powerplant:	one V-12 air-cooled turbocharged diesel, developing 750hp (559kW)
Performance:	maximum road speed: 45km/h (28.1mph); fording 1.45m (4ft 9in); vertical obstacle 0.9m (2ft 11in); trench 3.352m (11ft)

M60T Sabra main battle tank

Israel is a major operator of US-designed M60 Main Battle Tanks. They developed the Sabra as an upgrade to maintain their combat effectiveness against a new generation of armoured vehicles. The resulting tank was selected over the competing M60-2000 upgrade for service with the Turkish army, where it was designated M60T. The Sabra has an improved chassis and mounts a 120mm (4.72in) gun rather than the original 105mm (4.13in) cannon of the M60. It also has an internally-mounted 60mm (2.36in) mortar and three 7.62mm (0.3in) machine guns rather than the more usual one. Enhanced variants have already appeared. The Mk2 version uses modular armour, which makes upgrades or replacements of damaged sections easy, plus it can be fitted with reactive armour.

Country of origin:	Israel
Crew:	4
Weight:	60,610kg (133,622lb)
Dimentions:	length 6.95m (22ft 1in); width 3.63m (11ft 11in); height 3.27m (10ft 9in)
Range:	450km (279 miles)
Armour:	classified
Armament:	one 120mm (4.7in) smoothbore gun, one 60mm (2.3in) mortar, three 7.62mm (0.3in) machine guns
Powerplant:	671kW (900hp) Continental AVDS-1790-5A diesel
Performance:	maximum road speed 48km/h (29.8mph)

K2 Black Panther MBT

The K2 Black Panther is the most expensive tank in the world to date. Conceived as a replacement for the K1 MBT, using indigenous technology, it has been under development since 1995 and entered production in 2010–11. The Black Panther is protected by an advanced modular armour system, using easily replaced slabs of composite armour augmented by a countermeasures and active protection system. It is thought that the K2 has an equivalent level of protection to the M1 Abrams. The main gun is capable of delivering a range of munitions, including conventional anti-tank ammunition and the Korean Smart Top-Attack Munition (KSTAM), which can be fired from a concealed position at a range of up to 8km (4.97 miles). There are plans to export the K2, with Turkey as one of the first customers.

Country of origin:	South Korea
Crew:	3
Weight:	55,000kg (121,254lb)
Dimentions:	length 7.5m (24ft 7in); width 3.6m (11ft 9in); height 2.5m (8ft 2in)
Range:	430km (267 miles)
Armour:	classified, advanced composite
Armament:	one 120mm (4.7in) smoothbore cannon; one 12.7mm (0.5in) machine gun; one 7.62mm (0.3in) machine gun
Powerplant:	MTU MB-883 Ka500 diesel
Performance:	maximum road speed 70km/h (43mph)

Light Tanks

M551 Sheridan

The M551 was developed following a 1959 requirement for an air-portable tank to equip the US Army's airborne divisions. Between 1965 and 1970, 1700 vehicles were produced by General Motors and saw service in South Korea, Europe and Vietnam. It was in the latter that the M551's deficiencies were revealed when it proved highly susceptible to landmines, although its ability to fire canister ammunition was effective in beating off mass guerrilla attacks. As a result, it was withdrawn from most frontline units in the late 1970s, although many were modified by the National Training Center to resemble Soviet vehicles and used for training purposes. The main armament consisted of a 152mm weapon that fired a wire-guided Shilelagh missile.

Country of origin:	USA
Crew:	4
Weight:	15,830kg (34,826lb)
Dimensions:	length 6.299m (20ft 8in); width 2.819m (9ft 3in); height (overall) 2.946m (9ft 8in)
Range:	600km (310 miles)
Armour:	40-50mm (1.57-2in)
Armament:	one 152mm gun/missile launcher; one coaxial 7.62mm machine gun; one 12.7mm anti-aircraft machine gun
Powerplant:	one six-cylinder Detroit 6V-53T diesel, developing 300hp (224kW)
Performance:	maximum road speed 70km/h (43mph); fording amphibious; vertical obstacle 0.838m (2ft 9in); trench 2.54m (8ft 4in)

Scorpion

The first prototype of the Alvis Scorpion, officially named Combat Vehicle Reconnaissance (Tracked), appeared in 1969, following a British Army requirement for a tracked reconnaissance vehicle to replace the Saladin armoured car. It entered service in 1972 and was exported to countries all over the world, particularly Belgium, where it was produced under licence. It saw action in the Falklands in 1982, where its flotation screens giving amphibious capability were particularly useful during the landings. The Scorpion proved its worth in both reconnaissance and in high-speed advances, and remains a key part of the British armoured forces. The Scorpion chassis has been used for a complete range of tracked vehicles, such as the Sultan, Spartan and Scimitar.

Country of origin:	UK
Crew:	3
Weight:	8073kg (17,760lb)
Dimensions:	length 4.794m (15ft 8.75in); width 2.235m (7ft 4in); height 2.102m (6ft 10.75in)
Range:	644km (400 miles)
Armour:	12.7mm (0.5in)
Armament:	one 76mm gun; one coaxial 7.62mm machine gun
Powerplant:	one Jaguar 4.2-litre petrol engine developing 190hp (142kW)
Performance:	maximum road speed 80km/h (50mph); fording 1.067m (3ft 6in); vertical obstacle 0.50m (1ft 8in); trench 2.057m (6ft 9in)

Light Tanks

AMX-13

The AMX-13 was designed immediately after the end of World War II. Production began in 1952 and continued until the 1980s. Its design included an automatic loader in the turret bustle which included two revolver-type magazines, each holding six rounds of ammunition. The tank was widely exported, proving particularly popular with developing nations such as Chile, Djibouti and Nepal, as well as Israel, the Netherlands and Switzerland. One interesting feature is the oscillating turret in which the gun is fixed in the upper part, which in turn pivots on the lower part. The AMX-13 was extensively modified and used as the basis for a complete family of vehicles, from self-propelled guns and howitzers to engineer vehicles, recovery vehicles, bridgelayers and Infantry Fighting Vehicles.

Country of origin:	France
Crew:	3
Weight:	15,000kg (33,000lb)
Dimensions:	length 6.36m (20ft 10.3in); width 2.50m (8ft 2.5in); height 2.30m (7ft 6.5in)
Range:	400km (250 miles)
Armour:	10-40mm (0.4-1.57in)
Armament:	one 75mm gun; one 7.62mm machine gun
Powerplant:	one SOFAM eight-cylinder petrol engine developing 250hp (186kW)
Performance:	maximum road speed 60km/h (37mph); fording 0.60m (1ft 11.7in); vertical obstacle 0.65m (2ft 1.7in); trench 1.60m (5ft 3in)

PT-76

The PT-76 was designed in the immediate period after World War II. For many years it was the standard reconnaissance vehicle of the Soviet Red Army, before being replaced by heavier T-62s, and was exported to more than 25 countries, seeing action in the 1967 Six-Day War, Vietnam and Angola. Intended as an amphibious tank, its armour was only sufficient to withstand small-arms fire, in order to keep the weight to a minimum. The tank was equipped with bilge pumps and water jets to allow it to move efficiently through water and could travel up to 65km (40 miles) in this fashion. The chassis was used for a number of other vehicles, including the BTR-50 Armoured Personnel Carrier and the FROG missile launcher. Though old, it is still in Russian service.

Country of origin:	USSR
Crew:	3
Weight:	14,000kg (30,800lb)
Dimensions:	length 7.625m (25ft 0.25in); width 3.14m (10ft 3.7in); height 2.255m (7ft 4.75in)
Range:	260km (160 miles)
Armour:	5-17mm (0.19-0.66in)
Armament:	one 76mm gun; one coaxial 7.62mm machine gun; one 12.7mm anti-aircraft machine-gun
Powerplant:	one V-6 six-cylinder diesel engine developing 240hp (179kW)
Performance:	maximum road speed 44km/h (27mph); fording amphibious; vertical obstacle 1.10m (3ft 7.3in); trench 2.80m (9ft 2in)

Light Tanks

Scimitar

The Scimitar is a variant of the Scorpion FV101 tracked reconnaissance vehicle, one of the CVR(T) family of light armoured vehicles developed for the British Army. Entering service in 1978, it was intended mainly for a fire support role. The powerful RARDEN cannon is able to penetrate all light armoured vehicles, and the side armour of most main battle tanks. Its own armour protection is minimal, though, being barely sufficient to resist small-arms fire. The Scimitar can be fitted with night-vision sights, laser rangefinder and computerised fire-control system. Unusually for a 1970s combat vehicle, it runs on petrol rather than diesel. Amphibious capability is provided by a collapsible flotation screen, and the vehicle is propelled in the water by its tracks.

Country of origin:	UK
Crew:	3
Weight:	7800kg (17,160lb)
Dimensions:	length 4.8m (15ft 9in); width 2.24m (7ft 4in); height 2.1m (6ft 11in)
Range:	644km (402 miles)
Armour:	12.7mm (0.5in)
Armament:	one 30mm Rarden gun; one 12.7m machine gun
Powerplant:	one Jaguar 4.2-litre petrol engine developing 190hp (142kW)
Performance:	maximum road speed 80km/h (50mph); fording 1.067m (3ft 6in); vertical obstacle 0.50m (1ft 8in); trench 2.057m (6ft 9in)

Wiesel

The Wiesel was developed to a requirement for an air-portable light armoured tracked vehicle for use by airborne troops. Prototypes were built by Porsche and deliveries began at the end of the 1980s – a total of 345 vehicles will be delivered to the German Army (210 will be armed with a wire-guided anti-tank weapon). There are two main versions, one armed with a conventional cannon (complete with 20 rounds of ready use ammunition), the other with a missile launcher. Its compact nature, necessary for air transport, makes it very difficult to detect the Wiesel on the battlefield. A whole host of variants are possible such as ambulance, anti-aircraft (equipped with Stinger surface-to-air missiles), armoured personnel carrier, command vehicle and recovery vehicle.

Country of origin:	Germany
Crew:	3
Weight:	2750kg (6050lb)
Dimensions:	length 3.265m (10ft 8.5in); width 1.82m (5ft 11.7in); height 1.875m (6ft 1.8in)
Range:	200km (124 miles)
Armour:	classified
Armament:	one 20mm cannon or a Hughes anti-tank missile launcher
Powerplant:	one five-cylinder turbocharged diesel engine developing 86hp (64kW)
Performance:	maximum road speed 80km/h (50mph); vertical obstacle 0.4m (1ft 4in); trench 1.20m (3ft 11in)

Light Tanks

Stingray

The prototype of the Stingray was unveiled in 1984 by Cadillac Gage, who had foreseen the need for a light tank with good mobility and firepower which was simple to operate and maintain. Wherever possible, proven parts from other vehicles have been adapted to save development costs. The Stingray comes equipped with laser rangefinder, stabilisation devices for the gun, nuclear, biological and chemical (NBC) protection and has the firepower of a main battle tank. Its drawback is its light armour. However, given the power of modern high explosive anti-tank (HEAT) rounds, this may make little difference. The Stingray has performance and power at a much lower unit cost when compared to a main battle tank, and is thus the subject of great interest around the world.

Country of origin:	USA
Crew:	4
Weight:	19,051kg (41,912lb)
Dimensions:	length 9.35m (30ft 8in); width 2.71m (8ft 11in); height 2.54m (8ft 4in)
Range:	483km (300 miles)
Armour:	classified
Armament:	one 105mm rifled gun; one coaxial 7.62mm machine gun; one 7.62mm anti-aircraft machinegun
Powerplant:	one Diesel Model 8V-92 TA diesel engine developing 535hp (399kW)
Performance:	maximum road speed 69km/h (43mph); fording 1.22m (4ft); vertical obstacle 0.76m (2ft 6in); trench 1.69m (5ft 7in)

LARS II

The Light Artillery Rocket System (LARS) was developed in the mid-1960s and was accepted into West German service in 1969. Known as the Artillerie Raketenwerfer 110SF, the LARS was upgraded to the LARS II and mounted on the MAN 4 x 4 chassis. With 36 launcher tubes, the full complement could be launched in only 17.5 seconds and could be reloaded in around 15 minutes with a variety of different rounds, including parachute-retarded anti-tank mines. The launcher was supported by a resupply vehicle containing 144 rockets. 209 launchers were in service with the West German Army, one battery per division, until replaced by the MLRS in the late 1980s. No doubt the design and thinking behind the LARS was influenced by Soviet rocket launchers on the Eastern Front in World War II.

Country of origin:	Germany
Crew:	3
Weight:	17,480kg (38,537lb)
Dimensions:	length 8.28m (27ft 2in); width 2.5m (8ft 2in); height 2.99m (9ft 10in)
Range:	480km (300 miles)
Armour:	none
Armament:	36 110mm rocket tubes
Powerplant:	one V-8 liquid-cooled diesel engine developing 320hp (238kW)
Performance:	maximum road speed 100km/h (62.5mph); fording 1.4m (94ft 7in); vertical obstacle 0.6m (1ft 11in); trench1.6m (5ft 3in)

Multiple Rocket Launchers

BM-21

The BM-21 entered service in the early 1960s and became the standard multiple rocket-launcher of Warsaw Pact armies, as well as most Soviet client states. Variants were produced in China, India, Egypt and Romania. The 40-round launcher was mounted on a URAL-375 6 x 6 truck (later a on a ZIL-131 in a modified 36-round form). For airborne troops, a smaller 12-round version was developed to be mounted on a 4 x 4 truck. Most BM-21 variants have been used in action, particularly in Afghanistan. In addition, customised versions were used by the PLO in battles around Beirut from 1982 onwards. The BM-21 is symbolic of Russian multiple rocket launchers, being crude and simple to operate. Nevertheless, when used in batteries it could deliver devastating firepower.

Country of origin:	USSR
Crew:	6
Weight:	11,500kg (25,300lb)
Dimensions:	length 7.35m (24ft 1in); width 2.69m (8ft 9in); height 2.85m (9ft 4in)
Range:	405km (253 miles)
Armour:	none
Armament:	40 122mm rocket-launcher tubes
Powerplant:	one V-8 water-cooled petrol engine developing 180hp (134kW)
Performance:	maximum road speed 75km/h (46.8mph); fording 1.5m (4ft 11in); vertical obstacle 0.65m (2ft 1in); trench 0.875m (2ft 10in)

BM-24

The BM-24 was the BM-21's predecessor, introduced into service during the early 1950s. Originally mounted on a ZIL-151 6 x 6 truck, the system was later transferred to a ZIL-157. The system consisted of two rows of six tubular frame rails. Two stabiliser jacks were fitted which had to be lowered before firing. The BM-24 saw widespread use with Arab armies against the Israelis, the latter being so impressed with the system that they pressed the large numbers of captured launchers into service and designed a new rocket for it, with shorter range but a more effective warhead. This version saw service in the 1973 Yom Kippur War and in Lebanon in 1982. Rocket types include high-explosive, smoke and chemical, with a typical range being 11km (6.84 miles).

Country of origin:	USSR
Crew:	6
Weight:	9200kg (20,240lb)
Dimensions:	length 6.7m (21ft 11in); width 2.3m (7ft 6in); height 2.91m (9ft 6in)
Range:	430km (269 miles)
Armour:	none
Armament:	12 240mm rocket-launcher tubes
Powerplant:	one six-cylinder water-cooled petrol engine developing 109hp (81kW)
Performance:	maximum road speed 65km/h (40.6mph); fording 0.85m (2ft 9in); vertical obstacle 0.46m (1ft 6in); trench 0.69m (2ft 3in)

Multiple Rocket Launchers

BM-27

The BM-27 entered service with the Soviet Army in the mid-1970s. With similar operational characteristics to contemporary American multiple rocket-launchers, the vehicle was designed to provide fire-support to frontline troops using chemical, high explosive and incendiary munitions. The system comprises one layer of four tubes on top of two layers of six tubes. The whole system is mounted on a ZIL-135 8 x 8 truck chassis. Four stabiliser jacks are lowered to provide support when firing. Support vehicles can reload the launcher within five minutes. A few BM-27s were transferred to Syria, where they saw action against Israeli troops in 1982. The BM-27 is much more sophisticated than earlier Russian rocket launchers, and can fire projectiles to a range of 40km (24.85 miles).

Country of origin:	USSR
Crew:	6
Weight:	22,750kg (49,940lb)
Dimensions:	length 9.3m (30ft 6in); width 2.8m (9ft 2in); height 3.2m (10ft 6in)
Range:	500km (312 miles)
Armour:	none
Armament:	16 220mm rocket-launcher tubes
Powerplant:	one V-8 water-cooled diesel engine developing 260hp (194kW)
Performance:	maximum road speed 65km/h (40.65mph); fording 1m (3ft 4in); vertical obstacle 1.1m (3ft 7in); trench 2.8m (9ft 2in)

Brazilian MLRS

The Astros II is a conventional truck-based multiple rocket launcher built by Tectran in Brazil. The 10-tonnes (9.9-tons) 6 x 6 cross-country vehicle is equipped with armoured shutters to protect the crew cabin. In service with the Brazilian Army and exported in large numbers to Iraq during the Iran-Iraq War, the Astros system uses a common launcher, command and fire-control vehicle to deliver three different types of rocket, the SS-30, SS-40 and SS-60. The rockets range in weight from 68kg to 595kg (149.6lb to 1309lb), all of which are unguided. An ammunition resupply vehicle is always attached to the Astros system. Though less sophisticated than the MLRS, for example, the Astros does provide an excellent rocket launcher system for Third World and developing states.

Country of origin:	Brazil
Crew:	3
Weight:	10,000kg (22,000lb)
Dimensions:	length 7m (22ft 11in); width 2.9m (9ft 6in); height 2.6m (8ft 6in)
Range:	480km (300 miles)
Armour:	classified
Armament:	one battery of four, 16 or 32 rocket-launcher tubes
Powerplant:	one six-cylinder water-cooled diesel engine developing 212hp (158kW)
Performance:	maximum road speed 65km/h (40.62mph); fording 1.1m (3ft 7in); vertical obstacle 1m (3ft 4in); trench 2.29m (7ft 6in)

Multiple Rocket Launchers

MLRS

The Vought Multiple Launch Rocket System (MLRS) had its origins in a 1976 feasibility study into what was known as a General Support Rocket System. Following trials the Vought system was chosen and entered service with the US Army in 1982. These Self-Propelled Launcher Loaders on the chassis of the M2 Infantry Fighting Vehicle carry two pods of six rounds each. These rounds might consist of fragmentation bomblets, anti-tank mines, chemical warheads or mine-dispensing munitions. The Vought MLRS was licensed to the UK, France, Italy, West Germany and the Netherlands for production. It saw action during the 1991 Gulf War, when Allied MLRS batteries tore large holes in Iraqi defence lines prior to the ground offensive to free Kuwait.

Country of origin:	USA
Crew:	3
Weight:	25,191kg (55,420lb)
Dimensions:	length 6.8m (22ft 4in); width 2.92m (9ft 7in); height 2.6m (8ft 6in)
Range:	483km (302 miles)
Armour:	classified
Armament:	two rocket pod containers, each holding six rockets
Powerplant:	one Cummings VTA-903 turbo-charged eight-cylinder diesel engine developing 500hp 373kW)
Performance:	maximum road speed 64km/h (40mph); fording 1.1m (3ft 7in); vertical obstacle 1m (3ft 4in); trench 2.29m (7ft 6in)

Valkiri

South Africa began development of an indigenous multiple rocket launcher in 1977 as a counter to the various Soviet systems in service with neighbouring African countries. The Valkiri entered service in 1981, deployed in batteries of eight, to be used against guerrilla camps, troop concentrations and soft-skinned vehicle convoys. Mounted on a 4 x 4 SAMIL truck chassis, the full 24-round complement could be fired in 24 seconds, with a 10-minute reloading time. Highly mobile and with minimal launch signature, the Valkiri proved an ideal weapon for cross-border raids and counter-insurgency work, especially as the system could be easily camouflaged to resemble a standard truck. Each of the rockets the system fired had a maximum range of 22km (13.67 miles).

Country of origin:	South Africa
Crew:	2
Weight:	6440kg (14,168lb)
Dimensions:	length 5.41m (17ft 9in); width 1.985m (6ft 6in), height 3.2m (10ft 6in)
Range:	650km (406 miles)
Armour:	none
Armament:	24 127mm rocket-launcher tubes
Powerplant:	one six-cylinder diesel engine developing 120hp (89kW)
Performance:	maximum road speed 80km/h (50mph); fording 0.5m (1ft 7in); vertical obstacle 0.6m (1ft 11in); trench 0.6m (1ft 11in)

Multiple Rocket Launchers

Walid

The Egyptian Army has relied in the main on copies of Soviet-produced multiple rocket launcher systems, reflecting the heavy Russian influence in the country in the 1950s and 1960s. However, since Egypt has moved closer to the West, a number of indigenous programmes have been initiated, in particular the Sakr-18 and Sakr-30 Multiple Rocket Launchers, as well as a specialised system for laying down smoke screens. Based on the Walid 4 x 4 armoured personnel carrier, a full salvo of D-3000 rockets is able to produce a smoke screen 1000m (3280ft) long, lasting for up to 15 minutes, sufficient to cover most activities on the battlefield. The same system can be mounted onto a T-62 tank. The rockets are carried in a ready-to-launch position (there is also a six-round version).

Country of origin:	Egypt
Crew:	2
Weight:	unknown
Dimensions:	length 6.12m (20ft); width 2.57m (8ft 5in); height 2.3m (7ft 6in)
Range:	800km (500 miles)
Armour:	8mm (0.31in)
Armament:	12 80mm rocket-launcher tubes
Powerplant:	one diesel engine developing 168hp (125kW)
Performance:	maximum road speed 86km/h (54mph); fording 0.8m (2ft 7in); vertical obstacle 0.5m (1ft 7in)

Type 70

The Type 63 was developed in the late 1950s. It consisted of three rows of four barrels. For firing the wheels were removed and the launcher was supported by two legs at the front, with a spade attached at the rear to absorb recoil. It could be fired independently, or mounted on a 4 x 4 truck chassis, this version being known as the Type 81. A smaller version was developed for use by airborne forces, which could be broken down for transport by men or horses. The Type 63 has seen extensive combat service around the world, being used by the Mujahideen in Afghanistan, by the North Vietnamese in Vietnam, by the Iranians in the Iran-Iraq War and by the PLO against the Israelis. The Type 70 rocket launcher, shown above and specified below, uses components of the YW 531C armoured personnel carrier.

Country of origin:	China
Crew:	2
Weight:	12,600kg (27,720lb)
Dimensions:	5.4m (17ft 9in); width 3m (9ft 9in); height 2.58m (8ft 6in)
Range:	500km (312 miles)
Armour:	10mm (0.39in)
Armament:	12 107mm rocket-launcher tubes
Powerplant:	one V-8 diesel engine developing 320hp (238kW)
Performance:	maximum road speed 65km/h (38mph); fording amphibious; vertical obstacle 0.6m (1ft 11in); trench 2m (6ft 6in)

Marder II

By 1941, the PzKpfw II was becoming obsolete. However, the production line was still in operation, so in order not to waste resources, the decision was taken to convert the chassis to a tank destroyer to tackle the large numbers of Soviet tanks on the Eastern Front. The standard Pak 40 anti-tank gun was mounted on the PzKpfw II's chassis. The combination of firepower and mobility worked well and the Marder II as it was known remained in production until 1944, with 1217 being made. The Marder II saw action in all theatres, particularly on the Eastern front, where some were later equipped with infrared systems for night-fighting. The Marder II proved an effective and versatile weapon and was the most widely used German self-propelled gun of World War II.

Country of origin:	Germany
Crew:	3 or 4
Weight:	11,000kg (24,200lb)
Dimensions:	length 6.36m (20ft 10.4in); width 2.28m (7ft 5.8in); height 2.20m (7ft 2.6in)
Range:	190km (118 miles)
Armour:	10mm (0.39in)
Armament:	one 7.5cm Pak 40/2 gun; one 7.92mm MG34 machine gun
Powerplant:	one Maybach HL 62 petrol engine developing 140hp (104.4kW)
Performance:	maximum road speed 40km/h (24.8mph); fording 0.9m (2ft 11in); vertical obstacle 0.42m (1ft 4in); trench 1.8m (5ft 11in)

Hetzer

Most tank destroyer conversions of existing tank chassis were rather cumbersome and lacked finesse in design. In contrast, the various Sturmgeschütz artillery vehicles had proved very effective tank killers, so it was decided to produce a light tank destroyer along the lines of a Sturmgeschütz. Based on the PzKpfw 38(t) chassis, the new Hetzer was put into production in 1943. Small, well-protected, with good mobility and able to knock out all but the heaviest tanks, the Hetzer was a tremendous success. By the time the factories were overrun in May 1944, 1577 had been built, including flame-thrower and recovery versions. The Czech Army took over production of the Hetzer after World War II and exports were still in service with the Swiss in the 1970s.

Country of origin:	Germany
Crew:	4
Weight:	14,500kg (31,900lb)
Dimensions:	length 6.20m (20ft 4.1in); width 2.50m (8ft 2.4in); height 2.10m (6ft 10.7in)
Range:	250km (155 miles)
Armour:	10-60mm (0.39-2.36in)
Armament:	one 7.5cm Pak 39 gun; one 7.92mm MG34 machine gun
Powerplant:	one Praga AC/2800 petrol engine developing 150-160hp (111.9-119.3kW)
Performance:	maximum road speed 39km/h (24.2mph); fording 0.9m (2ft 11in); vertical obstacle 0.65m (2ft 1in); trench 1.3m (4ft 3.2in)

Jagdpanzer IV

Experience during 1942 suggested that the Sturmgeschütz vehicles would have to be upgunned if their role as tank destroyers was to continue. The armament of the Panther was selected, and while modifications were made to the Sturmgeschütz III to allow for this upgrade, the Panther gun was fitted to the chassis of the PzKpfw IV. Known as the Jagdpanzer IV, the first production models appeared in 1943. With a low silhouette and well-protected hull, the Jagdpanzer IV soon proved popular with crews, especially as the armament proved sufficient to knock out almost any enemy tank encountered. Under Hitler's instructions, some were later fitted with the more powerful L/70 gun, but the extra weight resulted in less mobility. A total of 1139 were produced between December 1943 and March 1945.

Country of origin:	Germany
Crew:	4
Weight:	25,800kg (56,933lb)
Dimensions:	length 8.58m (28ft 1.8in); width 2.93m (9ft 7.4in); height 1.96m (6ft 5.2in)
Range:	214km (133 miles)
Armour:	11-80mm (0.43-3.14in)
Armament:	one 7.5cm Pak 39 gun; two 7.92mm MG34 machine guns
Powerplant:	one Maybach HL 120 petrol engine developing 265hp (197.6kW)
Performance:	maximum road speed 35km/h (22mph); fording 1.2m (3ft 11in); vertical obstacle 0.6m (23.6in); trench 2.3m (7ft 6.6in);

Nashorn

In an effort to get sizeable numbers of tank destroyers into service on the Eastern Front, the Germans embarked on a series of hurried improvisations. A special weapon-carrier vehicle based on the PzKpfw IV chassis was adapted to take the 8.8cm Pak 43 gun. The first of these so-called Nashorns entered service in 1943. The Nashorn was a high vehicle which was difficult to conceal, a problem increased by poor armour with only the driver being fully protected. It was therefore used as a long-range weapon, in contrast to most other tank destroyers. Some 433 were built before production ceased in 1944. The powerful gun made the Nashorn a potent battlefield weapon, but it was too bulky for its prescribed role and only the lack of anything better kept it in production in Germany.

Country of origin:	Germany
Crew:	5
Weight:	24,400kg (53,680lb)
Dimensions:	length 8.44m (27ft 8.3in); width 2.86m (9ft 4.6in); height 2.65m (8ft 8.3in)
Range:	210km (130.5 miles)
Armour:	10-30mm (0.39-1.18in)
Armament:	one 8.8cm Pak 43 gun; one 7.92mm MG34 machine gun
Powerplant:	one Maybach HL 120 petrol engine developing 265hp (197.6kW)
Performance:	maximum road speed 40km/h (24.8mph); fording 0.8m (2ft 7.5in); vertical obstacle 0.6m (23.6in); trench 2.3m (7ft 6.6in)

Elefant

The Elefant stemmed from the Porsche design for the PzKpfw VI Tiger. Henschel was awarded the contract for the new tank, but it was decided to use the Porsche design as a tank destroyer. Hitler demanded that the new vehicle be ready for the 1943 offensive on the Russian Front, so development was rather hurried. As a result many broke down in their first action at the Battle of Kursk, and the lack of proper armour and ponderous mobility made them easy targets for Soviet gunners in the battle. In addition, the lack of machine guns meant that there was no defence against Soviet troops disabling them with explosive charges in close-quarter combat. The survivors were withdrawn to Italy, where unreliability and lack of spares ensured their continued ineffectiveness.

Country of origin:	Germany
Crew:	6
Weight:	65,000kg (143,000lb)
Dimensions:	length 8.128m (26ft 8in); width 3.378m (11ft 1in); height 2.997m (9ft 10in)
Range:	153km (95 miles)
Armour:	50-200mm (1.97-7.87in)
Armament:	one 8.8cm Pak 43/2 gun
Powerplant:	two Maybach HL 120 TRM V-12 petrol engines each developing 530hp (395.2kW)
Performance:	maximum road speed 20.1km/h (12.5mph); fording 1.0m (3ft 4in); vertical obstacle 0.8m (31.5in); trench 2.65m (8ft 3in)

Jagdpanther

The Jagdpanther was one of the first purpose-built tank destroyers, as opposed to a hasty tank-conversion. Using the Panther chassis, the prototype was demonstrated to Hitler in October 1943, who named it the Jagdpanther himself. The vehicle was superb. Fast, well-armoured and mounting a powerful gun, the Jagdpanther became one of the most famous of all World War II vehicles, able to knock out almost any tank it encountered. A machine gun and anti-magnetic mine paint helped with close-quarter defence. On all European fronts, the Jagdpanther became feared. Fortunately for the Allies, planned production levels were never reached, and by the time the factories were overrun in April 1945, only 382 had been completed, mainly due to the disruption caused by Allied bombing raids.

Country of origin:	Germany
Crew:	5
Weight:	46,000kg (101,200lb)
Dimensions:	length 9.90m (32ft 5.8in); width 3.27m (10ft 8.7in); height 2.715m (8ft 10.9in)
Range:	160km (99.4 miles)
Armour:	80-120mm (3.15-4.72in)
Armament:	one 8.8cm Pak 43/3 gun; one 7.92mm MG34 machine gun
Powerplant:	one Maybach HL 230 petrol engine developing 600-700hp (447.4-522kW)
Performance:	maximum road speed 55km/h (34.2mph); fording 1.7m (5ft 7in); vertical obstacle 0.9m (35in); trench 1.9m (6ft 3in)

Tank Destroyers

L.40

The Italians were ahead of tactical thinking in one aspect of armoured vehicle production, when they developed one of the first tank destroyers in the late 1930s. This thinking proved useful when it was realised that their light tanks were of little combat value in North Africa in 1941. The chassis of the Semovente M 40 was fitted with a Böhler 47mm gun, one of the hardest hitting anti-tank weapons of its day. Around 280 of the tank destroyer vehicles were produced, and they fared adequately against Allied armour from 1942 onwards. Pressed into service by the Germans after the Italian surrender in 1943, the vehicle was unsuited for much of the Italian terrain and saw little action. Many had their armament removed and were converted into mobile command posts.

Country of origin:	Italy
Crew:	2
Weight:	6500kg (14,300lb)
Dimensions:	length 4.00m (13ft 1.5in); width 1.92m (6ft 3.6in); height 1.63m (5ft 4.2in)
Range:	200km (124 miles)
Armour:	6-42mm (0.23-1.65in)
Armament:	one Böhler 47mm gun or 8mm Breda modelo 38 machine gun
Powerplant:	one SPA 18D four-cylinder petrol engine developing 68hp (50.7kW)
Performance:	maximum road speed 42.3km/h (26.3mph); fording 0.8m (2ft 7in); vertical obstacle 0.8m (2ft 7in); trench 1.7m (5ft 7in);

M.41

The M 41 was the only heavy tank destroyer produced by Italy during World War II. Using the chassis of the M 14/41 tank, designers mounted a powerful anti-aircraft gun on the vehicle. Designed to operate at long range, the M 41 was not considered to require armour protection. The first production vehicles appeared in 1941, but only 48 were ever built, mainly because Italy's industrial plant was limited, but also because the gun was required for regular anti-aircraft duties. The M 41 proved effective in the open spaces of North Africa, but after being seized by the Germans after the Italian surrender proved to have little value in the mountainous terrain of Italy, where few tanks could operate. Most were therefore used as long-range artillery.

Country of origin:	Italy
Crew:	2 (on gun)
Weight:	17,000kg (37,400lb)
Dimensions:	length 5.205m (17ft 0.9in); width 2.20m (7ft 2.6in); height 2.15m (7ft 0.6in)
Range:	200km (124 miles)
Armour:	none
Armament:	one 90mm cannon
Powerplant:	one SPA 15-TM-41 eight-cylinder petrol engine developing 145hp (108.1kW)
Performance:	maximum road speed 35.5km/h (22mph); fording 1.0m (3ft 3in); vertical obstacle 0.9m (35.4in); trench 2.1m (6ft 10.7in)

Tank Destroyers

M10

During the period immediately before its entry into World War II, the US Army developed a concept to defeat fast-moving armoured formations using powerfully armed tank destroyers deployed *en masse*. The M10 was a product of this concept. Based on the M4 Sherman tank chassis and using the M7 gun, developed from an anti-aircraft weapon, the M10 was lightly armed as it was not intended for close-quarter combat. Production ran from September to December 1942, with nearly 5000 being produced. The concept of separate tank destroyer battalions was soon proved ineffective, and thus most M10s were used more as assault forces. The M10 continued in service until the end of the war, but its large and bulky nature and the diminishing effect of its gun reduced its usefulness.

Country of origin:	USA
Crew:	5
Weight:	29,937kg (65,861lb)
Dimensions:	length 6.83m (22ft 5in); width 3.05m (10ft 0in); height 2.57m (8ft 5in)
Range:	322km (200 miles)
Armour:	12-37mm (0.47-1.46in)
Armament:	one 76.2mm M7 gun; one 12.7mm Browning machine gun
Powerplant:	two General Motors six-cylinder diesel engines each developing 375hp (276.6kW)
Performance:	maximum road speed 51km/h (32mph); fording 0.91m (3ft); vertical obstacle 0.46m (18in); trench 2.26m (7ft 5in)

M18

Whereas most tank destroyers of World War II were converted tanks, the M18 Hellcat was designed for the role from the outset. Development began in 1942 and the first production models appeared in 1943, over 2500 being produced before October 1944. The M18 proved to be one of the best US tank destroyers of the war. Much smaller than the M10, it carried a more powerful gun and was considerably faster, in fact being the fastest tracked vehicle of the war, a good power-to-weight ratio providing excellent agility and acceleration. More importantly, it was able to hold its own on the battlefield. Despite their success, the decline of enthusiasm for specialist tank destroyer units led to the M18 being used more as assault guns and artillery towards the end of the war.

Country of origin:	USA
Crew:	5
Weight:	17,036kg (37,557lb)
Dimensions:	length 6.65m (21ft 10in); width 2.87m (9ft 5in); height 2.58m (8ft 5.5in)
Range:	169km (105 miles)
Armour:	9-25mm (0.35-0.98in)
Armament:	one 76.2mm M1A1 gun; one 12.7mm machine gun
Powerplant:	one Continental R-975 C1 radial petrol engine developing 340hp (253.5kW)
Performance:	maximum road speed 88.5km/h (55mph); fording 1.22m (4ft); vertical obstacle 0.91m (3ft); trench 1.88m (6ft 2in)

Tank Destroyers

Archer

The Archer stemmed from a British decision to increase anti-tank gun calibres from 57mm to 76.2mm. The new guns were too heavy for tanks then in existence. An interim solution was found by adapting the Valentine tank chassis for use as a tank destroyer. The first production Archer, as the new vehicle was known, appeared in March 1943, but it was October 1944 before the Archer saw any action. Initial worries about the rear-facing gun proved groundless. The low silhouette was ideal for ambushes, and the rear-facing gun meant that the vehicle could be driven away quickly without having to turn round, thus avoiding retaliation. In total 655 were produced by the end of World War II, and the Archer continued in service with the British until the mid-1950s.

Country of origin:	UK
Crew:	4
Weight:	16,257kg (35,765lb)
Dimensions:	length 6.68m (21ft 11in); width 2.76m (9ft 0.5in); height 2.25m (7ft 4.5in)
Range:	225km (140 miles)
Armour:	8-60mm (0.31-2.36in)
Armament:	one 17-pounder gun; one 0.303in Bren gun
Powerplant:	one General Motors 6-71 six-cylinder diesel engine developing 192hp (143.2kW)
Performance:	maximum road speed 32.2km/h (20mph); fording 0.91m (3ft); vertical obstacle 0.84m (2ft 9in); trench 2.36m (7ft 9in)

T-34/100 Tank Destroyer

More than 84,000 T-34 medium tanks were made by the Soviet Union and many went on to be sold to Soviet-friendly nations during the Cold War. The T-34/100 was an Egyptian tank destroyer variant of the T-34. Utilizing the T-34 chassis, the Egyptians modified the turret with armour plate extensions and added a recoil mechanism. The gun was a late-war Soviet 100mm (3.9in) BS-3 (M1944) anti-tank/field gun, which protuded greatly over the hull of the vehicle, creating an effect described as 'barrel hang'. At the tip of the gun was a double-barrelled muzzle brake to reduce further the gun's recoil. Lacking the heavier armour protection of more recent tanks, the T-34/100 was mainly used in a defensive role from the 1973 Yom Kippur War onwards.

Country of origin:	USSR/Egypt
Crew:	4
Weight:	(40,000kg; 88,185lbs)
Dimensions:	length: 6m (19ft 7in); width: 3m (9ft 9in); height: 3m (9ft 10in)
Range:	360km (223 miles)
Armour:	n/k
Armament:	one 1000mm (3.9in) BS-3 anti-tank gun
Powerplant:	one 372kW (493hp) V-2 V12 diesel engine
Performance:	maximum road speed 55km/h (33mph)

Tank Destroyers

Hornet Malkara

The Hornet Malkara was developed in the 1950s to provide a long-range anti-tank capability. The vehicle was essentially a modified Humber one-tonne (0.98 tons) 4 x 4 truck chassis with a Malkara missile launcher mounted on the back. It was designed specifically to be dropped by parachute. The operator fired the missile from the cab and controlled it by means of a joystick attached to a wire unreeling from the missile sights, along which were sent electronic signals. The missile carried the largest warhead ever fitted to an anti-tank guided weapon even in modern times, and could destroy any tank in service at that time. It continued in service until being replaced by the Ferret Mk 5 in the 1970s. Although crude, it was an indicator of the way anti-tank weapons would develop towards the end of the century.

Country of origin:	UK
Crew:	3
Weight:	5700kg (12,540lb)
Dimensions:	length 5.05m (16ft 7in); width 2.22m (7ft 3.5in); height 2.34m (7ft 8in)
Range:	402km (250 miles)
Armour:	8-16mm (0.31-0.62in)
Armament:	two Malkara anti-tank missiles
Powerplant:	one Rolls-Royce B60 Mk 5A six-cylinder petrol engine developing 120hp (89kW)
Performance:	maximum road speed 64km/h (40mph); trench not applicable

Austro-Daimler

Developed in 1904, the Austro-Daimler armoured car was the first military application of four-wheel drive. Typical of the period, it combines a standard car chassis with crude bolt-on armour, in the Austro-Daimler's case 4mm (0.16in) thick. The engine was situated in the front of the vehicle with the driver sitting just behind using a viewing slit in the frontal armour for visibility. Combat potential was provided by a Maxim machine gun or, in later models, two Schwarzlose machine guns mounted in the turret over the rear section of the vehicle. Although the Austro-Daimler gave a respectable on- and off-road performance (by turn-of-the-century standards) the vehicle never entered into military service.

Country of origin:	Austria
Crew:	4
Weight:	2500kg (5500lb)
Dimensions:	length (hull): 4.86m (15.94ft); width: 1.76m (5.77ft); height: 2.74m (8.99ft)
Range:	250km (150 miles)
Armour:	4mm (0.16in)
Armament:	one 7.92mm (0.31in) Maxim MG or two 7.92mm (0.30in) Schwarzlose MGs
Powerplant:	Daimler 4-cylinder petrol, developing 40hp (30kW)
Performance:	maximum road speed: 45km/h (28mph)

Austin-Putilov

The Austin-Putilov was a British design, though mostly produced and used in Russia. The Russians took the basic chassis (all that could be supplied by the over-stretched British production lines) and modified it considerably to cope with the harsh Russian conditions, including later replacing the rear wheels with tracks and adding additional armour and rear steering. Both in terms of numbers and performance, the Austin-Putilov was the most important armoured car the Russians possessed during World War I. Many also saw action in the internal fighting surrounding the October revolution and afterwards in the Russian Civil War. After 1918 some saw service with the Polish Army, with a number being sold to Japan. It was an extremely rugged vehicle.

Country of origin:	UK/Russia
Crew:	5
Weight:	5200kg (11,440lb)
Dimensions:	length 4.88m (16ft 0in); width 1.95m (6ft 4.75in); height 2.40m (7ft 10.5in)
Range:	200km (125 miles)
Armour:	8mm (0.315in)
Armament:	two Maxim machine guns
Powerplant:	one 50hp (37.3kW) Austin petrol engine
Performance:	maximum speed 50km/h (31mph)

Rolls-Royce

In 1914, the Royal Naval Air Service noted how the Belgians were using armoured cars to carry out raids on the advancing German Army. They decided to convert some of the Rolls-Royce Silver Ghost cars in their possession. The conversion was a success, and the Admiralty gave permission for an official armoured car based on the Silver Ghost chassis. With strengthened suspension and added armour, the Rolls-Royce saw service all over the world from March 1915, notably in Africa and the Arabian peninsula, where they proved to have excellent cross-country mobility. They were most at home in terrain where they could roam far and wide. They continued in service until being replaced in British Army service in 1922, although some were used in India well into World War II.

Country of origin:	UK
Crew:	3 or 4
Weight:	3400kg (7480lb)
Dimensions:	length 5.03m (16ft 6in); width 1.91m (6ft 3in); height 2.55m (8ft 4.5in)
Range:	240km (150 miles)
Armour:	9mm (0.35in)
Armament:	Vickers 0.303in machine gun
Powerplant:	one 40/50hp (30/37.3kW) Rolls-Royce petrol engine
Performance:	maximum road speed 95km/h (60mph)

Lanchester

Originally designed to support air bases and retrieve downed pilots, the Lanchester was the most numerous armoured car in service after the Rolls-Royce by the end of 1914. A year later they were formed into armoured car squadrons. The engine of the original car was retained, but the hull was much modified. The army took control of operations at the end of 1915 and decided to use the Rolls-Royce as the standard armoured car, Lanchesters being phased out of service. However, many were sent with navy crews to the Russians, with whom they served with some distinction in terrain as varied as Persia, Romania and Galicia. Reliable and fast, they spearheaded armoured columns and were used for reconnaissance before being shipped back to the UK.

Country of origin:	UK
Crew:	4
Weight:	4700kg (10,340lb)
Dimensions:	length 4.88m (16ft); width 1.93m (6ft 4in); height 2.286m (7ft 6in)
Range:	290km (180 miles)
Armour:	unknown
Armament:	one Vickers 0.303in machine gun
Powerplant:	one 60hp (45kW) Lanchester petrol engine
Performance:	maximum speed 80km/h (50mph)

Autoblindo Mitragliatrice Lancia Ansaldo IZ

Based on the Lancia IZ truck, the IZ armoured car was quite an advanced design for its day. With a turret-mounted machine gun and later a further small turret on top with an additional machine gun, the vehicle had considerable firepower. Steel rails protruded over the bonnet for cutting wire (a feature that reflected the experience of World War I for European armies). Little used by the Italians in the mountainous fighting against the Austro-Hungarian Army, many were sent to North Africa for policing duties. Total production by 1918 was around 120, and after World War I some were sent to Albania where they formed the sole armoured force of that country for many years. Some were even used by the Italians in the Spanish Civil War, though by this time they were very outdated.

Country of origin:	Italy
Crew:	6
Weight:	3700kg (8140lb)
Dimensions:	length 5.40m (17ft 8.66in); width 1.824m (6ft 0in); height with single turret 2.40m (7ft 10.5in)
Range:	300km (186 miles)
Armour:	9mm (0.35in)
Armament:	two machine guns
Powerplant:	one 35/40hp (26/30kW) petrol engine
Performance:	maximum speed 60km/h (37mph)

Autoblindé Peugeot

Based on a commercial model, the first Peugeot armoured car was a rather hasty improvisation which appeared in 1914. Improvements followed quickly in terms of armament and firepower. With the development of trench warfare following the first year of World War I, there was a limited role for the Peugeot, since being confined to roads they could do little more than patrol rear areas. They were used to contain the German breakthrough of March 1918, being more suited to this type of fluid warfare, but their role was mainly overshadowed by the newly emerging tanks. The few Peugeots still in service at the end of World War I were handed over to the Polish Army, where they remained in service for some years, seeing action against the Russians.

Country of origin:	France
Crew:	4 or 5
Weight:	4900kg (10,780lb)
Dimensions:	length 4.8m (15ft 9in); width 1.80m (5ft 11in); height 2.80m (9ft 2.25in)
Range:	140km (87 miles)
Armour:	unknown
Armament:	one 37mm gun
Powerplant:	one 40hp (30kW) Peugeot petrol engine
Performance:	maximum speed 40km/h (25mph)

Daimler/15

In late 1914, the companies Daimler, Büssing and Ehrhardt were commissioned to develop a prototype armoured car for Germany. Because of other production commitments, Daimler was not able to field its prototype until December 1915, but following testing, prototype models of the Daimler/15 went on to serve on all fronts with reasonable success. The Daimler/15 consisted of an all-wheel-drive car chassis with an armoured structure of Krupp riveted chromium-nickel stainless steel plates. Dual tyres at the rear and sand rims on the front wheels prevented the vehicle sinking into soft ground. Armament was provided by three machine guns. In many ways the Daimler/15's carrying capacity of 10 men made it an incipient APC.

Country of origin:	Germany
Crew:	10
Weight:	9800kg (21,600lb)
Dimensions:	length: 5.61m (18.4ft); width: 2.03m (6.66ft); height: 3.85m (12.63ft)
Range:	250km (150 miles)
Armour:	not known
Armament:	three 7.92mm (0.31in) MG
Powerplant:	one Daimler Model 4-cylinder petrol, developing 80hp (60kW)
Performance:	maximum road speed: 38km/h (24mph)

Pavesi 35 PS

The Pavesi 35 PS emerged from Italian inter-war experiments as an alternative to tracked armoured vehicles. It was developed by the agricultural vehicle company Pavesi-Tolotti of Milan, and consisted of a small armoured car driven by four outsize spoked wheels. Each wheel had a 1.55m (5.09ft) diameter with broad metal rims for powerful cross-country movement. The clearance provided by the wheels was 0.75m (2.46ft) and trenches of 1.4m (4.6ft) width could be crossed. Armament was provided by a single machine gun mounted in the central rotating turret, and later experiments incorporated a 57mm (2.24in) cannon. In use until the late 1920s, it was manufactured in later years by the Fiat company.

Country of origin:	Italy
Crew:	2
Weight:	5000kg (11,000lb)
Dimensions:	length 4m (13.12ft); width 2.18m (7.15ft); height 2.2m (7.22ft)
Range:	not available
Armour:	not available
Armament:	one 8mm (0.31in) MG
Powerplant:	one Pavesi 4-cylinder petrol, developing 35hp (26kW)
Performance:	maximum road speed 30km/h (19mph)

Daimler DZVR 1919

The Daimler DZVR was one of several German vehicles created after the end of World War I under the terms of the Treaty of Versailles. Inter-war Germany required security vehicles to police internal civil unrest and problems on its eastern borders, and 38 DZVR vehicles were ordered for this purpose. The DZVR was based on the chassis of the KD1 artillery tractor, and 1000 of these vehicles were left over from the war. Armour plate, 12mm (0.47in) thick, encased the six-man crew compartment, and a revolving turret at the top held a searchlight. During the 1920s, the searchlight was replaced by a Maxim machine gun. The DZVR remained in police use until the early 1940s.

Country of origin:	Germany
Crew:	6
Weight:	10,500kg (23,200lb)
Dimensions:	length 5.9m (19.36ft); width 2.1m (6.89ft); height 3.1m (10.17ft)
Range:	150km (100 miles)
Armour:	(Steel) 12mm (0.47in)
Armament:	two 7.92mm (0.31in) Maxim MGs
Powerplant:	one Daimler M1574 4-cylinder petrol, developing 100hp (75kW)
Performance:	maximum road speed 43km/h (27mph)

Berliet VUDB

The Lyons based French firm Berliet began producing armoured cars between the wars. Its initial output included the Berliet VUDB, a 4x4 vehicle which saw extensive use in France's North African colonies. The VUDB was produced as a prototype in 1929. In tests, French military officers were impressed with its range of over 350km (220 miles) and speed of 75km/h (47mph), both ideally suited to operations in the North African terrain. In 1930, it entered into service with the French Army. Another 12 vehicles were also built for the Belgian Army. The VUDB featured windows which could be shuttered with armoured plates when under fire, and was armed with three machine guns.

Country of origin:	France
Crew:	3
Weight:	4000kg (8800lb)
Dimensions:	length 4.3m (14.11ft); width 1.96m (6.43ft); height 2.15m (7ft)
Range:	350km (220 miles)
Armour:	not available
Armament:	three machine guns
Powerplant:	one Berliet 6-cylinder petrol, developing 49hp (37kW)
Performance:	maximum road speed 75km/h (47mph)

M39 Armoured Car

The M39 was produced by the DAF company in the build-up to World War II, resisting Dutch Army requests to license-build British armoured cars. It was a well-made 6x4 armoured car with an all-welded hull, a rear-mounted Ford Mercury V8 engine and a well-sloped glacis plate. A useful set of driving controls at the rear of the vehicle allowed the rear machine-gunner to control the vehicle in reverse in an emergency. At the front of the hull, two small wheels prevented the forward edge of the glacis plate digging into the ground on rough terrain. After the fall of the Netherlands in 1940, M39s were pressed into German service as Pz. SpWg L202h.

Country of origin:	Netherlands
Crew:	5
Weight:	6000kg (13,200lb)
Dimensions:	length 4.75m (15.58ft); width 2.03m (6.66ft); height 2.16m (7.09ft)
Range:	320km (200 miles)
Armour:	12mm (0.47in)
Armament:	one 37mm (1.46in) cannon; three 8mm (0.31in) MGs
Powerplant:	one Ford Mercury V8 petrol, developing 95hp (71kW)
Performance:	maximum road speed 60km/h (37mph)

Armoured Cars
SdKfz 231

Although the SdKfz 231 was originally developed at the Kazan test centre in the Soviet Union, the vehicle was a German design intended for German use. A 6 x 4 Daimler-Benz truck chassis was used as the basis, and an armoured hull and turret added. Production ran from 1932-35, by which time around 1000 had been built. The hull was too heavy for the chassis, though, which resulted in poor cross-country performance. However, they were used on roads to good effect during the occupation of Czechoslovakia and the campaigns in Poland and France in 1939-40, their appearance alone having a good propaganda value. Their greatest achievement was to provide an invaluable training vehicle for the German Army's development during the 1930s.

Country of origin:	Germany
Crew:	4
Weight:	5700kg (12,540lb)
Dimensions:	length overall 5.57m (18ft 6.75in); width 1.82m (5ft 11.5in); height 2.25m (7ft 4.5in)
Range:	250km (150 miles)
Armour:	8mm (0.31in)
Armament:	one 20mm KwK 38 cannon; one coaxial 7.62mm machine gun
Powerplant:	one Daimler-Benz, Bussing-NAG or Magirus water-cooled petrol engine developing between 60 and 80hp (45 and 60kW)
Performance:	maximum road speed 65km/h (40mph); fording 0.6m (2ft)

SdKfz 234

The SdKfz 234 was produced by Büssing-NAG in response to a 1940 German Army requirement for an 8 x 8 armoured car suitable for operations in hot climates. More streamlined than the earlier 231 series and with thicker armour, the 234's excellent performance ensured its place as probably the best vehicle of its type to see service in World War II with any army. The most famous model was the 234/2 Puma, which used the turret intended for the Leopard light tank. This gave sufficient firepower to deal with most enemy reconnaissance armour encountered. The quality of the vehicle may be judged by the fact that, despite its high cost of manufacture, the vehicle was the only reconnaissance vehicle kept in production by the starved German war industry in 1945.

Country of origin:	Germany
Crew:	4
Weight:	11,740kg (25,828lb)
Dimensions:	length 6.80m (22ft 3.66in); width 2.33m (7ft 6.5in); height 2.38m (7ft 9.5in)
Range:	1000km (625 miles)
Armour:	5-15mm (0.19-0.59in)
Armament:	one 20mm KwK 30/50mm KwK 39/1 cannon; one coaxial 7.92mm machine gun
Powerplant:	one Tatra Model 103 diesel engine developing 210hp (157kW)
Performance:	maximum road speed 85km/h (53mph); fording 1.2m (3ft 10.75in); vertical obstacle 0.5m (1ft 7.75in); trench 1.35m (4ft 5in)

Armoured Cars

SdKfz 222

When the Nazis began to rearm the German Army in the mid-1930s, a request was made for a series of light armoured cars based on a standard chassis. The demanding requirements could not be met by adapting commercial models, so a new design was produced. The first production SdKfz 222 appeared in 1938, and thereafter became the standard armoured reconnaissance car of the Wehrmacht. A reliable and popular vehicle, the SdKfz 222 served the army well during the Blitzkrieg against Poland and France in 1939-40, and later in North Africa. However, its restricted range, made evident in the latter theatre, proved problematic during the invasion of the Soviet Union in 1941. That said, it remained in German service in western Europe until the end of World War II.

Country of origin:	Germany
Crew:	3
Weight:	4800kg (10,560lb)
Dimensions:	length 4.80m (14ft 8.5in); width 1.95m (6ft 4.75in); height 2.00m (6ft 6.75in) with grenade screen
Range:	300km (187 miles)
Armour:	14.5-30mm (0.6-1.2in)
Armament:	one 20mm KwK 30 cannon; one 7.92 MG34 machine gun
Powerplant:	one Horch/Auto-Union V8-108 water-cooled petrol engine developing 81hp (60kW)
Performance:	maximum road speed 80km/h (50mph); fording 0.6m (24in)

Panhard et Levassor Type 178

The Panhard 178 was designed in the mid-1930s as a 4x4 armoured reconnaissance vehicle for the French Army. Its most common armament was a single 25mm (0.98in) cannon or two 7.5mm (0.29in) machine guns. French production of the Panhard 178 ended with the German occupation in 1940. The Germans, however, were impressed with the design and used large numbers under the designation Panzerspähwagen P 204(f). Some of these were turned into anti-aircraft platforms by fitting them with 37mm (1.46in) anti-aircraft guns. French production of the 178 recommenced in August 1944 after the liberation of Paris, though with a larger turret and 47mm (1.85in) gun. These endured in French Army service until 1960.

Country of origin:	France
Crew:	4
Weight:	8300kg (18,300lb)
Dimensions:	length 4.8m (15.74ft); width 2.01m (6.59ft); height 2.33m (7.64ft)
Range:	300km (190 miles)
Armour:	18mm (0.7in)
Armament:	one 25mm (0.98in) cannon; one 7.5mm (0.29in) MG
Powerplant:	one Renault 4-cylinder petrol, developing 180hp (134kW)
Performance:	maximum road speed 72km/h (45mph); fording 0.6m (2ft); gradient 40 percent; vertical obstacle 0.3m (1ft); trench 0.6m (2ft)

Light Armoured Car M8

The M8 was developed following American observation of operational trends in Europe in 1940-41. A design by Ford was accepted for service, and production of the M8 began in March 1943, continuing until the last month of World War II, by which time over 11,000 had been built. Despite British worries over its thin armour (it was known to British forces rather unkindly as the Greyhound), the M8 was a superb vehicle and widely used. A low silhouette made concealment easy and the vehicle had excellent cross-country mobility, plus the firepower to deal with any similar enemy vehicle (the 37mm gun was a tank armament at the beginning of the war). The M8 became the most important American armoured car, not just because of its excellent qualities, but because it was produced in enormous quantities.

Country of origin:	USA
Crew:	4
Weight:	7940kg (17,468lb)
Dimensions:	length 5.00m (16ft 5in); width 2.54m (8ft 4in); height 2.248m (7ft 4.5in)
Range:	563km (350 miles)
Armour:	8mm (0.31in)
Armament:	one 37mm gun; one 7.62 coaxial machine gun; one 12.7mm anti-aircraft machine gun
Powerplant:	one Hercules JDX six-cylinder petrol engine developing 110hp (82kW)
Performance:	maximum road speed 89km/h (55mph); fording 0.61m (24in); vertical obstacle 0.3m (12in)

T17E1 Staghound

The Staghound was developed in response to a US Army requirement for a Light Armoured Car in the early years of World War II. However, by the time the vehicle was ready for production, the American requirement had changed and so all production models were shipped to British and Commonwealth forces. The vehicle was fast, manoeuvrable and easy to operate and maintain, faring well in its initial combat in Italy in 1943, where small and nimble vehicles were at a premium. The Mk II was fitted with a tank howitzer and the Mk III with the turret from a Crusader tank. Other variants included a mine-clearer and command car. A well-liked vehicle, the Staghound continued in service with the British for several years after the end of World War II.

Country of origin:	USA
Crew:	5
Weight:	13,920kg (30,624lb)
Dimensions:	length 5.486m (18ft 0in); width 2.69m (8ft 10in); height 2.36m (7ft 9in)
Range:	724km (450 miles)
Armour:	8mm (0.31in)
Armament:	one 37mm gun; three 7.62mm machine guns
Powerplant:	two GMC six-cylinder petrol engines each developing 97hp (72kW)
Performance:	maximum speed 89km/h (55mph); fording 0.8m (2ft 8in); vertical obstacle 0.533m (1ft 9in)

Armoured Cars

Marmon Herrington

In 1938, the South African government ordered the development of an armoured car, based on foreign components but to be assembled in South Africa. The chassis and engine were made by Ford, the transmission by Marmon Herrington in the USA and the armament was imported from the UK. At the time it was first produced, the Marmon Herrington was the only armoured car available to British and South African forces in any numbers, and it saw extensive service in the Western Desert in the campaign against Rommel's *Afrika Korps*. Well-liked and sturdy, the vehicle was surprisingly effective despite light armour and armament, being relatively easy to maintain under operational conditions. The vehicles were much modified to suit local conditions, and were fitted in the field with many different weapons.

Country of origin:	South Africa
Crew:	4
Weight:	6000kg (13,200lb)
Dimensions:	length 4.88m (16ft); width 1.93m (6ft 4in); height 2.286m (7ft 6in)
Range:	322kg (200 miles)
Armour:	12mm (0.47in)
Armament:	one Vickers 7.7mm machine gun; one Boys 0.55in anti-tank rifle; one Bren Gun
Powerplant:	one Ford V-8 petrol engine
Performance:	maximum speed 80.5km/h (50mph)

Humber Mk I

Numerically, the Humber was the most important British armoured car of World War II, a total of 5400 being produced. Based on a pre-war wheeled light tank design by Guy, the Humber was initially fitted only with machine guns, which meant it was outgunned by the opposition. It was later upgunned and was used in North Africa from 1941 onwards, and wherever British troops were in action thereafter. Variants included a special radio carrier, known as Rear Link vehicle, which was fitted with a dummy gun, and an anti-aircraft version fitted with a special machine gun mounting. The vehicle gave excellent service, and was still being used by some armies in the Far East in the early 1960s. Like most British-produced armoured vehicles, the Humber was rugged, reliable and operationally sound.

Country of origin:	UK
Crew:	3 (4 in Mk III)
Weight:	6850kg (15,070lb)
Dimensions:	length 4.572m (15ft); width 2.184m (7ft 2in); height 2.34m (7ft 10in)
Range:	402km (250 miles)
Armour:	14.5-30mm (0.6-1.2in)
Armament:	one 15mm gun; one 7.92mm Besa machine gun
Powerplant:	one Rootes six-cylinder water-cooled petrol engine developing 90hp (77kW)
Performance:	maximum speed 72km/h (45mph); fording 0.6m (2ft); vertical obstacle 0.533m (1ft 9in); trench 1.22m (4ft)

Armoured Cars

Daimler Mk I

The Daimler armoured car was based on the same design as the Daimler scout car. Outwardly similar, it weighed almost twice as much and had a two-man turret. Work began in August 1939, but initial problems meant that the first production vehicles did not appear until April 1941. A total of 2694 were built. The turret was the same as that designed for the Tetrarch light airborne tank. The vehicle was equipped with hydraulic disc brakes, one of the earliest vehicles to be fitted with the system. First employed in North Africa, the vehicle established itself as an excellent addition to reconnaissance units, despite its limited combat capability, giving good all-round performance and reliability. The Daimler continued to serve for many years after the end of World War II.

Country of origin:	UK
Crew:	3
Weight:	7500kg (16,500lb)
Dimentions:	length 3.96m (13ft); width 2.44m (8ft); height 2.235m (7ft 4in)
Range:	330km (205 miles)
Armour:	14.5-30mm (0.6-1.2in)
Armament:	one 2-pounder gun; one Besa 7.92mm coaxial machine gun
Powerplant:	one Daimler six-cylinder petrol engine developing 95hp (71kW)
Performance:	maximum speed 80.5km/h (50mph); fording 0.6m (2ft); vertical obstacle 0.533m (1ft 9in); trench 1.22m (4ft)

Daimler Scout Car

When the British Army was forming its first armoured divisions in the late 1930s, a requirement was issued for a 4 x 4 scout car for reconnaissance purposes. The Daimler Scout Car was the result. Entering production just prior to the start of World War II, it was still being made at the end of the war and was to prove one of the most successful reconnaissance vehicles in use by any army in the war. Its inconspicuous nature and excellent mobility compensated for lack of armour and armament, deficiencies that are not necessarily fatal to vehicles that move fast on the battlefield and do not stand and engage in firefights with enemy armour. The folding roof was removed on later models, as experience showed it was rarely used operationally and gave minimal cover in any case.

Country of origin:	UK
Crew:	2
Weight:	3000kg (6600lb)
Dimensions:	length 3.226m (10ft 5in); width 1.715m (5ft 7.5in); height 1.50m (4ft 11in)
Range:	322km (200 miles)
Armour:	14.5-30mm (0.6-1.2in)
Armament:	one 0.303in Bren machine gun
Powerplant:	one Daimler six-cylinder petrol engine developing 55hp (41kW)
Performance:	maximum speed 88.5km/h (55mph); fording 0.6m (2ft); vertical obstacle 0.533m (1ft 9in); trench 1.22m (4ft)

Autoblinda 41

The Autoblinda had its origins in a dual requirement by the Italians for an armoured car for the cavalry divisions and a high-performance car for use in policing Italy's numerous African colonies. The Autoblinda 40 was produced to meet both these needs. The Autoblinda 41 was fitted with the turret of the L 6/40 light tank, complete with its 20mm cannon. This was a more effective combination, and thus production centred on this version. The vehicle could be adapted for desert use, with special sand tyres, and could also be adapted to run on railway tracks, being extensively used in this capacity for anti-partisan duties in the Balkans. One of the most numerous Italian armoured cars of World War II, the vehicle also saw action in the Western Desert and Tunisia.

Country of origin:	Italy
Crew:	4
Weight:	7500kg (16,500lb)
Dimensions:	length 5.20m (17ft 1.5in); width 1.92m (6ft 4.5in); height 2.48m (7ft 11.5in)
Range:	400km (248 miles)
Armour:	6-40mm (0.23-1.57in)
Armament:	one 20mm Breda cannon; two 8mm machine guns
Powerplant:	one SAP Abm 1 six-cylinder water-cooled inline petrol engine developing 80hp (60kW)
Performance:	maximum road speed 78km/h (49mph); fording 0.7m (28in); vertical obstacle 0.3m (12in); trench 0.4m (1ft 4in)

BA-10

The BA-10 was built on the chassis of the GAZ-AAA commercial truck (which was modified and reinforced to cope with the extra weight) and first appeared in 1932. It was a bulky, functional piece of equipment whose World War I ancestry was evident from its outmoded appearance. Despite its weight, the BA-10 proved well-suited to the terrain and distances of the Soviet Union, and its main armament was as good as many tanks. The Germans captured large numbers of the vehicle after the invasion of Russian in June 1941 and used them for anti-partisan duties both in the USSR and in the Balkans, a role in which it excelled. Those that remained in Soviet hands were replaced in frontline service after 1942 and stripped down, to be used as armoured personnel carriers.

Country of origin:	USSR
Crew:	4
Weight:	7500kg (16,500lb)
Dimensions:	length 4.70m (15ft 5in); width 2.09m (6ft 10.5in); height 2.42m (7ft 11.25in)
Range:	320km (199 miles)
Armour:	up to 25mm (0.98in)
Armament:	one 37mm/45mm gun; one 7.62mm machine gun
Powerplant:	one GAZ-M 14-cylinder water-cooled petrol engine developing 85hp (63kW)
Performance:	maximum speed 87km/h (54mph); fording 0.6m (1ft 11in); vertical obstacle 0.38m (1ft 3in); 0.5m (1ft 7in)

Armoured Cars

BA-64

With the onset of the German–Soviet war in 1941, the Red Army discovered that most of its armoured cars were inadequately armoured and outclassed by German vehicles. The BA-64 was an attempt to remedy these problems. Its armoured plates were angled steeply to increase bullet and missile deflection, the suspension was strengthened over previous vehicles to improve off-road durability and it had bullet-proof tyres and bullet-proof glass in the driver's observation visor. Most significantly, it had four-wheel drive which enabled it to climb 30-degree slopes. Armament remained light – a single 7.62mm (0.3in) Degtyarev machine gun mounted in the turret.

Country of origin:	Russia/Soviet Union
Crew:	2
Weight:	2360kg (5200lb)
Dimensions:	length: 3.67m (12.04ft); width: 1.52m (4.99ft); height: 1.88m (6.17ft)
Range:	560km (350 miles)
Armour:	(Steel) 4–15mm (0.16–0.59in)
Armament:	one 7.62mm (0.3in) machine gun
Powerplant:	one GAZ-MM 4-cylinder petrol, developing 54hp (40kW)
Performance:	maximum road speed: 80km/h (50mph)

Daimler Ferret Mk 2/3

Following a 1946 British requirement for a scout car, the first prototype of the Ferret was built by Daimler in 1949. Thereafter the ferret remained in production until 1971, by which time nearly 4500 vehicles had been built for over 30 countries. The Mk I version was armed simply with a machine gun mounted on its open top. By the time the vehicle had reached the Mk V stage, the vehicle had acquired a turret and the ability to mount the Swingfire anti-tank missile. It also carried smoke dischargers. Metal channels were often carried on the front of the hull to facilitate movement across ditches or sandy terrain. The Ferret was still in use with the British Army in the 1980s, and had been widely used around the world for internal security roles.

Country of origin:	UK
Crew:	2
Weight:	4400kg (9680lb)
Dimentions:	length 3.835m (12ft 10in); width 1.905m (6ft 3in); height 1.879m (6ft 2in)
Range:	306km (191 miles)
Armour:	8-16mm (0.31-0.63in)
Armament:	one 7.62mm machine gun
Powerplant:	one Rolls-Royce six-cylinder petrol engine developing 129hp (96kW)
Performance:	maximum road speed 93km/h (58mph); fording 0.914m (3ft); vertical obstacle 0.406m (1ft 4in); trench 1.22m (4ft)

Panhard EBR/FL-11

The distinction between the FL-10 and the FL-11 variants of the Panhard EBR lies in the turrets. The FL-10 turret is fitted to the AMX-13 light tank, and features a 75mm (2.95in) cannon fed from two revolver-type magazines, each holding six rounds. Gun elevation is +13 degrees and depression is -6 degrees. The FL-11 turret is specific to the EBR. Initial FL-11 models were armed with a 75mm (2.95mm) gun conventionally loaded and had an elevation of +15 degrees and a depression of -10 degrees. However, in the 1960s, the FL-11 turret received a new 90mm (3.54in) gun. The gun had the advantage of firing fin-stabilized rounds with better accuracy and an armour penetration of up to 320mm (12.6in).

Country of origin:	France
Crew:	4
Weight:	13,500kg (29,800lb)
Dimensions:	length (gun forwards) 6.15m (20.17ft); width 2.42m (7.94ft); height 2.32m (7.61ft)
Range:	600km (370 miles)
Armour:	40mm (1.57in)
Armament:	one 75mm (2.95in) cannon or one 90mm (3.54in); two 7.5mm (0.29in) or 7.62mm (0.3in) machine guns
Powerplant:	one Panhard 12-cylinder petrol, developing 200hp (149kW)
Performance:	maximum road speed 105km/h (65mph); fording 1.2m (3.9ft); gradient 60 percent; vertical obstacle 0.4m (1.3ft)

Saladin

The chassis of the Saladin is similar to that of the Saracen armoured personnel carrier, which was developed at the same time. Because of the requirements of the British forces in Malaya during the 1950s, the Saracen was given precedence and it was not until 1958 that production of the Saladin began. By 1972, when production ceased, 1177 had been built and they had been widely exported, particularly to Africa and the Middle East. A few Saladins were still in service with the British in Cyprus in the 1980s. One interesting feature was that all six wheels were powered, with steering on the front four, so the vehicle could be driven even if one wheel was blown off. Alvis has modified some Saladins, replacing the petrol engine with a more fuel-efficient model.

Country of origin:	UK
Crew:	3
Weight:	11,500kg (25,300lb)
Dimensions:	length 5.284m (17ft 4in); width 2.54m (8ft 4in); height 2.93m (9ft 7.3in)
Range:	400km (250 miles)
Armour:	8-32mm (0.31-1.25in)
Armament:	one 76mm gun; one 7.62mm coaxial machine gun; one 7.62mm anti-aircraft machine gun
Powerplant:	one eight-cylinder petrol engine developing 170hp (127kW)
Performance:	maximum road speed 72km/h (45mph); fording 1.07m (3ft 6in); vertical obstacle 0.46m (1ft 6in); trench 1.52m (5ft 0in)

Panhard AML 90

The Panhard Automitrailleuse Légère (AML) is currently in service worldwide in over 40 countries. It was originally developed in the late 1950s, entering service in 1961. The AML is a versatile vehicle, lighter in weight than the EBR, simple to maintain and drive, and easily modified with new turret configurations. Typical of French armoured cars, the basic AML with a H90 or Lynx turret has heavy firepower – a 90mm (3.54in) gun. Other turret versions include the HE-60-7 fitted with a 60mm (2.36in) mortar and the S 530 featuring twin 20mm (0.78in) anti-aircraft guns. The AML is also manufactured under licence in South Africa where it is called the Eland.

Country of origin:	France
Crew:	3
Weight:	5500kg (12,100lb)
Dimensions:	length (gun forwards) 5.11m (16ft 9in); width 1.97m (6ft 5in); height 2.07m (6ft 9in)
Range:	600km (370 miles)
Armour:	8–12mm (0.31–0.47in)
Armament:	one 90mm (3.54in) cannon; one 7.62mm (0.3in) coaxial MG; two smoke grenade launchers
Powerplant:	one Panhard Model 4 HD 4-cylinder petrol engine
Performance:	maximum speed 90km/h (56mph); fording 1.1m (3ft 7in); gradient 60 percent; vertical obstacle 0.3m (1ft); trench 0.8m (2ft 7in)

Eland Armoured Car

The Eland armoured car is actually the French Panhard AML, though modified for the South African Army. Production of the Mk 1 Eland began in 1962. Since then, the vehicle has been steadily updated. Marks 2 to 4 had improved brakes, fuel delivery and clutch. The Mark 5 of 1972 introduced a South African diesel engine and suspension and tyres more suited to the South African terrain. The latest model, the Mk 7, entered service in 1979. It features a turbo diesel engine of standard commercial type, thus reducing the logistical problems of finding spare parts. It works in permanent 4x4 mode and is armed with either a 90mm (3.54in) gun or a 60mm (2.36in) breech-loading mortar.

Country of origin:	South Africa
Crew:	3
Weight:	5300kg (11,700lb)
Dimensions:	length 3.79m (12ft 5in); width 2.02m (6ft 8in); height 1.88m (6ft 2in)
Range:	500km (310 miles)
Armour:	classified
Armament:	one 90mm (3.54in) gun; or one 60mm (2.36in) breech-loading mortar; two 7.62mm (0.3in) machine guns
Powerplant:	one 4-cylinder turbo diesel, developing 103hp (79kW)
Performance:	maximum road speed 85km/h (53mph)

Armoured Cars

AMX-10

In the 1950s, the French Army issued a requirement for a replacement for the standard Panhard EBR armoured car with a more powerful armament. The first prototype of the AMX-10 was completed in 1971, and the vehicle entered service in 1979. The two main drawbacks were cost (being more expensive to build than some main battle tanks) and level of sophistication, particularly important for a conscript army. The suspension could be adjusted for different types of terrain and the fire-control system was the most sophisticated installed in any vehicle of its class, with a laser rangefinder, computer and low-light TV system and complete amphibious capability. The internal layout is conventional, with driver at the front, a three-man turret and engine and transmission at the rear.

Country of origin:	France
Crew:	4
Weight:	15,400kg (33,880lb)
Dimensions:	length 9.15m (30ft 0.25in); width 2.95m (9ft 8in); height 2.68m (8ft 9.5in)
Range:	800km (500 miles)
Armour:	8-32mm (0.31-1.25in)
Armament:	one 105mm gun; one 7.62mm machine gun
Powerplant:	one Baudouin Model 6F 11 SRX eight-cylinder diesel developing 260hp (194kW)
Performance:	maximum road speed 85km/h (53mph); fording amphibious; vertical obstacle 0.70m (2ft 3.25in); trench 1.15m (3ft 9in)

Cougar

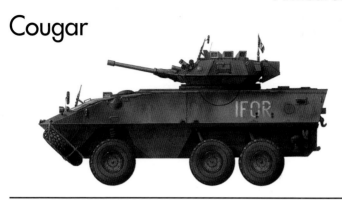

The Cougar is essentially a Swiss MOWAG Piranha produced by the Diesel Division of General Motors of Canada between 1979 and 1982. Three basic variants exist. The Cougar Gun Wheeled Fire Support Vehicle (WFSV) is fitted with the turret of an Alvis Scorpion with 76mm (2.99in) gun. An APC variant, the Grizzly APC, has the capacity to carry three crew and six other personnel. Finally, the Husky Wheeled Maintenance and Recovery Vehicle features a roof-mounted crane for engineering projects. All variants are amphibious. The Cougars are still in service today with the Canadian Army, though most have been upgraded to an 8x8 configuration. Specifications relate to the Wheeled Fire Support Vehicle variant.

Country of origin:	Canada
Crew:	3
Weight:	9526kg (21,004lb)
Dimensions:	length 5.97m (19ft 7in); width 2.53m (8ft 4in); height 2.62m (8ft 7in)
Range:	602km (374 miles)
Armour:	10mm (0.39in)
Armament:	one 76.2mm (3in) cannon; one 7.62mm (0.3in) coaxial machine gun
Powerplant:	one Detroit Diesel 6V-53T 6-cylinder diesel developing 215hp (160kW)
Performance:	maximum road speed 102km/h (63mph); fording amphibious; gradient 60 percent; vertical obstacle 0.5m (1ft 7in)

EGESA EE-9 Cascavel

The EE-9 was produced by the Brazilian armaments company ENGESA in the early 1970s as an attempt to replace obsolete US 6x6 M8 Greyhound armoured cars. It is itself a 6x6 vehicle, and originally utilized the M8 turret on the Mk I Cascavel. Subsequent indigenous models featured an ENGESA turret with 90mm (3.54in) gun, though the Mk II export model had the French Hispano-Suiza H-90 turret. Most modern Cascavels are fitted with computerized fire-control systems and laser range-finders. NBC protection is a further option. The Cascavel also has excellent lightweight armour developed by ENGESA and the University of São Paulo in a joint programme.

Country of origin:	Brazil
Crew:	3
Weight:	13,400kg (29,500lb)
Dimensions:	length (with gun) 6.2m (20ft 4in); width 2.59m (8ft 6in); height 2.68m (8ft 9in)
Range:	880km (545 miles)
Armour:	16mm (0.62in)
Armament:	one 90mm (3.54in) cannon; one coaxial MG, some versions one 12.7mm (0.5in) or 7.62mm (0.3in) turret-mounted machine gun
Powerplant:	one Detroit Diesel 6V-53 6-cylinder diesel
Performance:	maximum road speed 100km/h (60mph); fording 1m (3ft 4in); gradient 60 percent; vertical obstacle 0.6m (2ft)

Fiat-OTOBREDA Type 6616 Armoured Car

The Type 6616 began its production life in 1972 as a joint venture between Fiat and OTO-Melara. Despite the end of production in the late 1980s, it is still in service today with the Italian Carabinieri and several Latin American and African countries. The three-man crew are seated in an amphibious all-welded steel armoured hull with a maximum thickness of 8mm (0.31in). Vision is provided in a 200-degree arc by five vision blocks, while the driver has a dedicated hatch and a roof aperture for a night-vision periscope. Standard main armament is a Rheinmetall 20mm (0.78in) Mk 20 Rh 202 cannon. A further option is a 90mm (3.54in) gun mounted in an OTOBREDA OTO T 90 CKL turret.

Country of origin:	Italy
Crew:	3
Weight:	8000kg (17,600lb)
Dimensions:	length 5.37m (17ft 7in); width 2.5m (8ft 2in); height 2.03m (6ft 8in)
Range:	700km (450 miles)
Armour:	(Steel) 6–8mm (0.24–0.31in)
Armament:	one Rheinmetall 20mm (0.78in) Mk 20 Rh 202 cannon; one 7.62mm (0.3in) coaxial machine gun
Powerplant:	one Fiat Model 8062.24 supercharged diesel engine
Performance:	maximum road speed 100km/h (75mph); fording amphibious; gradient 60 percent; vertical obstacle 0.45m (1ft 6in)

Armoured Cars

FV 721 Fox

The FV 721 Fox entered service with the British Army in 1973, having undergone development since 1965 as the replacement for the Ferret armoured car. Armament received a major upgrade from the Ferret's machine guns. The 30mm (1.18in) Rarden cannon was introduced, which when loaded with Armour-Piercing Discarding-Sabot Tracer (APDST) rounds can destroy light armoured vehicles at 1000m (3300ft) and even penetrate weaker armour points of MBTs. The Fox is a quick vehicle with a road speed of 104km/h (65mph) and can be made fully amphibious by fitting an external float screen. The wheels then power and steer the vehicle through the water.

Country of origin:	UK
Crew:	3
Weight:	6120kg (13,500lb)
Dimensions:	length (gun included) 5.08m (16ft 8in); width 2.13m (6ft 11in); height 1.98m (6ft 6in)
Range:	434km (270 miles)
Armour:	aluminium (details classified)
Armament:	one 30mm (1.18in) Rarden cannon; one coaxial 7.62mm (0.3in) machine gun; two x 4 smoke grenade launchers
Powerplant:	one Jaguar XK 4.2-litre 6-cylinder petrol engine
Performance:	max speed 104km/h (65mph); fording 1m (3ft 4in)/amphibious; gradient 46 percent; vertical obstacle 0.5m (1ft 7in); trench 1.22m (4ft)

Panhard ERC

The first Panhard ERC appeared in 1977, based on technology developed for a 1970 French Army requirement but not used. Production began in 1979 and the vehicle was quickly exported to Nigeria, Argentina and Iraq amongst others, with the French using it as part of their Rapid Intervention Force. The vehicle was fully amphibious, with six-wheel drive capability. One interesting feature was that the centre wheels could be raised or lowered to deal with different types of terrain. Other features included laser rangefinder, night vision equipment, nuclear, biological and chemical (NBC) defence systems and a land navigation system, essential for desert operations. The Panhard is fully amphibious, being propelled in the water by its wheels.

Country of origin:	France
Crew:	3
Weight:	7400kg (16,280lb)
Dimensions:	length 7.693m (25ft 2.75in); width 2.495m (8ft 2.25in); height 2.254m (7ft 4.75in)
Range:	800km (500 miles)
Armour:	10mm (0.39in)
Armament:	one 90mm gun; one 7.62mm coaxial machine gun
Powerplant:	one Peugeot V-6 petrol engine developing 166hp (116kW)
Performance:	maximum road speed 100km/h (62mph); fording amphibious; vertical obstacle 0.80m (2ft 7.5in); trench 1.10m (3ft 7.5in)

BRDM-2

The BRDM-2 entered service in the early 1960s, being seen in public for the first time in 1966. It was an improvement in every way over its predecessor, the BRDM-1, with better range, armour and armament (including an improved missile launcher), as well as heightened performance. The vehicle was equipped with two extra wheels which could be lowered to assist cross-country mobility, as well as a tyre-pressure regulation system. Standard equipment includes decontamination kit and winch. Variants include a chemical warfare reconnaissance vehicle and a turretless command vehicle. The chassis forms the basis for the SA-9 missile launcher. The BRDM-2 has been exported to almost 40 countries and has seen combat in Angola, Egypt, Syria, Vietnam and Iraq.

Country of origin:	UK
Crew:	4
Weight:	11,500kg (25,300lb)
Dimentions:	length 5.75m (18ft 10.3in); width 2.35m (7ft 8.5in); height 2.31m (7ft 7in)
Range:	750km (465 miles)
Armour:	2-14mm (0.08-0.55in)
Armament:	six 'Sagger' ATGWs; one 7.62mm coaxial machine gun; one 14.5mm KPV machine gun
Powerplant:	one V-8 petrol engine developing 140hp (104kW)
Performance:	maximum road speed 100km/h (62mph); fording amphibious; vertical obstacle 0.40m (1ft 3.75in); trench 1.25m (4ft 1in)

Spähpanzer 2 Luchs

Having previously relied on American or European imports, West Germany began to develop a range of indigenous armoured vehicles during the 1960s. From 1975, Thyssen Henschel began production of an 8 x 8 armoured reconnaissance vehicle – the Luchs – completing 408 before 1978. Too expensive for significant export success, the vehicle was well-armoured and came with a range of extras such as power steering to reduce driver fatigue, night vision, a nuclear, biological and chemical (NBC) system and pre-heating for the engine, essential for winter operations. Fully amphibious, the vehicle has an exceptional operational range. In the water it is powered by two propellers mounted at the rear of the vehicle. The turret has full power traverse through 360 degrees.

Country of origin:	West Germany
Crew:	4
Weight:	19,500kg (42,900lb)
Dimensions:	length 7.743m (25ft 4.75in); width 2.98m (9ft 9.3in); height (including anti-aircraft machine gun) 2.905m (9ft 6.3in)
Range:	800km (500 miles)
Armour:	classified
Armament:	one 20mm cannon; one 7.62 machine gun
Powerplant:	one Daimler-Benz OM 403 A 10-cylinder diesel engine developing 390hp (291kW)
Performance:	maximum road speed 90km/h (56mph); fording amphibious; vertical obstacle 0.60m (1ft 11.7in); trench 1.90m (6ft 3in)

ERC 90 F4 Sagiae

Production of the Panhard ERC 90 F4 Sagiae armoured car began in 1979, and it remains in production today with successful export sales. The Panhard ERC 90 F4 Sagiae belongs to the French Army, whose own particular configuration of the ERC features a long-barrelled 90mm (3.54in) cannon. Twenty rounds of 90mm ammunition are stored on board. The latest ERCs have computerized fire control, full NBC systems, and a computerized land-navigation system. The ERC hull can be fitted with various turrets. The ERC 90 F1 Lynx, for example, has the Hispano-Suiza Lynx 90mm (3.54in) turret as used on the AML armoured car. An 81mm (3.19in) mortar and 20 or 25mm (0.78 or 0.98in) twin anti-aircraft turrets are also available.

Country of origin:	France
Crew:	3
Weight:	8300kg (18,300lb)
Dimensions:	length (gun forwards) 7.69m (25ft 3in); width 2.5m (8ft 2in); height 2.25m (7ft 5in)
Range:	700km (430 miles)
Armour:	10mm (0.39in)
Armament:	one 90mm (3.54in) cannon; or one 7.62mm (0.3in) coaxial machine guns; two x 2 smoke grenade launchers
Powerplant:	one Peugeot V6 petrol, developing 155hp (116kW)
Performance:	maximum speed 100km/h (62mph); fording amphibious; gradient 60 percent; vertical obstacle 0.8m (2ft 7in); trench 1.1m (3ft 7in)

Renault VBC 90

The Renault Vehicule Blindé de Combat 90 (VBC 90) was produced mainly for export markets. Sales of the vehicle have, however, been disappointing and it is currently in service with only the French gendarmerie and Omani military forces. Unlike many other nations, France commonly fits large-calibre guns to its armoured cars. The VBC 90 mounts a powerful 90mm (3.54in) weapon on its Giat TS-90 turret. Computerized fire-control systems and laser range-finders are also fitted, and today, VBC 90s in service have NBC technology and night-vision devices. Production of the VBC 90 is complete and no variants other than the basic model have been produced.

Country of origin:	France
Crew:	3
Weight:	13,500kg (29,800lb)
Dimensions:	length (gun forwards) 8.8m (28ft 10in); width 2.5m (8ft 2in); height 2.55m (8ft 4in)
Range:	1000km (620 miles)
Armour:	classified
Armament:	one 90mm (3.54in) cannon; one 7.62mm (0.3in) coaxial MG; one 7.62mm (0.3in) turret-mounted MG (option); two x 2 smoke grenade launchers
Powerplant:	one Renault MIDS 06.20.45 turbo diesel, developing 220hp (164kW)
Performance:	max speed 92km/h (57mph); fording 1.2m (3ft 11in); gradient 50 percent; vertical obstacle 0.5m (1ft 7in); trench 1m (3ft 4in)

Armoured Cars

VEC Cavalry Scout Vehicle

The Vehículo de Exploracíon de Caballereía (VEC) emerged in prototype stage in the late 1970s, before entering service with the Spanish Army in 1980. It is a fairly standard armoured car design, with an all-welded aluminium armour providing protection across its frontal section against small arms ammunition up to 7.62mm (0.3in) armour-piercing rounds. The VEC holds five crew comfortably; the engine is set at the rear to conserve interior space. The vehicle is defended by either a 20mm (0.78in) cannon in a FIAT-OTO Melara turret, or a 25mm (0.98in) Oerlikon cannon in an Oerlikon-Bührle GDB-COA turret. NBC options are available and the VEC is also fully amphibious.

Country of origin:	Spain
Crew:	5
Weight:	13,750kg (30,300lb)
Dimensions:	length 6.1m (20ft); width 2.5m (8ft 2in); height 3.3m (10ft 10in)
Range:	800km (500 miles)
Armour:	aluminium (details classified)
Armament:	one 20mm (0.78in) cannon; or one 25mm (0.98in) cannon; one coaxial 7.62mm (0.3in) MG; two x 3 smoke grenade launchers
Powerplant:	(latest models) one Scania DS9 diesel, developing 310hp (231kW)
Performance:	maximum road speed 103km/h (64mph); fording amphibious; gradient 60 percent; vertical obstacle 0.6m (2ft); trench 1.5m (4ft 11in)

Cardoen Piranha 6x6D

The Chilean Piranha is a Swiss MOWAG Piranha produced under licence by Carlos Cardoen since the early 1980s (FAMAE are also heavily involved with Piranha production). The Swiss and Chilean versions are almost the same, though Cardoen has upgraded its vehicle to a 400-litre (106-gal) fuel capacity instead of the Swiss model's 250 litres (66gal). Though most 6x6 Piranhas in Chile are APCs, a small number are produced as Fire Support Vehicles. These have a Cockerill 90mm (3.54in) MK3 gun mounted on an ENGESA ET-90 90mm turret or a Cardoen 90mm turret. Other trial versions have been fitted with ATGW launchers and even Oerlikon Contraves 20mm (0.78in) GAD-AOA anti-aircraft turrets.

Country of origin:	Chile
Crew:	3 or 4
Weight:	10,500kg (23,200lb)
Dimensions:	length 5.97m (19ft 7in); width 2.5m (8ft 2in); height 2.65m (89ft 8in)
Range:	700km (435 miles)
Armour:	Not available
Armament:	one 90mm (3.54in) cannon; one 12.7mm (0.5in) coaxial MG
Powerplant:	one Detroit Diesel 6V-53T diesel, developing 300hp (224kW)
Performance:	maximum road speed 100km/h (60mph); fording amphibious; gradient 70 percent; vertical obstacle 0.5m (1ft 7in)

OTO Melara R3 Capraia

The R3 Capraia is a heavily armoured Italian reconnaissance vehicle which entered production in 1982. The basic vehicle is 4x4 configuration, with a hull that features welded aluminium armour with a thickness up to 32mm (1.26in), strong enough to deflect small-arms rounds of 7.62mm (0.3in) calibre. Many optional turrets and externally mounted weapons are available for the R3. Seen here is the T20 FA-HS turret fitted with an Oerlikon KAD-B17 20mm (0.78in) cannon. Other turret configurations include the T 7.62 FA (7.62mm (0.3in) machine gun), T 12.7 FA (12.7mm (0.5in) machine gun), T 106x2 FA (twin M40 106mm (4.17in) recoilless rifles) and a TOW turret (mounted launcher for a Hughes TOW ATGW).

Country of origin:	Italy
Crew:	4 or 5
Weight:	3200kg (7100lb)
Dimensions:	length 4.86m (15ft 11in); width 1.78m (5ft 10in); height 1.55m (5ft 1in)
Range:	500km (300 miles)
Armour:	(Aluminium) 32mm (1.26in)
Armament:	(T 20 FA-HS turret) one Oerlikon KAD-B17 20mm (0.78in) cannon
Powerplant:	one Fiat Model 8144.81.200 4-cylinder diesel, developing 95hp (71kW) at 4200rpm
Performance:	maximum road speed 120km/h (75mph); fording amphibious; gradient 75 percent

RPX-90

T he Lohr RPX-90 is a 4x4 armoured car with a powerful Hispano-Suiza CNMP 90mm (3.54in) cannon as standard. This weapon enables it to tackle MBTs and fortified positions at close ranges, though armoured reconnaissance remains its primary role. Other turrets are available for the RPX-90, including variants with 20mm (0.78in) cannon, 60mm (2.36in) mortar and MATRA SATCP surface-to-air missiles. The vehicle has an all-welded steel hull and large low-pressure tyres to give good off-road traction. Wide bulletproof windows at the front provide the driver with broad visibility. These can be shuttered in combat. Despite its boat-like shape, the RPX-90 is not amphibious.

Country of origin:	France
Crew:	3
Weight:	11,000kg (24,300lb)
Dimensions:	length (gun forwards) 7.41m (24ft 4in); width 2.56m (8ft 5in); height 2.54m (8ft 4in)
Range:	1000km (620 miles)
Armour:	classified
Armament:	one 90mm (3.54in) cannon; one 7.62mm (0.3in) coaxial MG
Powerplant:	one BMW 6-cylinder turbo diesel, developing 310hp (231kW)
Performance:	maximum road speed 105km/h (65mph); fording 1.4m (4ft 7in); gradient 40 percent; vertical obstacle 0.6m (2ft)

Rooikat

The Rooikat is one of the world's most potent armoured cars. Its development programme began in 1978, but it took 12 years before it was ready to enter service in 1990. Two main versions are available. The Rooikat 76 has a stabilized 76mm (2.99in) gun, and the Rooikat 105 has an even more powerful 105mm (4.13in) anti-tank gun which can fire six rounds per minute. Such firepower allows the Rooikat to make aggressive seek-and-destroy missions as well as combat reconnaissance. The classified armoured type protects the crew from anti-tank mines and small arms ammunition up to 24mm (0.94in) calibre. All tyres have run-flat inserts – mobility is maintained even with loss of pressure in all eight tyres.

Country of origin:	South Africa
Crew:	4
Weight:	28,000kg (61,700lb)
Dimensions:	length 7.09m (23ft 3in); width 2.9m (9ft 6in); height 2.8m (9ft 2in)
Range:	1000km (620 miles)
Armour:	classified
Armament:	one 76mm (2.99in) gun (Rooikat 76); one 105mm (4.13in) gun (Rooikat 105); one coaxial 7.62mm (0.3in) MG; one turret-mounted 7.62mm (0.3in) MG; two x 4 smoke grenade launchers
Powerplant:	one V-10 diesel engine developing 563hp (420kW)
Performance:	max road speed 120km/h (75mph); fording 1.5m (4ft 11in); gradient 70 percent; vertical obstacle 1m (3ft 4in); trench 2m (6ft 7in)

T-37

The origins of the T-37 are to be found in the 1931 purchase by the USSR of a number of British Carden-Loyd amphibious tanks. The Soviets were duly impressed but realised that the tank was unsuited to fulfil all their requirements. Their version of the British design eventually became the T-37. The first production models appeared in late 1933. A small vehicle with a crew of just two, their buoyancy stemmed from pontoons attached to either side of the hull. Designed mainly for reconnaissance, and with only light armour and armament, they nevertheless were used in a combat role following the German invasion in 1941, where they fared badly and were replaced as quickly as possible. A few were retained for use as light tractors.

Country of origin:	USSR
Crew:	2
Weight:	3200kg (7040lb)
Dimensions:	length 3.75m (12ft 3.6in); width 2.10m (6ft 10.7in); height 1.82m (5ft 11.7in)
Range:	185km (115 miles)
Armour:	3-9mm (0.1-0.4in)
Armament:	one 7.62mm machine gun
Powerplant:	one GAZ AA petrol engine developing 40hp (29.8kW)
Performance:	maximum speed 56.3km/h (35mph); fording amphibious; vertical obstacle 0.787m (2ft 7in); trench 1.879m (6ft 2in)

Amphibious Vehicles

T-40

The T-40 was designed to replace the T-37, whose manifold deficiencies had become painfully apparent by 1938. To speed development, the design included as many automobile components as possible. Flotation tanks were fitted at the rear, giving the vehicle a rather bulky appearance. The T-40 was equipped with very thin armour and fared poorly as a result during the fighting in Finland in 1939. It was thus decided to dispense with the amphibious characteristics and use the vehicle as a land tank. This proved an impractical conversion and its use was minimal after that, seeing some service with armoured formations as a reconnaissance vehicle during 1941 against the Germans. Only around 225 T-40s were ever built, as light tanks were given low priority at that time.

Country of origin:	USSR
Crew:	2
Weight:	5900kg (12,980lb)
Dimensions:	length 4.11m (13ft 5.8in); width 2.33m (7ft 7.7in); height 1.95m (6ft 4.8in)
Range:	360km (224 miles)
Armour:	8-14mm (0.3-0.55in)
Armament:	one 12.7mm machine gun
Powerplant:	one GAZ-202 petrol engine developing 70hp (52.2kW)
Performance:	maximum speed 44km/h (27.3mph); fording amphibious; vertical obstacle 0.70m (2ft 3.6in); trench 3.12m (10ft 2.8in)

Terrapin Mk 1

The Terrapin was the British equivalent of the American DUKW, although never produced on the same scale. It did make a useful contribution, though, during the latter stages of the war, particularly during its first action, being used to open up the water approaches to Antwerp in 1944. The Terrapin had a number of defects, though. Its two engines each drove one side of the vehicle, thus if one engine broke down the Terrapin tended to swing round violently. The centrally located engines split the cargo compartment in two, preventing large loads such as guns or vehicles being carried. Rather slow and easily swamped in rough waters, the Terrapin was adequate but further development was abandoned due to the large numbers of American DUKWs available, an altogether machine.

Country of origin:	UK
Crew:	2
Weight:	12,015kg (26,411lb)
Dimensions:	length 7.01m (23ft); width 2.67m (8ft 9in); height 2.92m (9ft 7in)
Range:	240km (150 miles)
Armour:	8mm (0.31in)
Armament:	none
Powerplant:	two Ford V-8 petrol engines each developing 85hp (63.4kW)
Performance:	maximum land speed 24.14km/h (15mph); maximum water speed 8km/h (5mph); fording amphibious

DD Sherman

The Duplex Drive (DD) Sherman was born from a British concept, designed to allow tanks to float in water during amphibious operations. Development began in 1941, with a collapsible fabric screen and rubber air tubes being fitted to a boat-shaped platform welded onto a Sherman tank. The tank was powered in the water by two rear propellers. Once in shallow water, the screen could be collapsed and the tank was ready for conventional use. The vehicle was rather slow and could only be used in fairly calm waters. However, the Sherman's main gun proved very useful in supporting amphibious landings, in particular those on D-Day in June 1944, and the tank was a nasty surprise for the Germans, whose attempts to develop a similar concept had failed.

Country of origin:	USA
Crew:	5
Weight:	32,284kg (71,025lb)
Dimensions:	length 6.35m (20ft 10in); width 2.81m (9ft 3in); height 3.96m (13ft)
Range:	240km (149 miles)
Armour:	12-51mm (0.47-2in)
Armament:	one 75mm gun; two 0.3in machine guns
Powerplant:	one Ford GAA V-8 petrol engine developing 400 or 500hp (335.6 or 373kW)
Performance:	maximum water speed four knots; fording amphibious; vertical obstacle 0.61m (2ft 0in); trench 2.26m (7ft 5in)

DUKW

Universally known as the 'Duck', the DUKW first appeared in 1942. In essence it was a derivative of the GMC 6 x 6 truck with a boat-shaped hull for buoyancy. The simple design made it easy to operate and maintain and over 21,000 were built before the end of World War II, seeing service with all Allied forces. Designed to carry supplies from ships to the beach, it could in fact travel much farther inland, carrying troops or even light artillery. A number of weapons-carrying versions were produced, including the Scorpion, which could be used as a rocket launcher. Despite limited load-carrying capability and temperamental performance in rough seas, the DUKW was a sturdy and reliable vehicle and has often been described as an Allied war-winner.

Country of origin:	USA
Crew:	2
Weight:	9097kg (20,013lb)
Dimensions:	length 9.75m (32ft 0in); width 2.51m (8ft 2.9in); height 2.69m (8ft 10in)
Range:	120km (75 miles)
Armour:	none
Armament:	basic version – none.
Powerplant:	one GMC Model 270 engine developing 91.5hp (68.2kW)
Performance:	maximum land speed 80km/h (50mph); maximum water speed 9.7km/h (6mph); fording amphibious

Amphibious Vehicles

LVT 2

The LVT 2 was an improvement on the LVT 1, which was a civil design intended for use in the Florida swamps and not really suited for combat. The new vehicle used the engine and transmission of the M3 Light Tank. Initially the engine was mounted at the rear which restricted cargo space, but this was soon solved by moving the engine to the front in later versions. Steering and brake systems were also problematic for inexperienced crews. These vehicles were used widely in the early Pacific campaigns, from Guadalcanal onwards. They also saw action in northwest Europe during the latter stages of the war. Some versions had rocket-launchers, flame-throwers and light cannon, but their main role was to carry ashore the first wave of a landing force.

Country of origin:	USA
Crew:	3
Weight:	17,509kg (38,519lb)
Dimensions:	length 7.95m (26ft 1in); width 3.25m (10ft 8in); height 3.023m (9ft 11in)
Range:	road radius 241km (150 miles); water radius 120.7km (75 miles)
Armour:	12mm (0.47in)
Armament:	one 0.5in and two 0.3in machine-guns
Powerplant:	two Cadillac petrol engines developing a total of 220hp (164.1kW)
Performance:	maximum land speed 27.3km/h (17mph); maximum water speed 9.7km/h (6mph); fording amphibious

LVT (A)

The LVT (A) was an ordinary LVT adapted to mount an M3 light tank turret with a 37mm gun. The intention was that this vehicle should provide fire-support during the initial stages of an amphibious landing, giving a significant punch in the battles to establish a beachhead. It was common for LVT (A)s to fire their 37mm guns while still in the water, a waste considering the amount of naval gunfire which usually accompanied an amphibious landing. However, the 37mm gun proved to be too light for this task and so a 75mm howitzer was installed, mounted in the turret of the M8 Howitzer Motor Carriage. The LVT (A) was used extensively along with the rest of the LVT family during the island-hopping operations in the Pacific in World War II, as well as in parts of northwest Europe with British forces.

Country of origin:	USA
Crew:	2
Weight:	10,800kg (23,760lb)
Dimensions:	length 7.95m (26ft 1in); width 3.25m (10ft 8in); height 3.023m (9ft 11in)
Range:	road radius 241km (150 miles); water radius 120.7km (75 miles)
Armour:	up to 67mm (2.63in)
Armament:	one 37mm cannon (later 75mm howitzer); one 7.62mm machine gun
Powerplant:	two Cadillac petrol engines developing a total of 220hp (164.1kW)
Performance:	maximum land speed 27.3km/h (17mph); maximum water speed 9.7km/h (6mph); fording amphibious

Amphibious Vehicles

LVT 4

The LVT 4 was an improved LVT 2 with the engine moved forward and a ramp added at the rear for easier loading and unloading, giving the LVT 4 the capability to carry cargo such as jeeps and artillery. This was the most prolific of the series with over 8000 produced, four times as many as the LVT 2. Like the LVT 2, the LVT 4 was developed from the pre-war Roebling tractor, used in the Florida Everglades. Propelled in the water by its tracks, one problem was that the flotation chambers gave the vehicle a high silhouette and thus made it an easier target. The British Army received a number of LVTs, designating them as the Buffalo, and these were used for river-crossings in the final stages of the war in Europe, particularly the crossing of the River Rhine in March 1945.

Country of origin:	USA
Crew:	3
Weight:	17,509kg (38,519lb)
Dimensions:	length 7.95m (26ft 1in); width 3.25m (10ft 8in); height 3.023m (9ft 11in)
Range:	road radius 241km (150 miles); water radius 120.7km (75 miles)
Armour:	12mm (0.47in)
Armament:	one 0.5in and two 0.3in machine-guns
Powerplant:	two Cadillac petrol engines developing a total of 220hp (164.1kW)
Performance:	maximum land speed 27.3km/h (17mph); maximum water speed 9.7km/h (6mph); fording amphibious

Type 2 Ka-Mi

Development of the Type 2 began in the 1930s, with efforts to turn the Type 95 Kyu-Go light tank into an amphibious vehicle by adding flotation tanks. The unwieldy results prompted the designers to fit pontoons to the tank to provide buoyancy, retaining the main components of the tank. The new Type 2, as it was designated, went into production in 1942. The most commonly used Japanese amphibious tank, it contained several innovations including radio and telephone intercom system for the crew, as well as an onboard mechanic. It was used mainly for infantry support and often as just a land-based pillbox for island defence by 1944. This diminished their tactical effectiveness, and too few were built by the Japanese war machine to give this impressive design the impact it deserved.

Country of origin:	Japan
Crew:	5
Weight:	with pontoons 11,301kg (24,862lb); without pontoons 9571kg (21,056lb)
Dimensions:	length with pontoons 7.417m (24ft 4in); length without pontoons 4.826m (15ft 10in); width 2.79m (9ft 1.8in); height 2.337m (7ft 8in)
Range:	land radius 199.5km (125 miles); water radius 149.6km (93 miles)
Armour:	6-12mm (0.23-0.47in)
Armament:	one 37mm anti-tank gun; two 7.7mm machine gun
Powerplant:	one six-cylinder air-cooled diesel engine developing 110hp (82kW)
Performance:	maximum land speed 37km/h (23mph); maximum water speed 9.65km/h (6mph); fording amphibious

Land-Wasser-Schlepper

In 1936 the German Army contracted Rheimetall to build a special tractor for amphibious operations, which could tow behind it a cargo trailer also capable of floating. The Land-Wasser-Schlepper was essentially a motor tug fitted with tracks, capable of carrying up to 20 passengers. Its ungainly appearance belied its effective performance. However, it was rather cumbersome on land and suffered from a lack of armour. Even though designed for the calm waters of inland Europe, the project was pursued with enthusiasm while the invasion of England looked possible. After this was cancelled, interest waned and the project was cancelled in turn. Nevertheless, a pre-production series of seven vehicles was produced and some of them went on to serve on the Eastern Front after 1941.

Country of origin:	Germany
Crew:	3 + 20
Weight:	13,000kg (28,600lb)
Dimentions:	length 8.60m (28ft 2.6in); width 3.16m (10ft 4.4in); height 3.13m (10ft 3.3in)
Range:	240km (149 miles)
Armour:	unknown
Armament:	none
Powerplant:	one Maybach HL 120 TRM V-12 engine developing 265hp (197.6kW)
Performance:	maximum road speed 40km/h (24.85mph); maximum water speed unloaded 12.5km/h (7.8mph); fording amphibious

Type 6640A

As the largest manufacturer of wheeled vehicles in Italy, it was no surprise that Fiat was chosen to build an amphibious vehicle, following a requirement for the Italian Home Office for a civil protection and fire-fighting vehicle. The hull was constructed of aluminium for lightness and the vehicle could carry a maximum payload of 2.14 tonnes (two tons). A winch was provided at the rear for cargo loading. Once afloat, the vehicle could be powered either by its wheels or by a propeller, the rudder being coupled to the steering wheel. The Type 6640A bore a striking resemblance, as do many modern amphibious vehicles, to the American DUKW of World War II. Production ended in the early 1980s. Like most modern Italian amphibious vehicles, the Type 6640A was well built.

Country of origin:	Italy
Crew:	2
Weight:	6950kg (15,290lb)
Dimensions:	length 7.30m (23ft 11.4in); width 2.50m (8ft 2.4in); height 2.715m (8ft 10.9in)
Range:	750km (466 miles)
Armour:	4mm (0.16in)
Armament:	none
Powerplant:	one six-cylinder diesel engine developing 117hp (87kW)
Performance:	maximum road speed 90km/h (56mph); maximum water speed with propeller 11km/h (6.8mph) or with wheels 5km/h (3.1mph); fording amphibious; vertical obstacle 0.43m (1ft 5in); trench not applicable

PTS

The PTS entered service with the Soviet Red Army in the mid-1960s. On water, the PTS could carry up to 10 tonnes (9.8 tons) of equipment or 70 men, but the drawback was that the position of the exhaust pipes on top of the cargo compartment tended to allow fumes to blow back onto the troops behind – a potentially fatal flaw. The PTS was the first Soviet amphibious vehicle to have a fully enclosed crew compartment. A PKP boat-shaped trailer was specially developed for the PTS. A variant was used by Poland which mounted a rocket-propelled mine-clearing system in the rear. The PTS was used by most Warsaw Pact countries, Iraq, Syria and also Egypt, which used it to good effect during the Yom Kippur War, during the crossing of the Suez Canal.

Country of origin:	USSR
Crew:	2
Weight:	22,700kg (49,940lb)
Dimensions:	length 11.50m (37ft 8.8in); width 3.30m (10ft 10in); height 2.65m (8ft 8.3in)
Range:	300km (186miles)
Armour:	6-10mm (0.23-0.39in)
Armament:	none
Powerplant:	one V-54P diesel engine developing 359hp (261kW)
Performance:	maximum road speed 42km/h (26mph); maximum water speed 10.6km/h (6.5mph); fording amphibious; vertical obstacle 0.65m (2ft 1.6in); trench 2.5m (8ft 2.4in)

CAMANF

For many years, the Brazilian Marines relied on American DUKWs of World War II vintage for transportation from offshore boats to the beach. By the 1970s, these were becoming difficult to maintain. BVEI began work on a replacement in 1975, and the first production vehicles were delivered towards the end of the decade. The CAMANF is in essence a 6 x 6 F-7000 Ford chassis fitted with a watertight body. It is virtually identical to the DUKW with minor modifications, such as a stronger bow to cope with rougher water, to suit regional requirements. The payload is officially five tonnes (4.9 tons), but this is much reduced in rough waters. The Brazilians made the correct decision in selecting a tried and trusted design, and although the CAMANF is unexceptional, it is a reliable amphibian.

Country of origin:	Brazil
Crew:	3
Weight:	13,500kg (29,700lb)
Dimensions:	length 9.50m (31ft 2in); width 2.50m (8ft 2.4in); height 2.65m (8ft 8.3in)
Range:	430km (267miles)
Armour:	6-10mm (0.23-0.39in)
Armament:	one 12.7mm anti-aircraft machine gun
Powerplant:	one 190hp (142kW) Detroit-Diesel Model 40-54N diesel engine
Performance:	maximum road speed 72km/h (45mph); maximum water speed 14km/h (8.7mph); fording amphibious; vertical obstacle 0.40m (1ft 3.7in); trench not applicable

Amphibious Vehicles

LVTP7

In 1971, FMC completed the first production model of the LVTP7 designed specifically for the US Marine Corps. With an aluminium hull and propelled either by twin-waterjets or its tracks, the vehicle was capable of carrying up to 25 fully equipped troops, forming an important element in US power projection capabilities. The vehicle could be loaded alongside ships through an opening in the roof hatch, although troops usually exited through the rear. The vehicle was widely exported, notably to Argentina where it took part in the Falklands invasion in 1982. It also saw service on peacekeeping duties in Lebanon. Variants included a command vehicle and recovery vessel, and some vehicles in US Marine Corps service have been fitted with Enhanced Applique Armour for extra protection.

Country of origin:	USA
Crew:	3 + 25
Weight:	22,837kg (50,241lb)
Dimensions:	length 7.943m (26ft 0.7in); width 3.27m (10ft 8.7in); height 3.263m (10ft 8.5in)
Range:	482km (300miles)
Armour:	45mm (1.8in)
Armament:	one 12.7mm machine gun; optional 40mm grenade launcher
Powerplant:	one Detroit-Diesel Model 8V-53T engine, developing 400hp (298kW)
Performance:	maximum road speed 64km/h (40mph); maximum water speed 13.5km/h (8.5mph); fording amphibious; vertical obstacle 0.914m (3ft 0in); trench 2.438m (8ft)

LARC-5

The LARC-5 was developed to a US Army requirement for a vehicle capable of transporting cargo from ship to shore and then inland to supply bases. Around 950 were built between 1962 and 1968. The LARC-5 was a fairly basic vehicle with no proper suspension and power steering on the front wheels only. It could carry just under 4.5 tonnes (4.3 tons) of cargo or 20 fully equipped troops between the cabin at the front and the engine at the rear. It was exported to Australia, West Germany and Argentina, seeing action with the latter in the Falklands conflict. The influence of the World War II-vintage DUKW can clearly be seen – testimony to the excellence of the original vehicle. The good range of the LARC-5 is indicative of the more mobile nature of modern warfare when compared to World War II.

Country of origin:	USA
Crew:	1 + 2
Weight:	14,038kg (30,883lb)
Dimensions:	length 10.668m (35ft 0in); width 3.149m (10ft 4in); height 3.034m (9ft 11.4in)
Range:	402km (250miles)
Armour:	none
Armament:	none
Powerplant:	one V8 diesel engine developing 300hp (224kW)
Performance:	maximum road speed 48.2km/h (30mph); maximum water speed 16km/h (10mph); fording amphibious; vertical obstacle about 0.5m (1ft 7.7in); trench not applicable

EKW Bison

Developed originally as a civilian truck for use in underdeveloped regions, the EKW Bison 4 x 4 was first seen in public in 1982, having been adopted for military use. Fully amphibious, the Bison is equipped with side flotation bags and two propellers (which can be traversed through 360 degrees for maximum manoeuvrability), as well as automatically activated bilge pumps. For land use, the Bison has power-assisted steering and a tyre-pressure regulation system for rough terrain, a feature which Soviet designers have been particularly fond of since the end of World War II. The Bison has a fully enclosed forward control cab with the engine to the rear. The engine itself is coupled to a fully automatic transmision with six forward and one reverse gear.

Country of origin:	Germany
Crew:	2
Weight:	16,000kg (35,200lb)
Dimensions:	length 9.34m (30ft 7.7in); width 2.50m (8ft 2.4in); height to cab roof 2.964m (9ft 8.5in)
Range:	900km (559miles)
Armour:	none
Armament:	none
Powerplant:	one V8 air-cooled diesel engine developing 320hp (239kW)
Performance:	maximum road speed 80km/h (49.7mph); maximum water speed 12km/h (7.4mph); fording amphibious; vertical obstacle not available; trench not applicable

SdKfz 2

The SdKfz 2 was developed for use by German infantry and airborne units. It was designed to be an artillery tractor for very light weaponry. Known as the Kettenkrad, the first of these small tractors entered service in 1941. However, by this time German airborne troops were generally being used as regular infantry, so the vehicle's intended role was largely redundant. As a result, the SdKfz 2 was used mainly as a supply vehicle in difficult terrain, where other vehicles could not travel. Their impact was limited by their low cargo capacity and limited production numbers. By 1944, they were seen as an expensive luxury and production ceased. One interesting variant was a high-speed cable-laying vehicle for linking command posts and forward positions.

Country of origin:	Germany
Crew:	3
Weight:	1200kg (2640lb)
Dimensions:	length 2.74m (8ft 11.9in); width 1.00m (3ft 3.4in); height 1.01m (3ft 3.8in)
Range:	100km (62.5 miles)
Armour:	none
Armament:	none
Powerplant:	one Opel Olympia 38 petrol engine developing 36hp (26.8kW)
Performance:	maximum road speed 80km/h (49.7mph)

Maultier

German trucks proved totally unable of operating successfully during the first winter of the Russian campaign in 1941-1942. It was thus decided to produce a low-cost half-track to take over many of the trucks' duties. The Wehrmachtsschlepper could not be produced in sufficient numbers to fulfil this need so Opel and Daimler-Benz chassis were fixed to tracked assemblies from PzKpfw II tanks. The new Maultier as it was known was a reasonable success, although lacking the mobility of 'proper' halftracks. By late 1942, the Maultier was being pressed into service as a launch-vehicle for the Nebelwerfer rocket launcher, with over 3000 conversions being ordered by the German Army. In combat Maultiers were organised into Nebelwerfer brigades.

Country of origin:	Germany
Crew:	3
Weight:	7100kg (15,620lb)
Dimensions:	length 6.00m (19ft 8.2in); width 2.20m (7ft 2.6in); height 2.50m (8ft 6in)
Range:	130km (81.25 miles)
Armour:	8-10mm (0.31-0.39in)
Armament:	one 15cm Nebelwerfer (later versions); one 7.92mm machine gun
Powerplant:	one 3.6-litre six-cylinder petrol engine developing 91hp (68kW)
Performance:	maximum road speed 38km/h (30mph); fording 0.6m (2ft); vertical obstacle 2.0m (6ft 6.7in); trench 1m (3ft 3in)

SdKfz 250/10

The SdKfz 250 was developed following a mid-1930's requirement for a one-tonne (0.98 tons) halftrack to provide mobility for infantry and other units operating with panzer divisions. The first example appeared in 1939 and saw action for the first time in May 1940 during the invasion of France. Production continued until 1944, with later models having redesigned hulls to make manufacture easier and cut down on the amount of raw materials required, as the basic design was rather expensive. Variants included a communications vehicle and mobile observation post, as well as a number of specialised weapons carriers, mounting everything from anti-aircraft guns to anti-tank cannons. The vehicle remained in service until the end of the war proving to be a reliable and popular halftrack.

Country of origin:	Germany
Crew:	6
Weight:	5380kg (11,836lb)
Dimensions:	length 4.56m (14ft 11.5in); width 1.945m (6ft 4.6in); height 1.98m (6ft 6in)
Range:	299km (186 miles)
Armour:	6-14.5mm (0.23-0.6in)
Armament:	one 3.7cm Pak 35/36 anti-tank gun
Powerplant:	one six-cylinder petrol engine developing 100hp (74.6kW)
Performance:	maximum road speed 59.5km/h (37mph); fording 0.75m (29.5in); vertical obstacle 2.0m (6ft 6.7in)

Tracked Infantry Vehicles
SdKfz 11

The first versions of the SdKfz 11 appeared in 1934 and after a series of manufacturing changes, the vehicle entered full production in 1939. Primarily intended as an artillery tractor, it was used initially by 10.5cm howitzer batteries. The vehicle proved so successful that it was later used to tow a wide variety of guns at the expense of heavier purpose-built vehicles, eventually seeing most service with Nebelwerfer batteries to tow the rocket launchers. The vehicle was one of the few to remain in production right through the war, and a number of variants were produced, including two designed specifically for chemical warfare decontamination, but these were not produced in significant numbers as large-scale chemical warfare never occurred during World War II.

Country of origin:	Germany
Crew:	9
Weight:	7100kg (15,620lb)
Dimensions:	length 5.48m (17ft 11.7in); width 1.82m (5ft 11.7in); height 1.62m (5ft 3.8in)
Range:	122km (76 miles)
Armour:	8-14mm (0.31-0.55in)
Armament:	none
Powerplant:	one six-cylinder petrol engine developing 100hp (74.6kW)
Performance:	maximum road speed 53km/h (33mph); fording 0.75m (29.5in); vertical obstacle 2.0m (6ft 6.7in)

Bren Gun
Carrier

The Bren Carrier was more correctly known as the Universal (Bren Gun) Carrier. Produced between 1934 and 1960, it was used to transport a two-man Bren team, though initially it was designed as a gun tractor for a Vickers machine gun and a four-man crew. It was the advent of the Bren gun in 1936 which put an end to its gun tractor days. In effect, the Carrier was little more than an armoured metal box. The engine was placed in the centre of the vehicle next to the driver and gunner – the noise was apparently deafening. Despite their crudity, the Carriers were much used, and around 10 could be found in each infantry battalion. Various experimental models abounded, including versions mounting 25-pounder (87.6mm/3.45in) guns.

Country of origin:	UK
Crew:	2
Weight:	4000kg (8800lb)
Dimensions:	length 3.65m (12ft); width 2.11m (6ft 11in); height 1.57m (5ft 2in)
Range:	250km (150 miles)
Armour:	10mm (0.39in) maximum
Armament:	one 7.62mm (0.3in) Bren MG
Powerplant:	one Ford V8 petrol, developing 85hp (63kW) at 3500rpm
Performance:	maximum road speed 48km/h (30mph)

Tracked Infantry Vehicles
SdKfz 251/1

The SdKfz 251 had its origins in the same requirement as the SdKfz 250. However, the 251 series was a heavier vehicle. It entered service in 1939, intended as an armoured personnel carrier. The 250 was a useful vehicle, capable of keeping up with panzer formations. There were 22 special-purpose variants, including rocket-launcher (referred to as the 'infantry Stuka'), flame-thrower, anti-tank, communications vehicle, observation post and ambulance and infrared searchlight carrier. Early reliability problems did not prevent the vehicle being produced by the thousands, and it was a sturdy vehicle used on all fronts, becoming a virtual trademark of German panzer formations. The SdKfz 251/1 was the standard armoured personnel carrier for the panzergrenadier group.

Country of origin:	Germany
Crew:	12
Weight:	7810kg (17,182lb)
Dimensions:	length 5.80m (19ft 0.3in); width 2.10m (6ft 10.7in); height 1.75m (5ft 8.9in)
Range:	300km (186 miles)
Armour:	6-14.5mm (0.23-0.6in)
Armament:	two 7.92mm machine guns
Powerplant:	one Maybach six-cylinder petrol engine developing 100hp (74.6kW)
Performance:	maximum road speed 52.5km/h (32.5mph); fording 0.6m (2ft); vertical obstacle 2.0m (6ft 6.7in)

SdKfz 251/20

The SdKfz 251/20 was one of the seemingly endless variants of the basic 251 model. Known as the 'Uhu', it was produced towards the end of the World War II and was used mainly on the Eastern Front. Like all the other 251 models, it was designed to operate with, and as part of, the panzer divisions, needing to be speedy, tough and reliable. It carried an infrared searchlight and its primary purpose was to illuminate enemy targets and allow panzer units to attack at night. The fact that the German war machine was still churning out such specialised variants at the end of the war is testament to the durability and excellent qualities of the vehicle. The main searchlight had a 360-degree traverse and could be folded down when not in use. In total around 60 were built before the war ended.

Country of origin:	Germany
Crew:	4
Weight:	7824kg (17,248lb)
Dimensions:	length 5.80m (19ft 0.3in); width 2.10m (6ft 10.7in); height 1.75m (5ft 8.9in)
Range:	300km (186 miles)
Armour:	6-14.5mm (0.23-0.6in)
Armament:	none
Powerplant:	one Maybach six-cylinder petrol engine developing 100hp (74.6kW)
Performance:	maximum road speed 52.5km/h (32.5mph); fording 0.6m (2ft); vertical obstacle 2.0m (6ft 6.7in)

Tracked Infantry Vehicles
SdKfz 7

Development of the SdKfz 7 can be traced back to a 1934 requirement for an eight-tonne (7.87 tons) half-track. The vehicle first appeared in 1938 and was destined to be used mainly as the tractor for the 8.8cm flak guns. The vehicle could carry up to 12 men and a considerable quantity of supplies, as well as pulling up to 8000kg (17,600lb). Most were fitted with a winch, and the vehicle was widely admired as a useful vehicle, being also used as a weapons carrier, to particularly good effect with anti-aircraft weapons. They also saw service as observation and command posts for V2 rocket batteries. They were admired even by their enemies, with the British trying to make exact copies of captured vehicles and some vehicles being appropriated for use by the Allies after World War II.

Country of origin:	Germany
Crew:	12
Weight:	11,550kg (25,410lb)
Dimensions:	length 6.85m (20ft 3in); width 2.40m (7ft 10.5in); height 2.62m (8ft 7.1in)
Range:	250km (156 miles)
Armour:	8mm (0.31in)
Armament:	basic version – none.
Powerplant:	one Maybach HL 62 six-cylinder petrol engine developing 140hp (104.4kW)
Performance:	maximum road speed 50km/h (31mph); fording 0.5m (1ft 7in); vertical obstacle 2.0m (6ft 6.7in)

Schwerer Wehrmachtsschlepper

By 1941, the German Army was in need of a medium halftrack, but it had to be economical to produce as the German war machine was already stretched. The Schwerer Wehrmachtsschlepper, or army heavy tractor, was intended for use by infantry units as a general supply vehicle and personnel carrier. To keep costs down, luxuries like a closed cab and rubber-capped tracks were mainly dispensed with. Production was slow, partly due to the lack of priority accorded the vehicle and partly due to the attentions of RAF Bomber Command. However, production continued until the end of the World War II, with a few vehicles seeing service in the post-war Czech Army. Variants included a rocket launcher, anti-aircraft vehicle and a frontline supply vehicle fitted with an armoured cab.

Country of origin:	Germany
Crew:	2
Weight:	13,500kg (29,700lb)
Dimensions:	length 6.68m (21ft 11in); width 2.50m (8ft 2.4in); height 2.83m (9ft 3.4in)
Range:	300km (187 miles)
Armour:	8-15mm (0.31-0.59in)
Armament:	one 3.7cm gun; one 7.92mm machine gun
Powerplant:	one Maybach HL 42 six-cylinder petrol engine developing 100hp (74.6kW)
Performance:	maximum road speed 27km/h (16.8mph); fording 0.6m (2ft); vertical obstacle 2.0m (6ft 6.7in)

SdKfz 9

The SdKfz 9 was by far the largest of all World War II half-tracks. It originated as a result of a 1936 requirement for a heavy recovery vehicle to operate alongside panzer units. The vehicle was used both for recovery and for towing heavy artillery and bridging units. A weapons-carrying version was produced in 1943 mounting an 8.8cm anti-aircraft gun, where it saw action in Poland and France. The recovery version was fitted with a crane and stabilising legs to allow it to cope with heavy tanks. However, even with an earth spade at the back for extra traction, two SdKfz 9s were generally required to recover tanks such as the massive Tiger, and when the more capable Bergepanther arrived the SdKfz's role was diminished somewhat and therefore production ceased in 1944

Country of origin:	Germany
Crew:	9
Weight:	18,000kg (39,600lb)
Dimensions:	length 8.25m (27ft 0.8in); width 2.60m (8ft 6in); height 2.76m (9ft 0.7in)
Range:	260km (162 miles)
Armour:	8-14.5mm (0.31-0.57in)
Armament:	none, though sometimes one 8.8cm Flak gun
Powerplant:	one Maybach HL V-12 petrol engine developing 250hp (186.4kW)
Performance:	maximum road speed 50km/h (31mph); fording 0.6m (2ft); vertical obstacle 2.0m (6ft 6.7in)

Wasp Mk IIC

The Wasp was a flamethrower vehicle developed in the United Kingdom in the early 1940s. It was basically a Universal Carrier vehicle fitted with a flame-throwing device. Two fuel tanks and nitrogen pressure cylinders were fitted into the rear of the hull. The driver and co-driver sat in the front, a flamethrower nozzle jutting out of the front armoured wall. Aiming the flamethrower was a crude process of simply pointing the vehicle at the target, which could be engaged at about 100m (330ft). The Wasp Mk IIC was a Canadian variant. It added an extra crew member, the space acquired by reducing fuel capacity and relocating some fuel to a tank behind the hull.

Country of origin:	Canada/UK
Crew:	3
Weight:	3850kg (8500lb)
Dimensions:	length 3.65m (12ft); width 2.03m (6ft 8in); height 1.58m (5ft 2in)
Range:	180km (110 miles)
Armour:	(Steel) 10mm (0.39in) maximum
Armament:	1 x flamethrower; 1 x 7.7mm (0.303in) MG
Powerplant:	1 x Ford 9-cylinder petrol, developing 59hp (44kW)
Performance:	maximum road speed 48km/h (29mph)

Tracked Infantry Vehicles

M3

American half-track production began in earnest in 1941, and by the end of the war over 40,000 of all types had been produced. The M3 was widely used by all Allied forces, mainly as a personnel carrier, although also saw service as an ambulance, communications vehicle and artillery tractor. In fact, it was so prolific that it became something of a trademark of Allied forces, particularly after the D-Day landings of June 1944. After World War II, the M3 was gradually reduced to the role of recovery vehicle. However, vehicles supplied to the Soviet Union before 1945 continued to see service with some Warsaw Pact countries for many years. It also remained a frontline vehicle for the Israeli Defence Force until relatively recently, seeing service in all the Arab-Israeli wars.

Country of origin:	USA
Crew:	13
Weight:	9299kg (20,458lb)
Dimensions:	length 6.18m (20ft 3.5in); width 2.22m (7ft 3.5in); height 2.26m (7ft 5in)
Range:	282km (175 miles)
Armour:	8mm (0.31in)
Armament:	one 12.7mm machine gun; one 7.62mm machine gun
Powerplant:	one White 160AX six-cylinder petrol engine developing 147hp (109.6kW)
Performance:	maximum road speed 64.4km/h (40mph); fording 0.81m (2ft 8in)

P 107

The P 107 came in two basic variants: an artillery tractor for light field pieces and an engineer tractor. The latter had an open cargo body behind the cab and was used to tow trailers carrying combat engineer equipment. Following the fall of France to the Germans in 1940, the P 107 was pressed into Wehrmacht service, being used to tow field and anti-tank guns. Then the Germans stripped the vehicles of their superstructures and fitted armoured hulls in their place. Most of these conversions remained in France for training purposes and general duties, though they did see combat following the D-Day landings in June 1944. The Germans retained the mounted roller under the nose of the vehicle, which was used to assist the vehicle in and out of ditches.

Country of origin:	France
Crew:	5-7
Weight:	4050kg (8910lb)
Dimensions:	length 4.85m (15ft 10.9in); width 1.80m (5ft 10.9in); height 1.95m (6ft 4.8in)
Range:	400km (248.5 miles)
Armour:	none (original version)
Armament:	none
Powerplant:	one four-cylinder petrol engine developing 55hp (41.0kW)
Performance:	maximum road speed 45km/h (28mph)

Wurfgranate 41

Nebelwerfer units were originally formed to lay down smoke screens for tactical use. The launchers were later adapted to fire artillery rockets, whose droning sound led to the Allied nickname 'Moaning Minnie'. The 15cm-Nebelwerfer 41 was mounted on a 3.7cm anti-tank gun carriage, but in 1942 the launcher was fitted to the half-tracked SdKfz 4/1 Maultier. This was a more effective system, as rockets betrayed their location immediately on firing and thus tended to draw swift retaliation. The Panzerwerfer 42, as it was known, allowed rapid escape from the point of firing and thus greater survivability. In the main, the mobile launchers were used to give fire-support for armoured operations. Note that the specifications below relate to the 15cm Wurfgranate 41 rocket.

Country of origin:	Germany
Crew:	
Weight:	overall 31.8kg (70lb); propellant 6.35kg (14lb); filling 2.5kg (5.5lb)
Dimensions:	length 979mm (38.55in); diameter 158mm (6.22in)
Range:	7055m (23,145ft)
Armour:	–
Armament:	–
Powerplant:	–
Performance:	initial velocity 342m (1120ft) per second

Ram/Kangaroo

The Ram/Kangaroo was an expedient vehicle used to transport Canadian soldiers into action in Europe in late 1944. The vehicle was essentially a turretless Canadian Ram tank, which was developed in 1942 and 1943 but was quickly rendered obsolete by the introduction of the US Sherman tank. By mid-1944, 500 Rams were in storage in England, and these were converted into armoured personnel carriers. The turret was removed, benches were fixed in the interior alongside ammunition racks and a standard infantry No.19 wireless set was fitted. Ram/Kangaroos were light and mobile vehicles, and joined the ranks of several similar Allied tank conversions.

Country of origin:	Canada/UK
Crew:	2 + 8
Weight:	29,000kg (63,900lb)
Dimensions:	length 5.79m (19ft); width 2.78m (9ft 1in); height 2.47m (8ft 1in)
Range:	230km (140 miles)
Armour:	88mm (3.46in) maximum
Armament:	one 7.62mm (0.3in) MG
Powerplant:	one Continental R-975 9-cylinder diesel, developing 399hp (298kW)
Performance:	maximum road speed 40km/h (25mph); vertical obstacle 0.6m (2ft); trench 2.26m (7ft 5in)

Tracked Infantry Vehicles
Wurfkörper M F1 50

The Wurfkörper 28cm and 32cm rockets were amongst the first to be fitted to vehicles to provide mobile firepower. The vehicle most often used was the SdKfz 251, this combination being known as the Stuka-zu-Fuss ('Foot Stuka') or Heulende Kuh ('Howling Cow'). The combination saw action through World War II. The system was rather temperamental, as the rockets were highly inaccurate and aiming was achieved by simply pointing the vehicle in the general direction of the target. As a result, they tended to be used *en masse* where possible. They were still devastating weapons whenever they did hit the target, the high-explosive warhead being particularly well regarded for street fighting and demolishing houses. The specifications below relate to the Wurfkörper M FI 50 rocket.

Country of origin:	Germany
Crew:	–
Weight:	overall 79kg (174lb); propellant 6.6kg (14.56lb); filling 39.8kg (87.7lb)
Dimensions:	length 1.289m (50.75in); body diameter 320mm (12.6in)
Range:	2028m (6651ft)
Armour:	–
Armament:	–
Powerplant:	–
Performance:	–

M75

The International Harvester M75 was an initial US attempt to replace the wartime M3 half-track and produce a modern armoured personnel carrier. Its design was flawed in that it relied on expensive tank components for its production, especially the running gear, engine and transmission. Mainly for reasons of cost, only 1729 were produced between 1951 and 1954. The M75 looked towards the M113 in design concept. It featured a steel armoured box with a sloped glacis front big enough for two crew and 10 soldiers. Twin doors at the rear of the hull provided entry and exit. Armament consisted of one 12.7mm (0.5in) Browning M2 HB machine gun mounted on the roof.

Country of origin:	USA
Crew:	2 + 10
Weight:	18,828kg (41,516lb)
Dimensions:	length 5.19m (17ft); width 2.84m (9ft 4in); height 2.77m (9ft 1in)
Range:	185km (115 miles)
Armour:	(Steel) 15.9mm (0.63in)
Armament:	one 12.7mm (0.5in) Browning M2 HB
Powerplant:	one Continental AO-895-4 6-cylinder petrol, developing 295hp (220kW) at 2660rpm
Performance:	maximum road speed 71km/h (44mph); fording 1.22m (4ft); gradient 60 percent; vertical obstacle 0.46m (1ft 6in); trench 1.68m (5ft 6in)

Tracked Infantry Vehicles

BTR-50

Between 1957 and the early 1970s, the BTR-50 served as the standard Soviet armoured personnel carrier before it was superseded by the BMP-1. It was a lightly armed (1 x 7.62mm/0.3in machine gun) APC with a large carrying capacity of 20 personnel. The low-profile hull meant that the occupants entered and exited over the vehicle's side rather than through hatches and doors. A later version, the BTR-50K, had an enclosed armoured roof and roof hatches for access. The chassis of the vehicle was basically that of the PT-76 light tank and its engine was a modified version of that used in the T-54 main battle tank. Waterjets powered the vehicle when in amphibious mode.

Country of origin:	Russia/Soviet Union
Crew:	2 + 20
Weight:	14,200kg (31,300lb)
Dimensions:	length: 7.03m (23ft); width: 3.14m (10ft 4in); height: 2.07m (6ft 9in)
Range:	400km (250 miles)
Armour:	(Steel) 10mm (0.39in)
Armament:	one 7.62mm (0.3in) machine gun
Powerplant:	one Model V6 6-cylinder diesel, developing 240hp (179kW) at 1800rpm
Performance:	maximum road speed: 44km/h (27mph); fording: amphibious; gradient: 70 percent; vertical obstacle: 1.1m (3ft 7in); trench: 2.8m (9ft 2in)

AMX VCI

The AMX VCI (Véhicule de Combat d'Infanterie) went into production in 1957 to meet a French Army requirement to replace the cancelled Hotchkiss TT6 and TT9 armoured personnel carriers. As the name suggests, the vehicle is constructed around the modified chassis of the AMX-13 light tank. It carried three crew and 10 soldiers, the latter sitting back to back in a bisected internal compartment at the rear, accessible by double doors. Standard armament is a 12.7mm (0.5in) M2 HB machine gun pintle-mounted on the roof. Updated AMX VCIs have NBC and night-vision systems. The AMX VCI was developed into a large number of variants, ranging from TOW-armed anti-tank vehicles to the RATAC radar-carrier vehicle.

Country of origin:	France
Crew:	3 + 10
Weight:	15,000kg (33,100lb)
Dimensions:	length 5.7m (18ft 8in); width 2.67m (8ft 9in); height 2.41m (7ft 11in)
Range:	350km (220 miles)
Armour:	(Steel) 30mm (1.18in) maximum
Armament:	one 12.7mm (0.5in) M2 HB machine gun
Powerplant:	one SOFAM 8Gxb 8-cylinder petrol, developing 250hp (186kW) at 3200rpm
Performance:	max road speed 60km/h (37mph); fording 1m (3ft 4in); gradient 60 percent; vertical obstacle 1m (3ft 4in); trench 1.6m (5ft 4in)

Tracked Infantry Vehicles

AMX VTT/TB

The chassis of the AMX-13 light tank yielded a bewildering number of variants. Most prolific were the series of vehicles based upon the AMX VCI mechanized infantry combat vehicle, developed from the late 1950s onwards. The standard VCI was converted into, amongst other vehicles, an 81mm (3.19in) mortar vehicle, a battery command post, an ENTAC missile launcher, a Roland SAM vehicle, a TOW anti-tank missile vehicle, a combat engineer vehicle and an ambulance vehicle – this being the AMX VTT/TB. The VTT/TB was more of a battlefield rescue vehicle than an ambulance, as it had no facilities for advanced medical care. It could carry four sitting and three stretchered patients as well as two orderlies and the two-man crew.

Country of origin:	France
Crew:	2 + 9
Weight:	14,300kg (31,500lb)
Dimensions:	length 5.7m (18ft 8in); width 2.67m (8ft 9in); height 1.92m (6ft 3in)
Range:	350km (220 miles)
Armour:	(Steel) 30mm (1.18in) maximum
Armament:	none
Powerplant:	one SOFAM 8Gxb 8-cylinder petrol, developing 250hp (186kW) at 3200rpm
Performance:	max road speed 60km/h (37mph); fording 1m (3ft 4in); gradient 60 percent; vertical obstacle 1m (3ft 4in); trench 1.6m (5ft 4in)

Schützenpanzer SPz 11-2 kurz

The SPz kurz is actually a German version of a French vehicle, the Hotchkiss SP 1A. During the 1950s, Hotchkiss produced tracked armoured vehicles intended for the French Army, though ultimately the army placed no orders. West Germany, however, was at this time seeking to develop its armoured military forces. After testing the Hotchkiss prototypes, the German Army received 2374 Hotchkiss vehicles between 1958 and 1962. Redesignated the SPz 11-2, it featured an all-welded hull of APC type, with twin doors in the rear and escape hatch underneath. The SPz kurz was a reconnaissance vehicle variant of the 11-2, with the small turret carrying a Hispano-Suiza 20mm (0.78in) cannon.

Country of origin:	Germany
Crew:	5
Weight:	8200kg (18,100lb)
Dimensions:	length 4.51m (14ft 10in); width 2.28m (7ft 3in); height 1.97m (6ft 6in)
Range:	400km (250 miles)
Armour:	15mm (0.59in)
Armament:	one Hispano-Suiza 820/L35 20mm (0.78in) cannon; three smoke grenade launchers
Powerplant:	one Hotchkiss 6-cylinder petrol, developing 164hp (122kW)
Performance:	maximum speed 58km/h (36mph); fording 1m (3.3ft); gradient 60 percent; vertical obstacle 0.6m (2ft); trench 1.5m (4.9ft)

Tracked Infantry Vehicles

SPz lang HS30

The HS30 was destined to be blighted by technical problems throughout its active life. Consequently, only 2176 vehicles were built (out of a projected 4450) between 1958 and 1962. In the early 1970s, remaining HS30s were replaced with Marder mechanized infantry combat vehicles. The HS30 was a basic armoured personnel carrier which could carry five soldiers and a three-man crew inside an all-welded steel hull. It was not amphibious, neither did it have an NBC option, both serious deficits in the Cold War era. It was, however, well armed. A turret-mounted 20mm (0.78in) Hispano HS820 was the primary weapon, but ATGWs and M40A1 106mm (4.17in) recoilless rifles were further options.

Country of origin:	Germany
Crew:	3 + 5
Weight:	14,600kg (32,200lb)
Dimensions:	length 5.56m (18ft 3in); width 2.25m (7ft 5in); height 1.85m (67ft 1in)
Range:	270km (170 miles)
Armour:	(Steel) 30mm (1.18in) maximum
Armament:	one 20mm (0.78in) Hispano HS820 cannon and other options
Powerplant:	one Rolls-Royce 8-cylinder petrol, developing 235hp (175kW) at 3800rpm
Performance:	max road speed 51km/h (32mph); fording 0.7m (2ft 4in); gradient 60 percent; vertical obstacle 0.6m (2ft); trench 1.6m (5ft 4in)

M-80 MICV

Though indebted to Soviet armoured personnel carrier design, the M-80 Mechanised Infantry Combat Vehicle (MICV) is essentially a Yugoslav design. It is an amphibious APC with an all-welded steel armour hull, with NBC protection and night-vision devices fitted as standard. Its most distinctive feature is the configuration of turret armament. As well as two Yugoslav copies of the Soviet Sagger ATGW, the turret mounts a 30mm (1.18in) cannon and a 7.62mm (0.3in) machine gun. Both these weapons are set in turret slits to allow anti-aircraft engagement at an elevation of 75 degrees. Consequently, the M-80 is able to engage low-flying aircraft at ranges of up to 1500m (4900ft).

Country of origin:	Yugoslavia
Crew:	3 + 7
Weight:	13,700kg (30,200lb)
Dimensions:	length 6.4m (21ft); width 2.59m (8ft 6in); height 2.3m (7ft 7in)
Range:	500km (310 miles)
Armour:	(Steel) 30mm (1.18in)
Armament:	two Yugoslav Sagger ATGWs; one 30mm (1.18in) cannon; one 7.62mm (0.3in) MG
Powerplant:	one HS-115-2 8-cylinder turbo diesel, developing 260hp (194kW)
Performance:	maximum road speed 60km/h (37mph); fording amphibious; gradient 60 percent; vertical obstacle 0.8m (2ft 7in); trench 2.2m (7ft 2in)

Tracked Infantry Vehicles

SU-60

The SU-60 was Japan's first post-war tracked armoured personnel carrier. It entered service with the Japanese Ground Self Defence Force in 1960 and was eventually replaced by the Type 73 in the early 1970s. A general US M113 appearance belies a different crew configuration. The driver and bow machine-gunner sat at the front of the vehicle on the right and left respectively, with the commander between them. The final crew member sat just behind and to the right of the commander, and would operate the 12.7mm (0.5in) roof-mounted machine gun. Variants of the SU-60 include two mortar carriers, an NBC detection vehicle, an anti-tank vehicle and a bulldozer.

Country of origin:	Japan
Crew:	4 + 6
Weight:	11,800kg (26,000lb)
Dimensions:	length 4.85m (15ft 11in); width 2.4m (7ft 10in); height 1.7m (5ft 7in)
Range:	300km (190 miles)
Armour:	Steel (details classified)
Armament:	one 12.7mm (0.5in) Browning M2 HB MG
Powerplant:	one Mitsubishi 8 HA 21 WT 8-cylinder diesel, developing 220hp (164kW) at 2400rpm
Performance:	max road speed 45km/h (28mph); fording 1m (3ft 4in); gradient 60 percent; vertical obstacle 0.6m (2ft); trench 1.82m (6ft)

AMX-10P

Designed in the mid-1960s, the first French AMX-10s rolled off the production line in 1973. With an all-aluminium hull, the AMX-10 was fully amphibious, being propelled by two waterjets. It also carried a nuclear, biological and chemical (NBC) defence system and night-vision equipment. Inside, there was capacity for eight troops. The vehicle has spawned a range of variants, including an ambulance, a repair vehicle, an anti-tank vehicle with four guided weapons and a mortar tractor for towing a Brandt 120mm mortar. The AMX-10 has been exported to many countries including Greece, Qatar, Mexico, Saudi Arabia and Indonesia, the vehicles for the latter having improved amphibious capability as they are designed to leave landing craft offshore and float in under their own power.

Country of origin:	France
Crew:	3 + 8
Weight:	14,200kg (31,240lb)
Dimensions:	length 5.778m (18ft 11in); width 2.78m (9ft 1in); height 2.57m (8ft 5in)
Range:	600km (373 miles)
Armour:	classified
Armament:	one 20mm cannon; one 7.62mm coaxial machine gun
Powerplant:	one HS-115 V-8 water-cooled diesel, developing 280hp (209kW)
Performance:	maximum road speed 65km/h (40mph); fording amphibious; vertical obstacle 0.70m (2ft 4in); trench 1.60m (5ft 3in)

Tracked Infantry Vehicles

FV432

In 1962, the FV432 was the first fully tracked armoured personnel carrier to be accepted into service by the British Army since World War II. Between 1963 and 1971 a total of 3000 were built by GKN Sankey. Few were exported, as the similar American M113 was a much cheaper option. At one time known as the Trojan, the FV432's main purpose was to transport fighting men to the battlefield, carrying 10 troops, the vehicle was one of the first to be fitted with a nuclear, biological and chemical (NBC) defence system. Initially the vehicles were fitted with flotation screens to give an amphibious capability, but these were removed as they were prone to damage. Variants included a command vehicle, ambulance, mortar carrier and mine-layer, as well as an anti-tank version armed with Swingfire missiles.

Country of origin:	UK
Crew:	2 + 10
Weight:	15,280kg (33,616lb)
Dimensions:	length 5.251m (17ft 7in); width 2.80m (9ft 2in); height (with machine gun) 2.286m (7ft 6in)
Range:	483km (300 miles)
Armour:	12mm (0.47in)
Armament:	one 7.62mm machine gun
Powerplant:	one Rolls-Royce K60 six-cylinder multi-fuel engine developing 240hp (170kW)
Performance:	maximum road speed 52.2km/h (32mph); fording 1.066m (3ft 6in); vertical obstacle 0.609m (2ft); trench 2.05m (6ft 9in)

M-60P

The M60P appears to look to the West and the US M113 for its inspiration rather than to the East and Soviet armoured personnel carriers. Like subsequent Yugoslav APCs, however, it is a medley of various foreign parts and design elements. The Soviet SU-76 self-propelled gun chassis provides the basis for the suspension, an Austrian Steyr-type engine gives the power, and Western APCs, such as the US M59 and British FV432, contribute to overall design. An M60PB anti-tank variant was later produced. This featured two 82mm (3.23in) recoilless rifles, though by the mid-1970s these were ineffective against modern main battle tank armour. The M60P only operated in Yugoslavia, and is still in service today.

Country of origin:	Yugoslavia
Crew:	3 + 10
Weight:	11,000kg (24,300lb)
Dimensions:	length 5.02m (16ft 6in); width 2.77m (9ft 1in); height 2.77m (9ft 1in)
Range:	400km (250 miles)
Armour:	(Steel) 25mm (0.98in)
Armament:	one 12.7mm (0.5in) MG; one 7.62mm (0.3in) MG
Powerplant:	one FAMOS 6-cylinder diesel, developing 140hp (104kW)
Performance:	maximum road speed 45km/h (28mph); fording 1.25m (4ft 1in); gradient 60 percent; vertical obstacle 0.6m (2ft); trench 2m (6ft 7in)

Tracked Infantry Vehicles

Marder

The Marder Schützenpanzer was the first mechanised infantry combat vehicle to enter service in the West, and was one of a family of vehicles based on the chassis of the Swiss SPX12-3. Production began in 1970, and by 1975 some 3000 had been built. At the time, it was the most advanced of its type in the world. With excellent armour and high cross-country speed, it was able to operate with Leopard main battle tanks in combined operations. The troops inside were able to use their weapons from inside by means of a periscope and firing ports. A remote-controlled machine gun was provided for local defence. Later versions carried the Milan anti-tank guided missile. Variants include a surface-to-air missile (SAM) launcher and a radar carrier. Over 6000 rounds of ammunition are carried in the vehicle.

Country of origin:	West Germany
Crew:	4 + 6
Weight:	28,200kg (62,040lb)
Dimensions:	length 6.79m (22ft 3in); width 3.24m (10ft 8in); height 2.95m (9ft 8in)
Range:	520km (323 miles)
Armour:	classified
Armament:	one 20mm Rh 202 cannon; one coaxial 7.62mm machine gun
Powerplant:	one MTU MB 833 six-cylinder diesel, developing 600hp (447kW)
Performance:	maximum road speed 75km/h (46.6mph); fording 1.50m (4ft 11in); vertical obstacle 1.00m (3ft 3in); trench 2.50m (8ft 2in)

Pbv

Design on the Pbv 302 began in 1961 and full-scale production began in 1966. The Pbv was similar in layout to the American M113 and was one of the first vehicles of its type with a fully enclosed weapon station. The troop compartment is at the rear with room for 10 fully equipped soldiers. There are no firing ports, but soldiers are able to fire through the hatches on the top. The turret is manually operated, and the 20mm cannon can be fed from a belt holding 135 rounds of from 10-round box magazines. Fully amphibious, the Pbv is propelled through the water by its tracks. Variants include a command vehicle, observation vehicle and ambulance. Few were exported, mainly because of the strict controls placed on exports of military equipment by the Swedish government.

Country of origin:	Sweden
Crew:	2 + 10
Weight:	13,500kg (29,700lb)
Dimensions:	length 5.35m (17ft 7in); width 2.86m (9ft 5in); height 2.50m (8ft 2in)
Range:	300km (186 miles)
Armour:	classified
Armament:	one 20mm Hispano cannon
Powerplant:	one Volvo-Penta Model THD 100B 6-cylinder inline diesel engine developing 280hp (209kW)
Performance:	maximum road speed 66km/h (41mph); fording amphibious; vertical obstacle 0.61m (2ft); trench 1.80m (5ft 11in)

M113A2

The M113 was the result of a mid-1950s US requirement for a lightweight, amphibious and airportable armoured infantry vehicle. Production began in the early 1960s, since when 70,000 have been built and exported to nearly 50 countries, the vehicle being constantly updated to meet modern requirements. In particular, the early versions afforded the gunner no protection at all, this being addressed as a priority following combat experience, notably in Vietnam, the Middle East, North Africa and the Far East. With many variants, including mortar carrier, command vehicle, anti-aircraft and flame-thrower vehicles, the M113 will stay in service well into the 21st century and will probably be the most widely used armoured vehicle ever built.

Country of origin:	USA
Crew:	2 + 11
Weight:	11,341kg (24,950lb)
Dimensions:	length 2.686m (8ft 9in); width 2.54m (8ft 4in); height 2.52m (8ft 3in)
Range:	483km (300 miles)
Armour:	up to 44mm (1.73in)
Armament:	one 12.7mm machine gun; two 7.62mm machine guns
Powerplant:	one six-cylinder water-cooled diesel, developing 215bhp (160kW)
Performance:	maximum road speed 67.59km/h (42mph); maximum water speed 5.8km/h (3.6mph); fording amphibious; vertical obstacle 0.61m (2ft); trench 1.68m (5ft 6in)

M2 Bradley

The M2 Bradley was the US Army's first mechanised infantry combat vehicle. The first production models appeared in 1981, and they were soon being produced at the rate of 600 per year. The hull of the M2 is made of aluminium, with a layer of spaced laminate armour for added protection. The 25mm cannon has a stabiliser to allow for firing on the move. The troop compartment in the rear is fitted with firing ports and periscopes to allow the troops to fire from within the vehicle. Night vision and a nuclear, biological and chemical (NBC) defence system are standard. The Bradley plays a key role in the US Army's combined arms concept, but critics say it is too big, too expensive and too difficult to maintain and is insufficiently armoured to operate with main battle tanks on the battlefield.

Country of origin:	USA
Crew:	3 + 7
Weight:	22,666kg (49,865lb)
Dimensions:	length 6.453m (21ft 2in); width 3.20m (10ft 6in); height; 2.972m (9ft 0in)
Range:	483km (300 miles)
Armour:	classified
Armament:	one Hughes Helicopter 25mm Chain Gun; one 7.62mm coaxial machine gun; two anti-tank launchers.
Powerplant:	one Cummins eight-cylinder diesel, developing 500hp (373kW)
Performance:	maximum road speed 66km/h (41mph); fording amphibious; vertical obstacle 0.914m (3ft); trench 2.54m (8ft 4in)

Tracked Infantry Vehicles

AIFV

The shortcomings of the M113 prompted the US Army to order a new vehicle with better protection for the gunner and firing ports for the troops in the rear. The FMC Corporation realised that the resulting M2 would be too heavy and expensive for most countries, and thus developed the AIFV primarily for export. Better armed and armoured (with steel appliqué armour layers) than the M113, the vehicle is fully amphibious. The main gun is enclosed for better protection and the seven troops in the back all have firing ports. Night-vision and nuclear, biological and chemical (NBC) systems are available. The AIFV is a good compromise between the M113 and the M2 and has proved popular with Turkey, Belgium, the Philippines and the Netherlands all ordering significant quantities.

Country of origin:	USA
Crew:	3 + 7
Weight:	13,687kg (30,111lb)
Dimensions:	length 5.258m (17ft 3in); width 2.819m (9ft 3in); height (overall) 2.794m (9ft 2in)
Range:	490km (305 miles)
Armour:	classified
Armament:	one 25mm Oerlikon cannon; one 7.62 coaxial machine gun
Powerplant:	one Detroit-Diesel 6V-53T V-6 diesel engine developing 264hp (197kW)
Performance:	maximum road speed 61.2km/h (38mph); fording amphibious; vertical obstacle 0.635m (2ft 1in); trench 1.625m (5ft 4in)

BMD

The BMD was designed specifically for Soviet airborne forces to give increased firepower and mobility for troops behind enemy lines once on the ground. This was particularly important as the Soviets had only sufficient air transport to deliver one airborne division at a time. It entered service in 1970, and 330 were destined for each airborne division. Based on the BMP-1, the vehicle was fitted with an unusual hydraulic suspension-adjustment system to alter the level of ground clearance. Fully amphibious, the vehicle had night vision and a nuclear, chemical and biological (NBC) defence system, plus a smoke generating system. Variants included a mortar carrier and command vehicle. The BMD was used to spearhead the Soviet invasion of Afghanistan in 1979.

Country of origin:	USSR
Crew:	3 + 4
Weight:	6700kg (14,740lb)
Dimensions:	length 5.40m (17ft 9in); width 2.63m (9ft 8in); height 1.97m (6ft 6in)
Range:	320km (200 miles)
Armour:	15-23mm (0.59-0.9in)
Armament:	one 73mm gun; one coaxial 7.62mm machine gun; two front-mounted 7.62mm machine guns; one AT-3 'Sagger' ATGW
Powerplant:	one V-6 liquid-cooled diesel engine developing 240hp (179kW)
Performance:	maximum road speed 70km/h (43mph); fording amphibious; vertical obstacle 0.80m (2ft 8in); trench 1.60m (5ft 3in)

Tracked Infantry Vehicles

MT-LB

The MT-LB was developed to fulfil a variety of roles, such as towing artillery and anti-tank guns, moving cargo and acting as an armoured personnel carrier. Fully amphibious, being propelled in the water by its tracks, the MT-LB had room in the back for 11 troops. On snow-covered ground, the tracks could be removed and much wider ones added. In swampy ground, the MT-LB was used in place of the BMP mechanised infantry combat vehicle. Variants included an engineer combat vehicle, a command vehicle with specialised radar and a repair vehicle. The MT-LB was also used as the basis for the 2S1 self-propelled howitzer which entered service in the 1970s and was widely exported. It was exported to Bulgaria, Czechoslovakia, Finland, Hungary, Poland, Sweden and the former Yugoslavia.

Country of origin:	USSR
Crew:	2 + 11
Weight:	11,900kg (26,180lb)
Dimensions:	length 6.454m (21ft 2in); width 2.85m (9ft 4in); height 1.865m (6ft 5in)
Range:	500km (310 miles)
Armour:	3-10mm (0.1-0.39in)
Armament:	one 7.62mm machine gun
Powerplant:	one YaMZ 238 V-8 diesel engine developing 240hp (179kW)
Performance:	maximum road speed 61.5km/h (38mph); fording amphibious; vertical obstacle 0.70m (2ft 3in); trench 2.70m (8ft 10in)

Sultan

The Sultan is part of a group of vehicles based on the same aluminium hull which form part of the British Army's battle group formation. It is designed to provide the commander with an armoured platform to allow him to keep up with his forward elements. There is a compartment in the back with a desk, map boards and radios. Space is a real problem, although there is a tent which can be extended from the rear to give more room, but at the expense of mobility. Its cramped conditions while on the move (particularly while closed down during a nuclear, biological and chemical [NBC] exercises) make this a difficult vehicle to work in. Like many such armoured fighting vehicles currently in service around the world, its crew is prone to severe motion sickness.

Country of origin:	UK
Crew:	3
Weight:	8172kg (17,978lb)
Dimensions:	length 5.12m (16ft 9in); width 2.24m (7ft 4in); height 2.6m (8ft 6in)
Range:	483km (301 miles)
Armour:	classified
Armament:	one 7.62mm machine gun
Powerplant:	one 4.2-litre petrol engine developing 190hp (141kW)
Performance:	maximum road speed 80km/h (50mph); fording 1.067m (3ft 6in); vertical obstacle 0.5m (1ft 7in); trench 2.057m (6ft 9in)

Tracked Infantry Vehicles

Spartan

Т he Alvis Spartan is a member of the Scorpion family and entered service with the British Army in 1978. It has specialised roles, such as carrying Javelin surface-to-air missiles (SAMs) or Royal Engineer assault teams. It has a three-man crew and room in the back for four fully equipped troops, though the vehicle has no firing ports. Flotation screens can be fitted around the top of the hull, which, when erected, makes the Spartan fully amphibious (in the water it is propelled by its tracks). The newest production models incorporate a number of improvements, including an upgraded suspension system and a more fuel-efficient Perkins diesel engine. By the end of 1995, a total of 960 Spartan vehicles had been built. As shown above, it can be fitted with a Milan anti-tank weapon.

Country of origin:	UK
Crew:	3 + 4
Weight:	8172kg (17,978lb)
Dimensions:	length 5.125m (16ft 9in); width 2.24m (7ft 4in); height 2.26m (7ft 5in)
Range:	483km (301 miles)
Armour:	classified
Armament:	one 7.62mm machine gun; one Milan missile launcher
Powerplant:	one Jaguar six-cylinder petrol engine developing 190hp (142kW)
Performance:	maximum road speed 80km/h (50mph); fording 1.067m (3ft 6in); vertical obstacle 0.5m 1ft 7in); trench 2.057m (6ft 9in)

Warrior

The Warrior Mechanised Combat Vehicle entered development in 1972 and entered service with the British Army in 1987. The Warrior was part of a movement to change armoured personnel carriers from their role of merely transporting troops to and from the battlefield into a more capable infantry combat vehicle, this concept being inspired by the success of the Soviet BMP. Designed to supplement the FV432, the Warrior is heavier and much more heavily armoured. It is treated as a mobile fire base from which troops can fight, rather than a mere transport vehicle. Variants include a command vehicle, recovery vehicle, engineer and observation vehicle. It has been sold to Kuwait, whose Warriors have anti-tank launchers each side of the turret and air conditioning.

Country of origin:	UK
Crew:	3 + 7
Weight:	25,700kg (56,540lb)
Dimensions:	length 6.34m (20ft 10in); width 3.034m (10ft); height 2.79m (9ft 2in)
Range:	660km (412 miles)
Armour:	classified
Armament:	one 30mm Rarden cannon; one 7.62mm co-axial machine gun; four smoke dischargers
Powerplant:	one Perkins V-8 diesel engine developing 550hp (410kW)
Performance:	maximum road speed 75km/h (46.8mph); fording 1.3m (4ft 3in); vertical obstacle 0.75m (2ft 5in); trench 2.5m (8ft 2in)

Tracked Infantry Vehicles

FV433 Stormer

The Stormer is another British vehicle to use the Alvis Scorpion hull as its foundation. Development of the Stormer ran through the 1970s and production itself began in 1981. It is a fairly standard armoured personnel carrier, carrying three crew and eight infantry with a good road speed of 80km/h (50mph). It has sold well in export, particularly to Indonesia, Malaysia and Oman. The Stormer's main credit is its versatility. The basic vehicle can be fitted with lots of optional equipment and weaponry, including NBC systems, a flotation screen, night-vision instruments and guns ranging from 12.7mm (0.5in) machine guns to 90mm (3.54in) cannon and Starstreak missiles.

Country of origin:	UK
Crew:	3 + 8
Weight:	12,700kg (28,000lb)
Dimensions:	length 5.33m (17ft 6in); width 2.4m (7ft 10in); height 2.27m (7ft 5in)
Range:	650km (400 miles)
Armour:	aluminium (details classified)
Armament:	various
Powerplant:	one Perkins T6/3544 6-cylinder turbo diesel, developing 250hp (186kW) at 2600rpm
Performance:	max road speed 80km/h (50mph); fording amphibious; gradient 60 percent; vertical obstacle 0.6m (2ft); trench 1.75m (5ft 9in)

BMP-2

First seen in public in 1982, the BMP-2 was designed to supplement rather than replace the BMP-1, having an almost identical chassis. Its low silhouette and long sloping front is useful in that it presents a small target. This is vital because its armour is extremely poor. One remarkable feature is that the rear doors are hollow and serve as fuel tanks, with obvious dangers for the troops inside. There are few concessions to comfort, the crew compartment being very crowded and uncomfortable, although the troops can fire their weapons from within. The two-man turret has the commander on the right and the gunner on the left, the 30mm cannon having a powered elevation for use against helicopters and slow-flying aircraft. The BMP-2 saw action in Afghanistan.

Country of origin:	USSR
Crew:	3 + 7
Weight:	14,600kg (32,120lb)
Dimensions:	length 6.71m (22ft); width 3.15m (10ft 4in); height 2m (6ft 7in)
Range:	600km (375 miles)
Armour:	classified
Armament:	one 30mm cannon; one At-5 anti-tank missile launcher; one 7.62mm coaxial machine gun
Powerplant:	one Model UTD-20 six-cylinder diesel engine developing 300hp (223kW)
Performance:	maximum road speed 65km/h (40.6mph); fording amphibious; vertical obstacle 0.7m (2ft 4in); trench 2.4m (8ft 2in)

Tracked Infantry Vehicles

KIFV K-200

The Korean Infantry Fighting Vehicle K-200 is the first of a series of South Korean fighting vehicles developed by the Dae Woo Industries company. Borrowing from the US AIFV, it has become a powerful and reliable armoured personnel carrier. It can carry nine infantry and its three-man crew into battle at speeds of 74km/h (46mph). In amphibious mode, it achieves 7km/h (4mph) on water, propelled by its tracks. Standard armament is usually two machine guns: a 12.7mm (0.5in) and a 7.62mm (0.3in) weapon. However, optional armament configurations include 20mm (0.78in) Vulcan cannon and two mortar carriers – 81mm (3.19in) and 106mm (4.17in). An NBC reconnaissance variant has also been developed.

Country of origin:	South Korea
Crew:	3 + 9
Weight:	12,900kg (28,400lb)
Dimensions:	length 5.48m (19ft 2in); width 2.84m (9ft 4in); height 2.51m (8ft 3in)
Range:	480km (300 miles)
Armour:	Aluminium and steel (details classified)
Armament:	1 x 12.7mm (0.5in) MG; 1 x 7.62mm (0.3in) MG
Powerplant:	1 x MAN D-284T V8 diesel, developing 280hp (208kW) at 2300rpm
Performance:	maximum road speed 74km/h (46mph); fording amphibious; gradient 60 percent; vertical obstacle 0.64m (2ft 1in); trench 1.68m (5ft 6in)

YW 531 VERSION OT

The YW 703 is actually a version of the Norinco YW 531H armoured personnel carrier, China's main APC type. A 25mm (0.98in) cannon separates the YW 703 from all the other YW 531H derivatives, of which there are many. Other combat versions include the Type 85, armed with a 120mm (4.72in) or 82mm (3.23in) mortar, and a 122mm (4.8in) self-propelled howitzer version. Non-combat variants include the Type 85 command-post vehicle, an armoured recovery vehicle, and an ambulance. The YW 531H can be confused with the YW 534, though the former does not have the bank of four smoke grenade launchers set on either side of the turret.

Country of origin:	China
Crew:	3 + 7
Weight:	15,400kg (31,000lb)
Dimensions:	length 6.15m (20ft 2in); width 3.13m (10ft 3in); height 1.88m (6ft 2in)
Range:	500km (310 miles)
Armour:	steel (details classified)
Armament:	one 25mm (0.98in) cannon
Powerplant:	one Deutz Type BF8L413F 8-cylinder diesel, developing 320hp (239kW)
Performance:	maximum road speed 65km/h (40mph); fording amphibious; vertical obstacle 0.6m (2ft); trench 2.2m (7ft 2in)

Tracked Infantry Vehicles

BMP-3

The BMP-3 entered service in 1990, and is the latest in the BMP range. Classified as an Infantry Combat Vehicle, its extensive armament almost places it in the category of small tank. Its turret boasts a 100mm (3.93in) gun which can fire either conventional shells or AT-10 laser-guided ATGWs. Alongside this weapon is a 30mm (1.18in) cannon, and the turret also bears a 7.62mm (0.3in) PKT coaxial machine gun. Another machine gun is set in the forward hull. Despite the increase in stored ammunition and the consequent extra space this takes up, the BMP-3 takes only one less soldier than the BMP-1 (seven instead of eight), though it is almost a metre (3.3ft) longer.

Country of origin:	Soviet Union/Russia
Crew:	3 + 7
Weight:	18,700kg (41,200lb)
Dimensions:	length 7.14m (23ft 5in); width 3.23m (10ft 7in); height 2.65m (8ft 8in)
Range:	600km (370 miles)
Armour:	steel (details classified)
Armament:	one 100mm (3.93in) gun; one 30mm (1.18in) cannon; two 7.62mm (0.3in) PKT MG
Powerplant:	one UTD-29M 10-cylinder diesel, developing 500hp (373kW)
Performance:	maximum speed 70km/h (43mph); fording amphibious; gradient 60 percent; vertical obstacle 0.8m (2ft 7in); trench 2.5m (8ft 2in)

Namer IFV

The Israeli approach to infantry mobility has traditionally been a little different from that used by other nations. After years of using converted T-55 tanks as APCs and mounting half-squads of infantry aboard Merkava main battle tanks, it became apparent that a dedicated, heavily-protected infantry combat vehicle with the same mobility as the tank force was needed. The first Namer IFVs were converted Merkava Mk 1 tanks, but it was soon decided to use the Merkava MkIV chassis instead. The Namer thus became a new vehicle rather than a conversion. Armed with a 60m (196ft 10in) mortar in addition to a remotely controlled weapons station mounting a heavy machinegun or an automatic grenade launcher, the Namer retains many features of the Merkava tank, including its heavy protection.

Country of origin:	Israel
Crew:	3 + 9 additional personnel
Weight:	60,000kg (132,277lb)
Dimensions:	not known
Range:	500km (311 miles)
Armour:	classified; modular composite
Armament:	one 40mm (1.57in) automatic grenade launcher or one 12.7mm (0.5in) machine gun; one 60 mortar; one 7.72mm (0.303in) machine gun
Powerplant:	continental AVDS-1790 V12 diesel
Performance:	60km/h (37mph)

Type 89

The Mitsubishi Type 89 Mechanised Infantry Combat Vehicle is a true fighting machine. With the dimensions of a small tank, it boasts one 35mm (1.38in) Oerlikon Contraves cannon, a coaxial 7.62mm (0.3in) machine gun, and two preloaded ATGWs (usually Jyu-MAT medium-range missiles). A crew of three man the forward section (which includes the engine) and turret of the vehicle, and seven other combat personnel can be transported in the rear. Six firing ports are provided around the sides and rear of the Type 89 to allow small arms to be deployed against infantry attack. Production of the Type 89 began in 1991, and continues today.

Country of origin:	Japan
Crew:	3 + 7
Weight:	26,500kg (58,400lb)
Dimensions:	length 6.8m (22ft 4in); width 3.2m (10ft 6in); height 2.5m (8ft 2in)
Range:	400km (250 miles)
Armour:	classified
Armament:	one 35mm (1.38in) Oerlikon Contraves cannon; one coaxial 7.62mm (0.3in) machine gun; two ATGWs (Jyu-MAT anti-tank missiles)
Powerplant:	one 6-cylinder diesel developing 600hp (447kW)
Performance:	max road speed 70km/h (43mph); fording 1m (3ft 4in); gradient 60 percent; vertical obstacle 0.8m (2ft 7in); trench 2.4m (7ft 11in)

Combat Vehicle (CV) 90

The CV90 family of armoured vehicles was developed for the Swedish military, but has achieved considerable export success, seeing active service in Afghanistan since 2007. The steel hull can receive additional armour, enabling the vehicle to resist 30mm (1.18in) anti-armour rounds, though it is primarily protected by its small size and manoeuvrability. The chassis can support a range of variants including a light tank armed with a 120mm (4.72in) smoothbore gun, an anti-aircraft vehicle, observation and command vehicles and an armoured recovery variant. Using a family of vehicles greatly simplifies support both in terms of parts, availability and personnel training, resulting in improved efficiency and reduced costs.

Country of origin:	Sweden
Crew:	3 + 7 additional personnel
Weight:	23,000kg (50.706lb)
Dimentions:	length 6.55m (21ft 6in); width 3.1m (10ft 2in); height 2.7m (8ft 10in)
Range:	320km (199 miles)
Armour:	varies
Armament:	tank version: one 120mm (4.7in) gun, one 7.62mm (0.3in) machine gun
Powerplant:	410kW (550hp) Scania DSI V8 diesel
Performance:	maximum road speed 70km/h (43mph)

Bionix 25

The Bionix 25 IFV entered service in 1997 with the Singapore Armoured Forces. It is one of the new generation of armoured combat vehicles – fast, manoeuvrable and with enhanced survivability. The tracked configuration supports six road wheels on each side, and the front-drive system can power the Bionix 25 to a 70km/h (43mph) maximum speed. While the vehicular technology is produced by Singapore Technologies Automotive, the turret-mounted 25mm (0.98in) cannon is from the Boeing Company. This is stabilized for accuracy in rough terrain while a thermal sight enables night firing. Seven infantry can ride in the Bionix 25, access provided by a power-operated ramp in the hull rear.

Country of origin:	Singapore
Crew:	3 + 7
Weight:	23,000kg (50,700lb)
Dimensions:	length 5.92m (19ft 5in); width 2.7m (8ft 10in); height 2.53m (8ft 4in)
Range:	415km (260 miles)
Armour:	classified
Armament:	one 25mm (0.98in) Boeing M242 cannon; one coaxial 7.62mm (0.3in) MG; one turret-mounted 7.62mm (0.3in) MG; two x 3 smoke grenade launchers
Powerplant:	one 475hp (354kW) Detroit Diesel Model 6V-92TA diesel
Performance:	max speed 70km/h (43mph); fording 1m (3.3ft); gradient 60 percent; vertical obstacle 0.6m (2ft); trench 2m (6ft 7in)

VCC-80/Dardo IFV

The Dardo IFV emerged on the world scene in 1998, but is actually derived from an earlier vehicle, the VCC-80 MICV. This entered production 10 years earlier, and is a tracked infantry vehicle armed with a 25mm (0.98in) Oerlikon Contraves KBA cannon. The Dardo is little different. Its main modification lies in the turret, which was adapted to mount TOW anti-tank missiles on either side. Sophisticated technology runs throughout the VCC-80/Dardo, though it has yet to be proven in combat. The armour is of the latest layered aluminium/steel type and laser range-finding and night-vision systems are standard. A highly sloped glacis plate at the front of the vehicle provides maximum deflection against projectiles.

Country of origin:	Italy
Crew:	2 + 7
Weight:	23,000kg (50,700lb)
Dimensions:	length 6.7m (22ft); width 3m (9ft 10in); height 2.64m (8ft 8in)
Range:	600km (370 miles)
Armour:	layered aluminium/steel (details classified)
Armament:	one 25mm (0.98in) Oerlikon Contraves KBA cannon; one 7.62mm (0.3in) coaxial machine gun; two TOW launchers; two x 3 smoke grenade launchers
Powerplant:	one IVECO 8260 V-6 turbo diesel, developing 520hp (388kW)
Performance:	maximum speed 70km/h (43mph); fording 1.5m (4ft 11in); gradient 60 percent; vertical obstacle 0.85m (2ft 9in); trench 2.5m (8ft 2in)

Bronco ATTC

The Bronco All-Terrain Tracked Carrier is a twin-chassis vehicle developed to support military, peacekeeping and humanitarian relief operations in very difficult terrain. A variant – designated Warthog – has been purchased by the British Army. The Bronco runs on rubber tracks and can cope with snow, soft sand and swampy terrain. Its articulated steering system allows operations in very tight conditions such as rocky or mountainous areas. Four further variants are planned by the British Army. Twelve soldiers can normally be transported by the basic troop carrier model, which can be customized to serve as a communications vehicle or to carry other specialist equipment. The repair/recovery variant can serve as a mobile workshop and conduct engineering tasks with its crane and winch.

Country of origin:	Singapore
Crew:	front car) 4; (rear car) 8
Weight:	18,000kg (39,683lb)
Dimensions:	length 8.6m (28ft 3in); width 2.3m (8ft 2in); height 2.2m (7ft 3in)
Range:	not known
Armour:	steel, AMAP-ADS active protection system
Armament:	one 7.62mm (0.3in) MG or one 5.56mm (0.22in)?MG
Powerplant:	261kW (350hp) Caterpillar 3126B
Performance:	speed (road) 65km/h (40mph); speed (water) 5km/h (3.1mph)

BVS 10 Viking Armoured Personnel Carrier

A collaborative design effort between Britain and Sweden, the BVS 10 entered service with the Royal Marines in 2005. Fully amphibious, the vehicle carries up to four soldiers in its front vehicle and up to eight in the trailer. It is protected by specialized armour and mounts a light machine gun. Variants include a Command Carrier, with the rear cab designed as an enhanced digital communications platform; a repair and recovery variant, which carries four specialist maintenance crewmen, a crane and a winch; and an ambulance variant. For the UK the Viking has served in Afghanistan and Somaliland. It is also in service with the Netherlands Marine Corps, and there are orders for BVS 10s for France.

Country of origin:	Britain/Sweden
Crew:	front car driver + 4 passengers; rear car 8 passengers
Weight:	10,600kg (23,369lb)
Dimensions:	length 7.5m (24ft 7in); width 2.1m (6ft 10.7in); height 2.2m (7ft 2.5in)
Range:	300km (186 miles)
Armour:	steel with additional modulat bolt-on plates
Armament:	capacity for one 12.7mm (0.5in) Browning HMG or one 7.62mm (0.3in) MG
Powerplant:	183kW (250bhp) Cummins 5.9l in-line
Performance:	maximum road speed: 50km/h (31mph); max cross-country speed 15km/h (9.3mph); max water speed 5km/h (3.1mph)

Wheeled Infantry Vehicles

VAB

In 1974 Renault was selected to build a wheeled armoured personnel carrier to complement the AMX-10 tracked vehicle being issued to infantry battalions. Produced in 4 x 4 and 6 x 6 versions, the vehicle is fully amphibious being propelled in water either by its wheels or by twin water jets. A nuclear, biological and chemical (NBC) defence system and night-vision capability are fitted as standard. Variants include an ambulance, internal security vehicle, command vehicle, anti-tank and mortar carrier. The vehicle has sold well abroad, in North Africa and the Middle East, in countries where France has a major influence, and in particular in Morocco, where it has been used in a counter-insurgency role against Polisario guerrillas. The VAB is a very rugged vehicle.

Country of origin:	France
Crew:	2 + 10
Weight:	13,000kg (28,660lb)
Dimensions:	length 5.98m (19ft 7.4in); width 2.49m (8ft 2in); height 2.063m (6ft 9in)
Range:	1000km (621 miles)
Armour:	classified
Armament:	one 7.62mm machine gun
Powerplant:	one MAN six-cylinder inline diesel engine developing 235hp (175kW)
Performance:	maximum road speed 92km/h (57mph); fording amphibious; vertical obstacle 0.6m (2ft); trench not applicable

Ratel 20

The Ratel was designed by the South Africans to replace the British Saracen, when it became clear that political considerations might place future supplies in jeopardy. The prototype appeared in 1976, with the first production vehicles arriving just a year later. Designed specifically for South African needs, the vehicle has an exceptional range (needed for large-scale anti-guerrilla operations in the vast expanses of Africa) with excellent mobility, armour and firepower. It has seen combat extensive service, being used for counter-insurgency raids in Namibia and Angola, and has been exported to Morocco for similar duties. Variants include the Ratel 60, which is equipped with a 60mm mortar, the Ratel 90, which mounts the 90mm gun, and the Ratel repair, which is optimised for field repairs.

Country of origin:	South Africa
Crew:	4 + 7
Weight:	19,000kg (41,800lb)
Dimensions:	length 7.212m (23ft 8.4in); width 2.516m (8ft 3in); height 2.915m (9ft 6.8in)
Range:	1000km (621 miles)
Armour:	20mm (0.78in)
Armament:	one 20mm cannon; two 7.62mm machine guns
Powerplant:	one D 3256 BTXF six-cylinder diesel engine developing 282hp (210kW)
Performance:	maximum road speed 105km/h (65mph); fording 1.2m (3ft 11.2in); vertical obstacle 0.35m (1ft 1.7in); trench 1.15m (3ft 9.3in)

Wheeled Infantry Vehicles
UR-416

The UR-416 was developed from the chassis of the civilian Unimog 4 x 4 which appeared in the 1950s. Work on the military version began in the early 1960s and production began in 1966. The UR-416 was a relatively inexpensive vehicle, easy to maintain and operate. Room was provided for eight troops in the rear compartment and there were firing ports to allow them to use their weapons from inside. Variants included a command vehicle, repair vehicle and an ambulance. The UR-416 has been widely exported, particularly to Africa and South America and is used by several European countries for such duties as airport security and riot control, the vehicles being fitted with public address systems, fire extinguishers and blades for removing obstacles when on anti-riot duties.

Country of origin:	West Germany
Crew:	2 + 8
Weight:	7600kg (16,720lb)
Dimensions:	length 5.21m (17ft 1in); width 2.30m (7ft 6.5in); height 2.225m (7ft 3.6in)
Range:	700km (435 miles)
Armour:	9mm (0.35in)
Armament:	one 7.62mm machine gun
Powerplant:	one Daimler-Benz OM 352 six-cylinder diesel engine developing 120hp (89kW)
Performance:	maximum road speed 85km/h (53mph); fording 1.4m (4ft 7in); vertical obstacle 0.55m (1ft 9.7in); trench not applicable

BTR-40

The BTR-40 entered service in 1951. Based on a GAZ-43 4 x 4 truck chassis, it was able to carry eight troops as part of the Soviet doctrine of armoured spearheads supported by mechanised infantry. The vehicle filled a variety of roles such as ambulance, reconnaissance and command vehicle, in addition to being an armoured personnel carrier. The BTR-40 lacked the tyre-pressure regulation system common to many post-World War II Soviet vehicles, nor did it have a nuclear, biological and chemical (NBC) defence system. There was a specialised chemical warfare variant, though, the BTR-40kh, which was used to mark clear lanes through contaminated areas. The BTR-40 was phased out of frontline Red Army service from the late 1950s onwards. It was exported extensively to Soviet client states.

Country of origin:	USSR
Crew:	2 + 8
Weight:	5300kg (11,660lb)
Dimensions:	length 5m (16ft 5in); width 1.9m (6ft 3in); height 1.75m (5ft 9in)
Range:	285km (178 miles)
Armour:	8mm (0.31in)
Armament:	one 7.62mm machine gun
Powerplant:	one GAZ-40 six-cylinder water-cooled petrol engine developing 80hp (60kW)
Performance:	maximum road speed 80km/h (50mph); fording 0.8m (2ft 8in); vertical obstacle 0.47m (1ft 6in); trench 0.7m (2ft 4in)

Wheeled Infantry Vehicles

PSZH-IV

The PSZH-IV was a development of the FUG 4 x 4 amphibious scout car designed for the Hungarian Army in the early 1960s. Appearing in the mid-1960s (when it was thought by the West to be a reconnaissance vehicle), the vehicle was of all-welded steel construction and was a fully amphibious armoured personnel carrier, being propelled in water by two water jets and able to carry six troops (though their only means of exit and entry are via the small two-part door in each side of the hull). It was equipped with a tyre-pressure regulation system, nuclear, biological and chemical (NBC) defence system and infrared night-vision equipment. Variants included a command vehicle, ambulance and a NBC reconnaissance vehicle. It is in service with the armies of Bulgaria, Hungary, the Czech Republic and Iraq.

Country of origin:	Hungary
Crew:	3 + 6
Weight:	7500kg (16,500lb)
Dimensions:	length 5.70m (18ft 8.4in); width 2.50m (8ft 2.4in); height 2.30m (7ft 7in)
Range:	500km (311 miles)
Armour:	14mm (0.55in)
Armament:	one 14.5mm machine gun; one coaxial 7.62mm machine gun
Powerplant:	one Caspel four-cylinder diesel engine developing 100hp (74.57kW)
Performance:	maximum road speed 80km/h (50mph); fording amphibious; vertical obstacle 0.4m (1ft 3.7in); trench 0.6m (1ft 11.6in)

BTR-152V1

The BTR-152 was one of the first Soviet armoured personnel carriers, as Soviet forces had not used the type during World War II. First seen in public in 1951, the vehicle consisted of a ZIL-157 truck chassis with an armoured body. The main drawback of the early vehicle was the open-topped compartment, which left troops vulnerable to overhead shell bursts. In addition, its cross-country mobility was poor and it had no amphibious capability. Late vehicles have the central tyre pressure regulation system that allows the driver to adjust tyre pressure to suit the terrain being driven on. It was replaced in frontline service in the early 1960s by the BTR-60, but was exported widely to around 30 countries, seeing combat in the Middle East (with Syria, Egypt and Iraq in the Arab-Israeli wars), Africa and the Far East.

Country of origin:	USSR
Crew:	2 + 17
Weight:	8950kg (19,690lb)
Dimensions:	length 6.83m (22ft 4.9in); width 2.32m (7ft 7.3in); height 2.05m (6ft 8.7in)
Range:	780km (485 miles)
Armour:	4-13.5mm (0.15-0.53in)
Armament:	one 7.62mm machine gun
Powerplant:	one ZIL-123 six-cylinder petrol engine developing 110hp (82kW)
Performance:	maximum road speed 75km/h (47mph); fording 0.8m (2ft 7.5in); vertical obstacle 0.6m (1ft 11.6in); trench 0.69m (2ft 3.2in)

Wheeled Infantry Vehicles

BTR-60PB

The BTR-60 was introduced into Red Army service in the late 1960s to replace the BTR-152. The early BTR-60s still had an open-topped compartment, but this was soon remedied. The vehicle was fully amphibious and was propelled in water by a single water jet. It carried 14 troops, who were able to fight from inside the vehicle by means of firing ports, but who had to enter and exit the vehicle through roof hatches, with the obvious exposure to danger that this carried. Exported to over 30 countries, the BTR-60 has seen action in many parts of the world, having an integral role in protecting Soviet convoys in Afghanistan during the Russian occupation of the country, and even taking on the Americans during the invasion of Grenada in 1983, although they were quickly knocked out.

Country of origin:	USSR
Crew:	2 + 14
Weight:	10,300kg (22,660lb)
Dimensions:	length 7.56m (24ft 9.6in); width 2.825m (9ft 3.2in); height 2.31m (7ft 6.9in)
Range:	500km (311 miles)
Armour:	7-9mm (0.27-0.35in)
Armament:	one 12.7mm machine gun; two 7.62mm machine guns
Powerplant:	two GAZ-49B six-cylinder petrol engines, each developing 90hp (67kW)
Performance:	maximum road speed 80km/h (50mph); fording amphibious; vertical obstacle 0.4m (1ft 3.7in); trench 2m (6ft 7in)

OT-64C(1)

The OT-64 was Czechoslovakia and Poland's answer to the Soviet BTR-60. The OT-64 entered service in 1964, with the advantage over its Soviet counterpart of having a fully enclosed compartment for troops and being diesel, rather than petrol-powered, which extended range and reduced the risk of fire. It was heavier, though, with a lower power-to-weight ratio. Fully amphibious with two propellers, entry was through the rear, and a winch, nuclear, biological and chemical (NBC) defence system and night vision capability were fitted as standard. There were command and recovery variants and some OT-64s were adapted for anti-aircraft and anti-tank capability, the latter being fitted with 'Sagger' anti-tank guided weapons. North African and Middle East countries were the main export customers.

Country of origin:	Czechoslovakia/Poland
Crew:	2 + 15
Weight:	14,500kg (31,900lb)
Dimensions:	length 7.44m (24ft 5in); width 2.55m (8ft 4.4in); height 2.06m (6ft 9in)
Range:	710km (441 miles)
Armour:	10mm (0.39in)
Armament:	one 7.62mm machine gun
Powerplant:	one Tatra V-8 diesel engine developing 180hp (134kW)
Performance:	maximum road speed 94.4km/h (59mph); fording amphibious; vertical obstacle 0.5m (1ft 7.7in); trench 2m (6ft 7in)

MOWAG

The MOWAG was designed by Kreuzlingen for easy conversion to a number of diverse roles, such as ambulance, command vehicle or armoured personnel carrier. The MOWAG entered production in 1964, and its small size (there was only room for three troops in the rear, plus the commander, machine gunner and driver) proved ideal for internal security duties, particularly when fitted with a blade for clearing obstacles, a public address system and wire mesh protection for the vision blocks and headlamps. The vehicle was also available with bullet-proof tyres (with metal disks attached to the outside of the tyre). Export customers included Greece, Argentina, Bolivia, Chile and Iraq, all of which no doubt saw the vehicle's value in internal suppression. Production is now complete.

Country of origin:	Switzerland
Crew:	3 + 3
Weight:	8200kg (18,040lb)
Dimensions:	length 5.31m (17ft 5in); width 2.2m (7ft 3in); height 1.88m (6ft 2in)
Range:	400km (248 miles)
Armour:	8mm (0.31in)
Armament:	one 12.7mm or 7.62mm machine gun
Powerplant:	one V-8 four-stroke water-cooled petrol engine developing 202hp (151kW)
Performance:	maximum road speed 80km/h (50mph); fording 1.1m (3ft 7in); vertical obstacle 0.4m (1ft 4in); trench not applicable

Chaimite V-200

The BRAVIA Chaimite armoured personnel carrier was a Portuguese-licensed version of the US Cadillac Gage Commando V-150 armoured car. It is a 4x4 vehicle with the usual amphibious capabilities and a steel armoured hull. Carrying capacity is nine soldiers. The V-200 is one of nine versions of the Chaimite available, each distinguished usually by its armament. The V-200 is armed simply with twin turret-mounted 7.62mm (0.3in) machine guns. Subsequent versions go up in denominations of 100. The V-400, for example, is fitted with a 90mm (3.54in) cannon, whereas the V-700 is armed with ATGW systems. 6x6 and 8x8 prototype versions of the Chaimite have also been produced.

Country of origin:	Portugal
Crew:	2 + 9
Weight:	7300kg (16,100lb)
Dimensions:	length 5.6m (18ft 4in); width 2.26m (7ft 5in); height 2.26m (7ft 5in)
Range:	950km (590 miles)
Armour:	(Steel) 7.94mm (0.31in) maximum
Armament:	two 7.62mm (0.3in) MGs
Powerplant:	one M75 V8 petrol, developing 210hp (157kW)
Performance:	maximum road speed 110km/h (68mph); fording amphibious; gradient 65 percent; vertical obstacle 0.9m (2.9ft)

Wheeled Infantry Vehicles

Grenadier

The MOWAG Grenadier was an armoured car/armoured personnel carrier from the late 1960s and early 1970s which demonstrated multi-tasking in military vehicles. As an APC, it could carry eight personnel plus the driver, protecting them from small-arms fire. Even bullet-proof tyres could be fitted. It was fully amphibious, powered by a three-blade propeller. Extensive weapons fittings made it a purposeful combat vehicle. Options included a turret-mounted 20mm (0.78in) cannon, 80mm (3.15in) multiple rocket launchers, various anti-tank weapons and remote-control 7.62mm (0.3in) machine guns. The Grenadier series was effectively replaced by MOWAG's Piranha series of armoured cars in the 1980s.

Country of origin:	Switzerland
Crew:	1 + 8
Weight:	6100kg (13,450lb)
Dimensions:	length 4.84m (15ft 11in); width 2.3m (7ft 6in); height 2.12m (7ft)
Range:	550km (340 miles)
Armour:	not disclosed
Armament:	various (see text)
Powerplant:	one MOWAG 8-cylinder petrol, developing 202hp (150kW) at 3900rpm
Performance:	maximum road speed 100km/h (62mph)

V-150 Commando

The V-150 Commando was the successor to the V-100 developed in the early 1960s. It first appeared in the early 1970s, containing a number of improvements on the V-100, its most significant being the installation of a diesel engine to provide a greater range and less risk of fire than with a petrol engine. The V-150 was easily adapted for a number of roles, ranging from armoured personnel carrier to riot control and recovery vehicle. A wide range of armaments could be fitted to give extra flexibility, from anti-aircraft cannon to mortars and anti-tank guided weapons. All versions are fully amphibious, propelled in the water by their wheels. In addition, a wide variety of armaments can be fitted. A popular export model, the V-150 has been sold to around 25 countries.

Country of origin:	USA
Crew:	3 + 2
Weight:	9888kg (21,753lb)
Dimensions:	length 5.689m (18ft 8in); width 2.26m (7ft 5in); height 1.981m (6ft 6in)
Range:	643km (400 miles)
Armour:	classified
Armament:	various, including one 25mm cannon; one 7.62mm machine gun
Powerplant:	one V-540 V-8 diesel engine developing 202hp (151kW)
Performance:	maximum road speed 88.5km/h (55mph); fording amphibious; vertical obstacle 0.609m (2ft 0in); trench not applicable

Wheeled Infantry Vehicles

M706

Cadillac Gage began design on a multi-purpose armoured vehicle at the beginning on the 1960s which, following successful trials, was put into production in 1964 as the V-100 Commando, powered by a Chrysler engine. The US Army later designated the vehicle as M706. The vehicle was primarily destined for export but the conflict in Vietnam in the 1960s soon required a vehicle to fill the dual patrol and escort roles. Significant numbers of M706s saw service with both South Vietnamese and US troops. In Vietnam it proved a versatile and effective counter-insurgency weapon, being ideal for rapid counterattack when attached to ambushed convoys. A scaled-up version, the V-200, was sold to Singapore, and 1971 the V-100 was replaced by the V-150.

Country of origin:	USA
Crew:	3 + 2
Weight:	9888kg (21,753lb)
Dimensions:	length 5.689m (18ft 8in); width 2.26m (7ft 5in); height 1.981m (6ft 6in)
Range:	643km (400 miles)
Armour:	classified
Armament:	two 7.62mm machine guns
Powerplant:	one V-8 diesel engine developing 202bhp (151kW)
Performance:	maximum road speed 88.5km/h (55mph); fording amphibious; vertical obstacle 0.609m (2ft 0in); trench not applicable

V-300 Commando

The V-300 was a 6 x 6 version of the Commando range. Built by Cadillac as a private venture to complement its 4 x 4 vehicles, the first production models were delivered in 1983 for export to Panama. The layout of the vehicle was different from that of the earlier V-150. Troops entered and exited the vehicle through rear doors only (the V-150 having side and rear doors), with additional hatches in the roof. A wide variety of armament could be fitted. Standard equipment includes a front-mounted winch with a capacity to lift 9072kg (19,958lb). Variants include a command post vehicle, ambulance (with a higher roof), a mortar carrier, anti-aircraft model and an anti-tank vehicle. Fully amphibious, the vehicle is propelled through the water by its wheels.

Country of origin:	USA
Crew:	3 + 9
Weight:	13,137kg (28,900lb)
Dimensions:	length 6.40m (21ft 0in); width 2.54m (8ft 4in); height 1.981m (6ft 6in)
Range:	700km (435 miles)
Armour:	classified
Armament:	one 25mm Hughes Helicopter Chain Gun; one 7.62mm coaxial machine gun
Powerplant:	one turbocharged diesel engine developing 235hp (175kW)
Performance:	maximum road speed 93km/h (58mph); fording amphibious; vertical obstacle 0.609m (2ft); trench not applicable

Commando Ranger

In 1979, Cadillac Gage was selected to meet the US Air Force's requirement for an armoured vehicle to provide security and protect its foreign air bases from attack by terrorists or other groups, and escort ordnance to and from bases. The Ranger entered service in 1980, based on a standard Chrysler truck chassis. The fully armoured compartment carried six men, who could fire from within the vehicle through firing ports, and this compartment was insulated and air-conditioned to reduce crew fatigue on lengthy patrols. Known to the USAF as the Peacekeeper, the vehicle was exported to Luxembourg and Indonesia. Optional equipment includes grenade launchers, spotlight and front-mounted winch. Variants included a command vehicle and an ambulance.

Country of origin:	USA
Crew:	2 + 6
Weight:	4536kg (9979lb)
Dimensions:	length 4.699m (15ft 5in); width 2.019 (6ft 7.5in); height 1.981m (6ft 6in)
Range:	556km (345 miles)
Armour:	7mm (0.27in)
Armament:	one or two 7.62mm machine guns
Powerplant:	one Dodge 360 CID V-8 petrol engine developing 180hp (134kW)
Performance:	maximum road speed 112.5km/h (70mph); fording 0.457 (1ft 6in); vertical obstacle 0.254m (10in); trench not applicable

Humber 'Pig'

Designed to supplement the Alvis Saracen, the Humber 'Pig' was based on the chassis of the Humber FV1600 truck chassis and entered service with the British Army in the 1950s. It was intended purely for transport to and from the battlefield rather than for any combat role. Carrying six men and equipped with firing ports, the Pig found itself being phased out with the arrival of the FV432 into service. However, the conflict in Northern Ireland rescued it from the scrapheap – the British needed a riot-control vehicle. It was given additional armour for the internal security role and equipped with barricade-removal equipment at the front. It remained in service in Northern Ireland until the 1980s. Variants included an ambulance and an anti-tank version equipped with Malkara missiles.

Country of origin:	UK
Crew:	2 + 6 (or 2 + 8)
Weight:	5790kg (12,738lb)
Dimensions:	length 4.926m (16ft 2in); width 2.044 (6ft 8.5in); height 2.12m (6ft 11.5in)
Range:	402km (250 miles)
Armour:	8mm (0.31in)
Armament:	2 x 4 smoke dischargers
Powerplant:	one Rolls-Royce B60 Mk 5A six-cylinder petrol engine developing 120hp (89kW)
Performance:	maximum road speed 64km/h (40mph); fording 0.5m (1ft 7in); vertical obstacle 0.23m (9in); trench not applicable

Alvis Saracen

The Saracen was part of the FV600 family of armoured vehicles developed for the British Army after World War II. The Saracen, first produced in 1952, was given priority because of its suitability for use in the guerrilla situation then occurring in Malaya. The vehicle was the only real British armoured personnel carrier in service during the 1950s, but began to be phased out in the 1960s in favour of the FV432 tracked vehicle, with its better armour range and mobility. It remained in service in Northern Ireland, however, into the 1980s, as well as in parts of Africa and the Middle East. It shares many components with the Alvis 6 x 6 Saladin. Variants included an ambulance and command vehicle, but radar-carrying, self-propelled gun and mine-clearing versions never entered service.

Country of origin:	UK
Crew:	2 + 10
Weight:	8640kg (19,008lb)
Dimensions:	length 5.233m (17ft 2in); width 2.539 (8ft 4in); height 2.463m (8ft 1in)
Range:	400km (248 miles)
Armour:	16mm (0.62in)
Armament:	two 7.62mm machine guns
Powerplant:	one Rolls-Royce B80 Mk 6A eight-cylinder petrol engine developing 160hp (119kW)
Performance:	maximum road speed 72km/h (44.7mph); fording 1.07m (3ft 6in); vertical obstacle 0.46m (1ft 6in); trench 1.52m (5ft 0in)

Saxon

The Saxon was developed in the early 1970s in response to a British Army requirement for a wheeled armoured personnel carrier for the 1980s and 1990s. Based on the Bedford Mk4 4 x 4, the standard truck of the British Army, production began in 1976 and the first models were delivered to British battalions in 1984. The Saxon was one of the best armoured vehicles of its type when it was introduced. One unusual feature was that the mudguards were designed to blow off in the event that the vehicle hit a mine, thus allowing the blast to escape sideways rather than up into the vehicle. The Saxon could be fitted with a range of armaments and variants included a command vehicle, an anti-riot vehicle and an ambulance. Some Saxons have a one-man 7.62mm machine-gun turret fitted.

Country of origin:	UK
Crew:	2 + 8
Weight:	10,670kg (23,474lb)
Dimensions:	length 5.169m (16ft 11.5in); width 2.489 (8ft 2in); height 2.86m (9ft 4.6in)
Range:	510km (317 miles)
Armour:	classified
Armament:	one 7.62mm machine gun
Powerplant:	one Bedford 500 six-cylinder diesel engine developing 164hp (122kW)
Performance:	maximum road speed 96km/h (60mph); fording 1.12m (3ft 8in); vertical obstacle 0.41m (1ft 4in); trench not applicable

Panhard M3

The Panhard M3 remains one of the world's most successful armoured personnel carriers, if only for its massive export sales to over 35 countries with particular concentrations in Africa and the Middle East. There is little exceptional about the M3, and consequently it is ideal for transforming into local variants. It is a 4x4 armoured vehicle which can carry 10 men as well as a two-man crew, and negotiate rough terrain with confidence. Access and exit are through two side and two rear doors. It is fully amphibious, and can maintain 4km/h (2.5mph) in water, propelled by its wheels. The many M3 variants include engineer vehicles, anti-aircraft vehicles, an ambulance and radar versions.

Country of origin:	France
Crew:	2 + 10
Weight:	6100kg (13,450lb)
Dimensions:	length: 4.45m (14ft 7in); width: 2.55m (8ft 4in); height: 2m (6ft 7in)
Range:	600km (370 miles)
Armour:	12mm (0.47in) maximum
Armament:	Various
Powerplant:	one Panhard M4 HD 4-cylinder petrol, developing 90hp (67kW)
Performance:	maximum road speed: 90km/h (56mph); fording: amphibious; gradient: 60 percent; vertical obstacle: 0.3m (1ft); trench: 0.8m (2ft 7in)

BTR-70

The BTR-70 is essentially an improved BTR-60. Its hull is slightly longer than that of the BTR-60, and it features triangular access doors to the troop compartment on both sides, set between the second and third axles. Two roof hatches provide additional access. The troop compartment holds nine infantrymen sitting back to back along a central bench. Three firing ports and a vision block are on each side of the compartment. The two-man crew sit towards the front of the vehicle, and each has three forward and one side-facing periscope. Armament is confined to the small forward turret, and consists of one 14.5mm (0.57in) KPVT machine gun with a coaxial 7.62mm (0.3in) machine gun.

Country of origin:	Russia/Soviet Union
Crew:	2 + 9
Weight:	11,500kg (25,400lb)
Dimensions:	length: 7.53m (24ft 8in); width: 2.8m (9ft 2in); height: 2.23m (7ft 4in)
Range:	600km (370 miles)
Armour:	Steel (details classified)
Armament:	one 14.5mm (0.57in) KPVT MG; one coaxial PKT 7.62mm (0.3in) MG
Powerplant:	one ZMZ-4905 8-cylinder petrol, developing 240hp (179kW) at 2100rpm
Performance:	maximum road speed: 80km/h (50mph); fording: amphibious; gradient: 60 percent; vertical obstacle: 0.7m (2ft 4in); trench: 2.7m (8ft 11in)

Wheeled Infantry Vehicles

VXB-170

The VXB-170 is a 4x4 armoured personnel carrier developed by the French military truck manufacturer Berliet in the mid-1960s. It went into production in 1973 and has mainly served with the French Gendarmerie, where it has been a useful multi-purpose armoured vehicle ideally suited for security use. It is fully amphibious and has a carrying capacity of 12 or 13 soldiers. Windows are bullet-proofed and can be opened to provide firing-ports if necessary. Four roof hatches and three side doors provide multiple entry and exit routes. An optional feature is a 4500kg (9900lb) capacity winch which can be installed in the front of the hull. Apart from France, it is in service in Gabon, Senegal, Tunisia and with the United Nations peacekeeping forces.

Country of origin:	France
Crew:	12
Weight:	12,700kg (28,000lb)
Dimensions:	length 5.99m (19.65ft); width 2.5m (8.2ft); height 2.05m (6.73ft)
Range:	750km (470 miles)
Armour:	7mm (0.28in)
Armament:	one 7.62mm (0.3in) MG
Powerplant:	one Berliet V800M 8-cylinder diesel, developing 170hp (127kW)
Performance:	maximum road speed 85km/h (53mph); fording amphibious; gradient 60 percent

BMR-600

The BMR-600 infantry fighting vehicle was developed for the Spanish Army during the 1970s, and has gone on to see export service in Egypt, Saudi Arabia and Peru. In many ways it is a conventional armoured personnel carrier. It is fully amphibious with two waterjets providing propulsion from the rear of the hull. Lightweight aluminium armour provides protection from small-arms fire and shell splinters for the two crew members and 11 other occupants. A cupola on the roof provides a weapon mount. In the Spanish Army, a 12.7mm (0.5in) Browning M2 HB is fitted as standard, though a 20mm (0.78in) cannon is optional. Other combat versions of the BMR-600 include ATGW launcher and 81mm (3.19in) mortar carrier.

Country of origin:	Spain
Crew:	2 + 11
Weight:	14,000kg (30,900lb)
Dimensions:	length 6.15m (20ft 2in); width 2.5m (8ft 2in); height 2m (6ft 7in)
Range:	1000km (620 miles)
Armour:	(aluminium) 38mm (1.49in) estimated
Armament:	one 12.7mm (0.5in) Browning M2 HB
Powerplant:	one Pegaso 9157/8 6-cylinder diesel, developing 310hp (231kW) at 2200rpm
Performance:	maximum road speed 103km/h (64mph); fording amphibious; gradient 60 percent; vertical obstacle 0.6m (2ft); trench 1.35m (4ft 5in)

EE-3 Jararaca

The EE-3 Jararaca was produced by the now-dissolved ENGESA company. It is basically a diminutive 4x4 scout car only 4.12m (13.52ft) in length and 1.56m (5.12ft) in height. Its small size and light weight give it excellent manoeuvrability and speed, qualities it can maintain over rough ground using a central tyre-pressure regulation system. All tyres are of run-flat type. The hull is constructed from double-layer steel armour plate. Inside is a three-man crew with the driver positioned centrally over the front glacis plate. Three periscopes provide him with hatch-down visibility. The EE-3 accepts various armament configurations ranging from the standard 12.7mm (0.5in) Browning machine gun to a MILAN ATGW.

Country of origin:	Brazil
Crew:	3
Weight:	5500kg (12,100lb)
Dimensions:	length 4.12m (13ft 6in); width 2.13m (7ft); height 1.56m (5ft 1in)
Range:	750km (470 miles)
Armour:	Double-layer steel (details classified)
Armament:	one 12.7mm (0.5in) Browning M2 HB as standard
Powerplant:	one Mercedes-Benz OM 314A 4-cylinder turbo diesel, developing 120hp (89kW) at 2800rpm
Performance:	Maximum road speed 100km/h (60mph); fording 0.6m (2ft); gradient 60 percent; vertical obstacle 0.4m (1ft 4in); trench 0.4m (1ft 4in)

EE-11

In 1970, ENGESA began work on an armoured 6 x 6 wheeled vehicle in response to a Brazilian armed forces requirement. Production of the Urutu armoured personnel vehicle began in 1974. The vehicle was fully amphibious, being fitted with a trim vane, bilge pumps and two propellers. The Urutu was fitted with tyre-pressure regulation system, night vision and nuclear, biological and chemical (NBC) defence system and could carry up to 12 troops in the rear (who exit via doors in each side and one in the rear). Firing ports were available to allow these troops to fight from within the vehicle. Variants included an ambulance, cargo-transport, command vehicle, anti-aircraft and anti-tank versions, the latter being fitted with Milan or HOT anti-tank guided weapons.

Country of origin:	Brazil
Crew:	1 + 12
Weight:	13,000kg (28,600lb)
Dimensions:	length 6.15m (20ft 2in); width 2.59 (8ft 6in); height 2.09m (6ft 10.3in)
Range:	850km (528 miles)
Armour:	classified
Armament:	one 12.7mm machine gun; one 7.62mm machine gun
Powerplant:	one Detroit Diesel 6V-53N six-cylinder diesel engine developing 212hp (158kW)
Performance:	maximum road speed 90km/h (56mph); fording amphibious; vertical obstacle 0.6m (1ft 11.6in); trench not applicable

SIBMAS

The SIBMAS 6 x 6 armoured personnel carrier started as a private venture in the mid-1970s by the Belgian company BN Constructions Ferroviaires et Métalliques, with the first vehicles being delivered in 1983 to the Royal Malaysian Army, who eventually bought nearly 200 as fire-support vehicles, armed with the 90mm Cockerill Mk III gun. As expected, the basic model is fully amphibious without preparation and is propelled in the water by its wheels or by two propellers. Night vision and nuclear, biological and chemical (NBC) systems can be fitted as well as a range of different armaments. There are three entry doors: one in each side and one at the rear. The troop compartment has firing ports. Variants include an ambulance, a command vehicle and a cargo vehicle.

Country of origin:	Belgium
Crew:	3 + 11
Weight:	16,500kg (36,300lb)
Dimensions:	length 7.32m (24ft 0in); width 2.50 (8ft 2.4in); height (hull) 2.24m (7ft 4.2in)
Range:	1000km (621 miles)
Armour:	classified
Armament:	one 90mm Cockerill Mk III gun; one coaxial 7.62mm machine gun; one anti-aircraft 7.62mm machine gun
Powerplant:	one six-cylinder turbocharged diesel developing 320hp (239kW)
Performance:	maximum road speed 100km/h (62mph); fording amphibious; vertical obstacle 0.6m (1ft 11.6in); trench 1.5m (4ft 11in)

RBY Mk1

The RBY Mk1 is a light reconnaissance vehicle first manufactured by Israel Aircraft Industries in the mid-1970s. Though the hull is all-welded steel with 8mm (0.31in) armour, there is no top cover for the crew compartment. Also, the front windscreen can be folded flat for unimpaired visibility. These features increase the RBY's vulnerability to small-arms and shell fire, but reduce the chances of occupant heat exhaustion in the hot Middle Eastern climate. A variety of machine guns and cannon, even a 106mm (4.17in) recoilless rifle, can be fitted to the rim of the hull. The RBY Mk1's bonnet and bumpers are made of fibre glass designed to disintegrate harmlessly if the vehicle strikes a mine.

Country of origin:	Israel
Crew:	2 + 6
Weight:	3600kg (7900lb)
Dimensions:	length 5.02m (16ft 6in); width 2.03m (6ft 8in); height 1.66m (5ft 5in)
Range:	550km (340 miles)
Armour:	(Steel) 8mm (0.31in)
Armament:	various MGs and cannons
Powerplant:	one Chrysler 6-cylinder petrol, developing 120hp (89kW)
Performance:	maximum road speed 100km/h (62mph); fording 0.4m (1ft 4in); gradient 60 percent

Scout

The Cadillac Gage Commando Scout, to give it its proper title, has a boat-like appearance which belies the fact that it is not amphibious (its maximum fording depth is 1.17m/3ft 11in). Its name suggests a reconnaissance role, which is its primary duty, but it can also perform anti-tank and command post missions with different fitments. Turret options include a TOW ATGW launcher, a combination of a 40mm (1.58in) grenade launcher and a 12.7mm (0.5in) machine gun, or a twin machine gun. Its light weight and aerodynamic shape give the Scout an operating range of 1290km (800 miles), greater than most reconnaissance vehicles. It also has run-flat tyres as standard.

Country of origin:	USA
Crew:	2–3
Weight:	7240kg (15,960lb)
Dimensions:	length 5m (16ft 5in); width 2.05m (6ft 8in); height 2.16m (7ft 2in)
Range:	1290km (800 miles)
Armour:	steel (details classified)
Armament:	one 7.62mm (0.3in) MG
Powerplant:	one Cummins V6 diesel, developing 155hp (115kW) at 3300rpm
Performance:	maximum road speed 96km/h (60mph); fording 1.17m (3ft 11in); gradient 60 percent; vertical obstacle 0.6m (2ft)

RAM V-2L

The RAM V-2L is one variant amongst many in a series of light vehicles built by RAMTA Structures and Systems, a subsidiary of Israel Aircraft Industries. The first of the RAM family was the V-1, a 4x4 light armoured fighting vehicle which held two crew, seven passengers, and was armed with 7.62mm (0.3in) machine guns and 106mm (4.17in) recoilless rifles. The key distinction between the RAM V-1 and the subsequent V-2 is that the former has an open-top hull, whereas the latter is fully enclosed. Both the V-2 and V-1 split into many sub-variants, including versions fitted with TOW ATGW launchers and 20mm (0.78in) cannon anti-aircraft turrets.

Country of origin:	Israel
Crew:	2 + 7 or 8
Weight:	5750kg (12,700lb)
Dimensions:	length 5.52m (18ft 1in); width 2.03m (6ft 8in); height 1.72m (5ft 7in)
Range:	800km (500 miles)
Armour:	(Steel) 8mm (0.31in)
Armament:	one 12.7mm (0.5in) machine gun; two 7.62mm (0.3in) machine guns
Powerplant:	one Deutz 6-cylinder diesel, developing 132hp (98kW)
Performance:	maximum road speed 96km/h (60mph); fording 1m (3ft 4in); gradient 64 percent; vertical obstacle 0.8m (2ft 7in)

Wheeled Infantry Vehicles

TM 125

In spite of its small appearance, the TM 125 can carry 12 personnel, the passengers sitting five abreast down each side of the hull. The hull features a total of six firing ports, while vision for driver and commander is provided by two windows. Armoured shutters can be closed over the windows if necessary. Operational durability is enhanced by using run-flat tyres – even with all tyres totally deflated the TM 125 can maintain 40km/h (25mph) for distances up to 80km (50 miles). TM 125s come with a variety of armament options, including Rheinmetall 20mm (0.78in) cannon and TOW ATGWs. The vehicle is also fully amphibious, powered by two propellers mounted at the rear of the hull and steered by the front wheels.

Country of origin:	Germany
Crew:	2 + 10
Weight:	7600kg (16,800lb)
Dimensions:	length 5.54m (18ft 2in); width 2.46m (8ft 1in); height 2.01m (6ft 7in)
Range:	700km (430 miles)
Armour:	not available
Armament:	optional
Powerplant:	one Daimler-Benz OM 352 4-cylinder turbo diesel, developing 125hp (93kW)
Performance:	maximum road speed 85km/h (53mph); fording amphibious; gradient 80 percent; vertical obstacle 0.55m (1ft 10in)

TPz-1 Fuchs

The Transportpanzer 1 Fuchs is still in production and nearly 1000 have been delivered to the German Army alone. Export versions are used in the UK, Israel, the Netherlands, the US and several other countries. Built by Henschel Wehrtechnik, this vehicle was selected from a long series of prototype German armoured personnel carriers developed throughout the 1960s and 1970s. It is a fully amphibious 6x6 vehicle with space for carrying 10 soldiers in a rear troop compartment. In water, it can attain speeds of 10.5km/h (6.5mph) using twin propellers set beneath the rear of the hull. Numerous variants exist, such as an NBC reconnaissance vehicle, an EOD vehicle and a RASIT radar carrier.

Country of origin:	Germany
Crew:	2 + 10
Weight:	18,300kg (40,350lb)
Dimensions:	length 6.76m (22ft 2in); width 2.98m (9ft 9in); height 2.3m (7ft 6in)
Range:	800km (500 miles)
Armour:	steel (details classified)
Armament:	one 7.62mm (0.3in) MG
Powerplant:	one Mercedes-Benz OM402A 8-cylinder diesel, developing 320hp (239kW) at 2500rpm
Performance:	maximum road speed 105km/h (65mph); fording amphibious; gradient 70 percent; trench 1.6m (5ft 4in)

Wheeled Infantry Vehicles

VTP-1 Orca

The VTP-1 Orca ('Killer Whale') was developed by Industrias Cardoen SA in the early 1980s to fulfil its own brief for a multi-purpose armoured vehicle. With a carrying capacity of 16 fully armed men and a total length of 7.84m (25.72ft), the Orca stands as possibly the largest 6x6 armoured personnel carrier in the world. It has an all-welded steel hull with armour of 6 to 12mm (0.24–0.47in). Multiple mounts for machine guns are set around the top of the hull over the troop compartment. Even with its great size, the Orca can maintain a high road speed of 120km/h (75mph), and its 6x6 configuration also gives good cross-country mobility and performance.

Country of origin:	Chile
Crew:	2 + 16
Weight:	18,000kg (39,700lb)
Dimensions:	length 7.84m (25ft 9in); width 2.5m (8ft 2in); height 2.5m (8ft 2in)
Range:	1000km (620 miles)
Armour:	6–12mm (0.24–0.47in)
Armament:	multiple MGs
Powerplant:	one General Motors 6V-53T 6-cylinder diesel, developing 260hp (194kW) at 2400rpm
Performance:	maximum road speed 120km/h (75mph); gradient 60 percent

MOWAG Spy

The MOWAG Spy is a 4x4 version of the excellent Piranha series of vehicles. It has a basic armoured personnel carrier shape, though the sides of the hull are angled steeply to deflect both small-arms fire and the force of mine explosions, aided by a ground clearance of 0.5m (1ft 7in). Armament is located in a small turret at the rear of the vehicle. Standard fitment is a 12.7mm (0.5in) Browning M2 HB with a coaxial 7.62mm (0.3in) general-purpose machine gun. The latter can be mounted in a pair to provide extra firepower and dispense with the Browning. Other options include a 20mm (0.78in) Oerlikon GAS-AOA cannon. All weapons are remotely operated from inside the crew compartment.

Country of origin:	Switzerland
Crew:	3
Weight:	7500kg (16,500lb)
Dimensions:	length 4.52m (14ft 10in); width 2.5m (8ft 2in); height 1.66m (5ft 5in)
Range:	700km (430 miles)
Armour:	details classified
Armament:	one 12.7mm (0.5in) MG; one 7.62mm (0.3in) coaxial MG
Powerplant:	one Detroit or Cummins 8-cylinder petrol, developing 216hp (161kW) at 2800rpm
Performance:	maximum road speed 110km/h (68mph); fording amphibious; gradient 70 percent

Patria XA-180

The Patria XA-180 is a 6x6 armoured personnel carrier used mainly by Nordic military forces and the Republic of Ireland. It was developed in the early 1980s and entered service in 1983 with the Finnish Army. Its bow-like front testifies to a fully amphibious capability, something essential in the wet climes of northern Europe, though a trim vane has to be fitted prior to amphibious operations. The hull is all-welded steel armour with double doors in the rear providing entry and exit for up to 10 soldiers. Standard armament on the XA-180 is a roof-mounted machine gun, but variants include an ATGW carrier and an air-defence version fitted with the Crotale New Generation SAM system.

Country of origin:	Finland
Crew:	2 + 10
Weight:	15,000kg (33,100lb)
Dimensions:	length 7.35m (24ft 1in); width 2.89m (9ft 6in); height 2.47m (8ft 1in)
Range:	800km (500 miles)
Armour:	steel (details classified)
Armament:	one 7.62mm (0.3in) or 12.7mm (0.5in) MG
Powerplant:	one Valmet 6-cylinder turbo diesel, developing 236hp (175kW)
Performance:	maximum road speed 105km/h (65mph); fording amphibious; gradient 70 percent; vertical obstacle 0.6m (2ft); trench 1m (3ft 4in)

FS100 Simba

Alvis, the company responsible for the production of the Simba, defines the vehicle as 'a 4x4 wheeled armoured personnel carrier, primarily used in internal security and counter-insurgency roles'. The Simba is characteristic of a climate in which peacekeeping and anti-terrorism duties occupy much of the military timetable. It comes in several variants. An armoured personnel version can transport eight fully armed soldiers, and is armed with a single turret-mounted machine gun. The armoured infantry fighting vehicle version has a 20 or 25mm (0.78 or 0.98in) cannon. Other variants include ATGW vehicles and 81mm (3.19in) mortar carriers. Only the Philippines have bought the Simba, choosing the APC.

Country of origin:	UK
Crew:	2 + 8
Weight:	10,000kg (22,100lb)
Dimensions:	length 5.35m (17.55ft); width 2.5m (8ft 7in); height 2.59m (8ft 6in)
Range:	660km (410 miles)
Armour:	(steel) 8mm (0.31in) estimated maximum
Armament:	Various (see text)
Powerplant:	one Perkins 210Ti 8-cylinder diesel, developing 210hp (157kW) at 2500rpm
Performance:	maximum road speed 100km/h (62mph); fording 1m (3ft 4in); gradient 60 percent; vertical obstacle 0.45m (1ft 6in)

Condor

The Condor armoured personnel carrier was developed as a replacement for the UR-416 APC. Since it entered production in 1981, it has achieved good export sales, particularly in Malaysia. Two crew pilot the vehicle, the driver sitting at the front of the vehicle behind bullet-proof windows (shuttered in action), and the commander sitting behind him under a forward hatch cover in the roof. Twelve infantry occupy seats in the rear compartment. The hull is of all-welded steel armour. Armament fittings vary. They include 7.62mm (0.3in) and 12.7mm (0.5in) machine guns, 20mm (0.78in) cannon and ATGW systems. The Condor is fully amphibious, though a trim vane needs to be fitted before entering the water.

Country of origin:	Germany
Crew:	2 + 12
Weight:	12,400kg (27,300lb)
Dimensions:	length 6.13m (20ft 1in); width 2.47m (8ft 1in); height 2.18m (7ft 2in)
Range:	900km (560 miles)
Armour:	steel (details classified)
Armament:	varied (see text)
Powerplant:	one Daimler-Benz OM 352A 6-cylinder supercharged diesel, developing 168hp (125kW)
Performance:	maximum road speed 100km/h (62mph); fording amphibious; gradient 60 percent; vertical obstacle 0.55m (1ft 9in)

Casspir

After more than 30 years of service, the Casspir remains one of South Africa's most dependable armoured personnel carriers. It is instantly recognizable by its high ground clearance of 0.41m (1.35ft) at the axles. This is part of the Casspir's defence against anti-tank mines. Also, the belly of the hull is V-shaped to deflect any explosive forces away from the troop compartment. To suit the rough South African terrain, the Casspir has a long-range fuel tank for an 850km (530 mile) maximum range. It also contains a drinking water tank. Since its introduction, the Casspir has been heavily used for security and riot control work. Consequently all windows have protective shutters and rubber bullet and CS gas launchers can be fitted.

Country of origin:	South Africa
Crew:	2 + 10
Weight:	12,580kg (27,700lb)
Dimensions:	length 6.87m (22ft 6in); width 2.5m (8ft 2in); height 2.85m (9ft 4in)
Range:	850km (530 miles)
Armour:	Steel (details classified)
Armament:	one–three 7.62mm (0.3in) machine guns
Powerplant:	one ADE-325T 6-cylinder diesel, developing 170hp (127kW) at 2800rpm
Performance:	maximum road speed 90km/h (56mph); fording 1m (3ft 4in); gradient 65 percent; vertical obstacle 0.5m (1ft 7in); trench 1.06m (3ft 6in)

Wheeled Infantry Vehicles

LAV-25

The Light Armoured Vehicle 25 (LAV-25) is in most ways a copy of the Swiss MOWAG Piranha, one of the world's most successful armoured personnel carriers. Built by General Motors of Canada, it is an 8x8 armoured vehicle with capacity for three crew and six passengers, the latter sitting back to back in the hull rear. Like the Piranha, the LAV-25 has evolved into a large number of variants, including maintenance and recovery vehicles, ATGW carriers, Mobile Electronic Warfare Support System and even an Assault Gun Vehicle armed with a 105mm (4.13in) cannon. The standard turret is usually fitted with a 25mm (0.98in) M242 chain gun and a 7.62mm (0.3in) coaxial machine gun.

Country of origin:	Canada
Crew:	3 + 6
Weight:	12,882kg (28,405lb)
Dimensions:	length 6.39m (21ft); width 2.5m (8ft 2in); height 2.56m (8ft 5in)
Range:	668km (414 miles)
Armour:	Classified
Armament:	one 25mm (0.98in) M242 chain gun; one 7.62mm (0.3in) coaxial MG; various other options available (see text)
Powerplant:	one Detroit Diesel 6-cylinder diesel, developing 275hp (205kW)
Performance:	maximum road speed 100km/h (60mph); fording amphibious; gradient 60 percent; vertical obstacle 0.5m (1ft 7in); trench 2.06m (6ft 9in)

BTR-80

The BTR-80 was part of the steady development of the BTR family which entered production in 1984. Its key contribution to the series was to switch from the two petrol engines of the BTR-60 and BTR-70 to a single powerful V8 diesel. Seven fully laden soldiers can travel in the BTR-80 as well as the three-man crew, and the troop compartment has a total of six firing ports. The main weaponry is a turret-mounted 14.5m (0.57in) KPVT machine gun and a coaxial 7.62mm (0.3in) PKT machine gun. Sophisticated features of the BTR-80 include central tyre-pressure regulation, NBC fittings, and front four wheels steering. It is also fully amphibious, powered by a single waterjet.

Country of origin:	Russia/Soviet Union
Crew:	3 + 7
Weight:	13,600kg (23,000lb)
Dimensions:	length 7.65m (25ft 1in); width 2.9m (9ft 6in); height 2.46m (8ft 1in)
Range:	600km (370 miles)
Armour:	(Steel) 9mm (0.35in)
Armament:	one 14.5m (0.57in) KPVT MG; one coaxial 7.62mm (0.3in) PKT MG
Powerplant:	one V8 diesel, developing 260hp (193kW)
Performance:	maximum road speed 90km/h (56mph); fording amphibious; gradient 60 percent; vertical obstacle 0.5m (1ft 7in); trench 2m (6ft 7in)

Dragoon

The Dragoon Armoured Fighting Vehicle is a fast 4x4 vehicle armed with a turret-mounted 90mm (3.54in) KEnerga gun and coaxial 7.62mm (0.3in) machine gun. Wheels are recessed for travel over rough terrain and the steel hull is designed for fully amphibious operations. Since 1984, when production was taken over by the merger-created AV Technology Corporation, variants have emerged including an 81mm (3.19in) Armoured Mortar Carrier, a turretless APC carrying six infantry, a TOW ATGW launcher and an ambulance. Turret armament can be altered to 40mm (1.57in) cannon or 12.7mm (0.5in) machine gun. The Dragoon is in service with security forces in the US, Thailand, Turkey and various Latin American countries.

Country of origin:	USA
Crew:	3 + 6
Weight:	12,700kg (28,000lb)
Dimensions:	length 5.89m (19ft 4in); width 2.44m (8ft); height 2.13m (6ft 12in)
Range:	1045km (650 miles)
Armour:	steel (details classified)
Armament:	one 90mm (3.54in) KEnerga gun; one coaxial 7.62mm (0.3in) MG
Powerplant:	one Detroit 6V-53T 6-cylinder turbo diesel, developing 300hp (223kW) at 2800rpm
Performance:	maximum road speed 116km/h (72mph); fording amphibious; gradient 60 percent; vertical obstacle 0.6m (2ft)

Pandur

The Pandur 6x6 armoured vehicle was developed by Steyr-Daimler-Puch in the mid-1980s. It entered service with the Austrian Army in 1994 and many other armies since. A common chassis is produced in either 'A' or 'B' variants: 'A' with a raised centre roof and 'B' with a flat roof. Both house a two-man crew. The APC variant has additional space for eight personnel. Pandurs come in a range of variants according to turret or armament configuration. The Pandur Armoured Reconnaissance Fire Support Vehicle, for example, has a Mark 8 90mm (3.5in) gun mounted in a Cockerill LCTS turret, while the Light Armoured Vehicle features the MultiGun Turreted System with 25, 30 or 35mm (0.98, 1.18 or 1.38in) cannon.

Country of origin:	Austria
Crew:	2 + 8
Weight:	13,500kg (29,800lb)
Dimensions:	length 5.7m (18ft 8in); width 2.5m (8ft 2in); height 1.82m (6ft)
Range:	700km (430 miles)
Armour:	8mm (0.31in)
Armament:	one 12.7mm (0.5in) MG; two x 3 smoke grenades launchers; various other configurations
Powerplant:	Steyr WD 612.95 6-cylinder turbo diesel, developing 240hp (179kW)
Performance:	maximum road speed 100km/h (60mph); fording 1.2m (3ft 11in); gradient 70 percent; vertical obstacle 0.5m (1ft 7in)

Wheeled Infantry Vehicles

Fahd

The Fahd is a large armoured personnel carrier able to carry 10 fully armed soldiers as well as the two-man crew. Though an Egyptian vehicle, it was designed in Germany and actually uses a Mercedes-Benz truck chassis. The armoured hull provides the usual APC protection against small-arms fire and shell splinters, and steel shutters close over the windows when in combat. A standard Fahd is completely unarmed but there are many options for roof-mounted machine guns, cannons and ATGW launchers. A variant has even been produced fitted with the 30mm (1.18in) cannon turret from the Russian BMP-2. Firing ports are provided on both sides of the troop compartment.

Country of origin:	Egypt
Crew:	2 + 10
Weight:	10,900kg (24,000lb)
Dimensions:	length 6m (19ft 8in); width 2.45m (8ft 0.4in); height 2.1m (6ft 11in)
Range:	800km (500 miles)
Armour:	steel (details classified)
Armament:	none as standard (see text)
Powerplant:	one Mercedes-Benz OM-352 A 6-cylinder turbo diesel, developing 168hp (125kW) at 2800rpm
Performance:	max road speed 90km/h (56mph); fording 0.7m (2ft 3in); gradient 70 percent; vertical obstacle 0.5m (1ft 7in); trench 0.9m (2ft 11in)

Pandur II APC

The Pandur light armoured vehicle is available in 6 x 6 and 8 x 8 configurations. The larger version offers more internal space and can carry heavier weapon systems. These vary depending on the role the vehicle is expected to fulfil and include a light turret mounting a 30mm (1.18in) cannon and a 105mm (4.13in) gun system capable of dealing with heavy armoured vehicles. The Pandur's basic armour protects the occupants against small arms and can be upgraded to cope with heavy machine-gun fire. The vehicle can be converted to full amphibious capability if deemed necessary. The eight wheels have independent suspension and a tyre pressure regulation system for crossing rough or soft ground. A self-recovery winch allows a bogged-down Pandur to extricate itself.

Country of origin:	Austria
Crew:	2 + 12
Weight:	15,000kg (33,069lb)
Dimensions:	length 6.57m (21ft 7in); width 2.67m (8ft 9in); height 2.06m (6ft 9in)
Range:	600km (373 miles)
Armour:	classified
Armament:	depends on variant
Powerplant:	Cumins ISC 350 diesel developing 213kW (285hp)
Performance:	maximum road speed 105km/h (65mph)

Australian Light Armoured Vehicle (ASLAV)

The Australian Light Armoured Vehicle (ASLAV) is one of many wheeled multirole combat vehicles that have entered service in recent years, reflecting changes in the strategic situation. Wheeled vehicles are not quite as mobile in rough terrain as their tracked equivalents, but require less maintenance and have better strategic mobility as they can make better use of civilian roads. The ASLAV is a version of the Canadian-built LAV (Light Armoured Vehicle), modified for Australian conditions, notably the very hot temperatures encountered in northern Australia. It can be configured for a variety of roles, such as ambulance, reconnaissance, engineering, armoured recovery and command versions as well as an Armoured Personnel Carrier variant. A very similar vehicle is in New Zealand service.

Country of origin:	Australia
Crew:	depends on variant; usually 2–3
Weight:	13,200kg (29,101lb)
Dimensions:	length 6.53m (21ft 5in); width 2.62m (8ft 7in); height 2.69m (8ft 10in)
Range:	600km (373 miles)
Armour:	classified
Armament:	one M242 25mm (0.98in) chain gun, two 7.62mm (0.3in) machine gun (reconnaissance variant)
Powerplant:	Detroit diesel 6V-53T, developing 205kW (275hp)
Performance:	maximum road speed 100km/h (62mph)

BTR-90

3eBTR-90

BTR-90

The BTR-90 is Russia's next generation of Infantry Combat Vehicles, and its service status is only just being defined. It is similar to the BTR-80 in general appearance, and can carry 10 fully armed soldiers within its armoured and amphibious hull. What makes it distinctive is its armament. All its weaponry is mounted in a single turret located towards the front of the vehicle, and it consists of one 30mm (1.18in) 2A42 automatic cannon, a coaxial 7.62mm (0.3in) PKT machine gun, an automatic grenade launcher, and four AT-5 Spandrel anti-tank missiles. The spectrum of weaponry allows it to engage the enemy infantry, armour and aircraft equally.

Country of origin:	Russia/Soviet Union
Crew:	3 + 10
Weight:	17,000kg (37,500lb)
Dimensions:	length 7.64m (25ft); width 3.2m (10ft 6in); height 2.97m (9ft 9in)
Range:	600km (370 miles)
Armour:	welded steel plating
Armament:	one 30mm (1.18in) 2A42 automatic cannon; one coaxial 7.62mm (0.3in) PKT MG; one automatic grenade launcher; four AT-5 Spandrel ATGWs
Powerplant:	one V8 diesel, developing 210hp (157kW))
Performance:	maximum road speed 80km/h (50mph); fording amphibious

Al-Faris AF-40-8-1

The Al-Faris AF-40-8-1 is a conventionally designed 8x8 armoured personnel carrier. There are actually two versions of the vehicle on the market: the AF-40-8-1, the APC version, and the AF-40-8-2, an armoured reconnaissance vehicle. Both have the same steel hull and basic features, but the latter is usually more heavily armed. The Al-Faris has many armament options ranging from TOW ATGWs and 106mm (4.17in) recoilless rifles to turrets fitted with 120mm (4.72in) heavy mortars and 25mm (0.98in) cannon. An ingenious feature of the Al Faris is its adjustable suspension, which can be used to alter ground clearance from 150mm (5.91in) to 600mm (23.62in).

Country of origin:	Saudi Arabia
Crew:	1 + 11
Weight:	19,500kg (43,000lb)
Dimensions:	length 7.9m (25ft 11in); width 2.94m (9ft 8in); height 2.36m (7ft 9in)
Range:	800km (500 miles)
Armour:	Steel (details classified)
Armament:	various (see text)
Powerplant:	one Deutz BF 10L513 10-cylinder diesel, developing 400hp (298kW)
Performance:	maximum road speed 90km/h (55mph); fording amphibious; gradient 80 percent; vertical obstacle 1.52m (5ft); trench 2.5m (8ft 2in)

GTK/MRAV

The Gepanzerten Transportkraftfahrzeug/Multi-Role Armoured Vehicle (GTK/MRAV) is a joint German/United Kingdom/Netherlands project to develop a versatile next-generation armoured personnel carrier. The 6x6 base vehicle is the operator compartment and chassis. Onto this permanent base fit different interchangeable mission modules – such as a command-and-control module and a field-ambulance module – to form the rear compartment. The modules can be changed in less than one hour. Consequently, the GTK/MRAV can be many different vehicles within the remit of a single operation. The base vehicle is made of steel armour and the hull is shaped to deflect mine explosions.

Country of origin:	Germany/UK/Netherlands
Crew:	Up to 10 men, depending on module
Weight:	26,500kg (58,400lb)
Dimensions:	length 7.23m (23ft 9in); width 2.99m (9ft 10in); height 2.37m (7ft 9in)
Range:	1050km (625 miles)
Armour:	classified
Armament:	various depending on module
Powerplant:	one MTU 8-cylinder diesel, developing 710hp (530kW)
Performance:	maximum road speed 103km/h (64mph)

Light Armoured Vehicle (LAV) III

The LAV (Light Armoured Vehicle) III is based on the Piranha family constructed by the Swiss firm MOWAG. Suspension is hydropneumatic and the vehicle is fitted with a tyre pressure regulation system. This allows tyres to be deflated slightly, reducing ground pressure for improved mobility over soft terrain such as mud or snow. The LAV III is armed with a 25mm (0.98in) chain gun capable of dealing with most light armoured vehicles and has a thermal imaging system for night fighting. The vehicle can carry seven troops when acting as an armoured personnel carrier and can be adapted to other roles such as a field ambulance or command vehicle. The basic armour fit protects the vehicle from 7.62mm (0.3in) rounds and can be upgraded at a cost of increased weight.

Country of origin:	Canada
Crew:	3 + additional personnel
Weight:	16500kg (36.376lb)
Dimentions:	length 6.98m (22ft 11in); width 2.7m (8ft 10in); height 2.8m (9ft 2in)
Range:	450km (280 miles)
Armour:	classified
Armament:	one 25mm (0.98in) M242 chain gun; 2 x 7.62mm (0.3in) machine guns
Powerplant:	Caterpillar 3126 diesel developing 261kW (350hp)
Performance:	maximum road speed 100km/h (62mph)

GTK Boxer

The Boxer was developed under a joint UK/German project, which the Netherlands later joined, to develop a multi-role armoured vehicle. It is designed to serve as an armoured personnel carrier, field ambulance and command vehicle to equip rapid-deployment forces. The Boxer is constructed using a modular system and can accommodate mission-specific modules, which can be swapped out in under an hour. The vehicle itself is protected against shell fragments and heavy machine-gun fire in addition to blast and mines. The armour takes the form of a ceramic layer sandwiched between sheets of steel and can be upgraded in the future by replacing the central layer with more advanced compounds. Armament can be varied according to mission.

Country of origin:	UK/Germany/Netherlands
Crew:	3 + 8 additional personnel
Weight:	25,200kg (55,556lb)
Dimensions:	length 7.93m (26ft); width 2.99m (9ft 10in); height 2.37m (7ft 9in)
Range:	1050km (652 miles)
Armour:	classified
Armament:	one 12.7mm (0.5in) heavy machine gun or one 40mm (1.57in) automatic grenade launcher
Powerplant:	MTU V8 199 TE20 diesel
Performance:	road speed 103km/h (64mph)

ATF 2 Dingo

The ATF 2 Dingo is one of the more recent additions to German military vehicle ranks. Its carrying capacity is only four soldiers, apart from the one-man crew, but the occupants are well protected by the mine deflector system in the hull. This diverts the force of both anti-personnel and anti-tank mine explosions away from the troop and operator compartments. Air conditioning, onboard intercom, a rear driving camera, and NBC protection make the Dingo a particularly user-friendly vehicle to operate in hostile areas. Its chassis is that of the Unimog U1550L, which provides the Dingo with excellent off-road mobility. The Dingo is in service with the German Army and police, as well as the Czech, Norwegian and Austrian armies.

Country of origin:	Germany
Crew:	1 + 4
Weight:	8800kg (19,400lb)
Dimensions:	length 5.23m (17ft 2in); width 2.31m (7ft 7in); height 2.38m (7ft 10in)
Range:	700km (430 miles)
Armour:	not available
Armament:	one 7.62mm (0.3in) MG
Powerplant:	one Mercedes-Benz OM 366LA 6-cylinder turbo diesel, developing 237hp (177kW)
Performance:	maximum road speed 106km/h (66mph)

Stryker ICV

The eight-wheeled Stryker armoured fighting vehicle entered service with the US Army in 2002. Its mobility and protection have been instrumental during operations in Iraq. Its weapons systems are remotely controlled from inside the vehicle. The basic Stryker is a fast, advanced armoured personnel carrier capable of carrying nine troops and supporting them in action. It is protected against rockets and machine-gun fire; additional armour can be applied when necessary. Several variants are available including command, engineering support, mortar carrier and anti-tank missile versions, plus a Mobile Gun System armed with a 105mm (4.13in) gun. This is too lightly protected to serve as a replacement for main battle tanks, but offers direct fire support to a Stryker-mobile force.

Country of origin:	USA
Crew:	2 + 9
Weight:	16,470kg (36,234lb)
Dimensions:	length 6.95m (22ft 10in); width 2.72m (8ft 11in); height 2.64m (8ft 8in)
Range:	500km (310 miles)
Armour:	Stryker reactive armour tiles (SRAT)
Armament:	M2 12.7mm (0.5in) machine gun or Mk 19 40mm (1.57in) grenade launcher mounted in a PROTECTOR M151 Remote Weapon Station (RWS) (ICV)
Powerplant:	260kW (350hp) Caterpillar C7 diesel
Performance:	maximum speed 100km/h (62mph)

Mastiff PPV

The Mastiff PPV is the British variant of the basic Cougar armoured fighting vehicle built by Force Protection Inc. Acquired by both the British and US Armies, the Cougar is designed specifically to safeguard against mines and improvised explosive devices. The Mastiff entered service with British forces in 2007. The Mastiff was upgraded for British service with additional armour plates, anti-blast seats and a thermal imaging system for the driver. It also has increased troop and equipment stowage capacity. Primarily a 'protected patrol vehicle', the Mastiff can also function as a communications or command post or an ambulance and can transport bomb-disposal robots. Armament is optional, depending on circumstances.

Country of origin:	UK
Crew:	2 + 4
Weight:	17,000kg (38,000lb)
Dimensions:	length 5.91m (19ft 5in); width 2.74m (9ft); height 2.64m (8ft 8in)
Range:	966km (600 miles)
Armour:	ballistic protection offer against small arms calibre and mine protection against IED
Armament:	optional remote weapons station
Powerplant:	243kW (330hp) Caterpillar C-7 diesel
Performance:	maximum road speed 105km/h (65mph)

Jackal 2 (MWMIK)

The Jackal was introduced to replace vehicles such as the Land Rover in the light patrol and fire support roles. It was designed to be far more resistant to mines and improvised explosive devices while maintaining the levels of smallarms protection offered by current vehicles. An improved version, designated Jackal 2, was introduced as a result of experiences in Afghanistan. It features an improved chassis, which increases damage resistance as well as offering improved load-bearing and crew capacity, carrying four instead of three personnel. The Jackal can be armed with a range of light support weapons, notably heavy machineguns and automatic grenade launchers. A related vehicle, the six-wheeled Coyote, has been developed for the fire support and transport role.

Country of origin:	UK
Crew:	2 + 1–2 additional personnel
Weight:	6650kg (14,661lb)
Dimentions:	length 5.39m (17ft 8in); width 2m (6ft 7in); height 1.97m (6ft 6in)
Range:	800km (497 miles)
Armour:	classified
Armament:	one 40mm (1.57in) automatic grenade launcher or one 12.7mm (0.5in) heavy machine gun or one 7.62mm (0.3in) machine gun
Powerplant:	Cumins ISBe Euro3
Performance:	maximum road speed 129km/h (80mph)

Churchill AVRE

The Churchill (Assault Vehicle Royal Engineers) AVRE was borne out of the failure of the 1942 Dieppe raid where engineers were prevented from clearing obstacles by enemy fire. The tank was developed to transport engineers to the required spot and give protection, as well as carrying a heavy demolition weapon (special fittings were placed on the sides at the front for attaching devices). With a stripped interior to give extra storage space and a mortar capable of firing a heavy demolition charge, they performed excellently during their first action, clearing the way for the Normandy landings on D-Day (6 June 1944). They remained in service with the British Army until the 1960s but the concept was so successful that AVREs are still used, the current model being the Centurion AVRE.

Country of origin:	UK
Crew:	6
Weight:	38,000kg (83,600lb)
Dimensions:	length 7.67m (25ft 2in); width 3.25m (10ft 8in); height 2.79m (9ft 2in)
Range:	193km (120 miles)
Armour:	16-102mm (0.6-4in)
Armament:	one Petard 290mm spigot mortar; one 7.92mm Besa machine-gun
Powerplant:	one Bedford Twin-Six petrol engine developing 350hp (261kW)
Performance:	maximum road speed 24.9km/h (15.5mph); fording 1.016m (3ft 4in); vertical obstacle 0.76m (2ft 6in); trench 3.048m (10ft)

Canal Defence Light

The basic idea behind the the Canal Defence Light (a name chosen to preserve secrecy) was to replace the turret of a tank with a powerful searchlight to illuminate battlefields at night. The idea was first mooted in the mid-1930s, and by late 1939 a turret was ready for production. Initially attached to Matilda II tanks and then Grants, some 300 turrets were ordered. Two British brigades were equipped, one in the UK and one in North Africa. The light was positioned behind a shutter which was opened and closed to provide a flickering impression. Somehow, the opportunity to use the CDL never arose and they were confined to providing light for night river crossings and the like. This was probably just as well, for similar Russian experiments proved disastrous in battle.

Country of origin:	UK
Crew:	3 or 4
Weight:	26,000kg (57,200lb)
Dimensions:	length 5.61m (18ft 5in); width 2.59m (8ft 6in); height 2.51m (8ft 3in)
Range:	257km (160 miles)
Armour:	12-38mm (0.47-1.5in)
Armament:	one 7.92mm Besa machine gun
Powerplant:	two Leyland E148/E149 diesel engines each developing 95hp (70.8kW)
Performance:	maximum road speed 24km/h (15mph); fording 1.02m (3ft 4in); vertical obstacle 0.61m (2ft); trench 1.91m (6ft 3in)

Engineer Vehicles

ARK

The British Army produced its first bridging tank at the end of World War I and experimented throughout the inter-war period, seeing the need to have vehicles to facilitate the crossing of obstacles. The first Armoured Ramp Carrier, the ARK Mk I, appeared in 1943. This was a converted Churchill tank with the turret removed and a blanking plate welded over the aperture and timbered trackways across the top. The ARK could be driven into ditches or against obstacles and when the two folding ramps were lowered it could be used as a bridge for other vehicles. Variants included the Churchill Woodlark, which used rockets to open up the ramps and put them into position, and the Churchill Great Eastern which used a raised ramp system, but neither was very successful.

Country of origin:	UK
Crew:	4
Weight:	38,385kg (84,450lb)
Dimensions:	length 7.442m (24ft 5in); width 2.43m (8ft); height 2.13m (7ft)
Range:	144km (90 miles)
Armour:	16mm (0.6in)
Armament:	none
Powerplant:	one Bedford twin-six petrol engine developing 350hp (261kW)
Performance:	maximum road speed 20km/h (12.5mph); maximum cross-country speed about 12.8km/h (8mph); fording 1.016m (3ft 4in); vertical obstacle 0.76m (2ft 6in); trench 3.048m (10ft)

Churchill AVRE Fascine-
and Mat-Layer

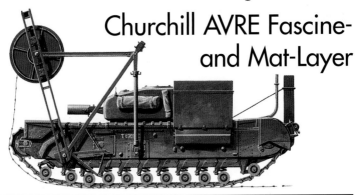

The fascine-layer was developed from a technique used in ancient times and resurrected during World War I to allow tanks and other vehicles to cross ditches or soft ground, generally using bundles of brushwood to fill gaps or mats made of bundles of chespaling or hessian, linked up and laid out behind the tank using a roller mechanism. The tank was a standard Churchill AVRE with the devices attached to the front. The Bobbin Carpet used a hessian mat to cover wire obstacles and allow troops forward to assault the defences. The bobbins were carried well above the ground. When required the weighted free end of the carpet was dropped to the ground, the bobbin automatically unwinding itself as the tank rolled forward. This was first used during the 1942 Dieppe raid.

Country of origin:	UK
Crew:	5
Weight:	42,000kg (92,400lb)
Dimensions:	length 7.442m (24ft 5in); width 2.438m (8ft); height 5.49m (18ft)
Range:	130km (81.25 miles)
Armour:	16-102mm (0.6-4in)
Armament:	one Petard 290mm spigot mortar; one 7.92mm Besa machine gun
Powerplant:	one Bedford twin-six petrol engine developing 350hp (261kW)
Performance:	maximum road speed 20km/h (12.5mph); maximum cross-country speed about 12.8km/h (8mph); fording 1.016m (3ft 4in); vertical obstacle 0.76m (2ft 6in); trench 3.048m (10ft)

Churchill AVRE with Log Carpet

A similar arrangement was developed using linked logs. The roadway was laid under the front tracks and was pulled from its carrying frame as the AVRE moved forward. Like the Bobbin Carpet, the Log Carpet was intended to be a temporary measure only. After World War II, flexible metal roadways were developed to replace these earlier devices. The log carpet itself consisted of 100 152mm (6in) diameter logs, each 4.26m (14ft) long, bound together with wire rope. A removable steel frame was fitted above the AVRE superstructure carrying the looped mat, which was released over the front of the vehicle by detonating a light charge. The vehicle was one of a number developed for laying tracks over marshy ground or barbed wire for wheeled vehicles and infantry.

Country of origin:	UK
Crew:	5
Weight:	40,727kg (89,600lb)
Dimensions:	length 7.442m (24ft 5in); width 2.438m (8ft); height 3.454m (11ft 4in) – log carpet mounted above tank
Range:	144.8km (90 miles)
Armour:	16-102mm (0.6-4in)
Armament:	one Petard 290mm spigot mortar; one 7.92mm Besa machine gun
Powerplant:	one Bedford twin-six petrol engine developing 350hp (261kW)
Performance:	maximum road speed 20km/h (12.5mph); maximum cross-country speed about 12.8km/h (8mph); fording 1.016m (3ft 4in); vertical obstacle 0.76m (2ft 6in); trench 3.048m (10ft)

Sherman BARV

The BARV was developed during the planning for the D-Day landings when it was deemed prudent to have deep-wading recovery vehicles available to rescue vehicles stranded in the water. Trials in December 1943 were successful, and by D-Day there were 55 ready for action, the rough weather giving them plenty of work to do. The BARV was in essence a standard Sherman, but with the turret replaced by a tall superstructure with extensive waterproofing. The crew generally included a diver for securing towing cables. The BARV could either tow or push but suffered a little from the lack of a winch. The BARV was eventually christened the Sea Lion during a long post-war service record. It was standard procedure for the crew to be issued with life jackets, and for one of their number to be a diver.

Country of origin:	USA
Crew:	5
Weight:	unknown
Dimensions:	length 6.2m (20ft 4in); width 2.68m (8ft 9in); height 2.97m (9ft 9in)
Range:	136-160km (85-100 miles)
Armour:	12mm – 62mm (0.4in – 2.4in)
Armament:	none
Powerplant:	twin General Motors 6-71 engines
Performance:	maximum road speed 47km/h (29mph); fording amphibious; vertical obstacle 0.61m (2ft); trench 2.26m (7ft 5in)

Engineer Vehicles

Bergepanther

With the advent of the heavier Tiger and Panther tanks, standard German recovery vehicles such as the SdKfz 9/1 proved inadequate. The Panther tank was therefore used as the basis for a new heavy recovery vehicle. The Bergepanther first appeared in 1943. The Panther's turret was removed and replaced by an open superstructure containing a winch. A large anchor at the back dug into the ground to give the vehicle extra stability when winching. There was also an open machine-gun mounting on the front of the vehicle for self-defence. Bergepanthers entered full service in the spring of 1944, concentrated in the heavy tank battalions, and by the end of the war almost 300 had been produced. It proved to be the best recovery vehicle of World War II.

Country of origin:	Germany
Crew:	5
Weight:	42,000kg (92,400lb)
Dimensions:	length 8.153m (26ft 9in); width 3.276m (10ft 9in); height 2.74m (9ft)
Range:	169km (105 miles)
Armour:	8-40mm (0.3-1.57in)
Armament:	one 20mm cannon and one 7.92mm machine gun
Powerplant:	one Maybach HL210 P.30 petrol engine developing 642hp (478.7kW)
Performance:	maximum road speed 32km/h (20mph); fording 1.70m (5ft 7in); vertical obstacle 0.91m (3ft 0in); trench 1.91m (6ft 3in)

Karl Ammunition Carrier

The Karl Ammunition Carrier was designed to supply the massive Karl Siege Howitzers, the sheer weight of the projectiles (over two tonnes [1.96 tons] each) necessitating a new vehicle. The basic tank hull of the PzKpfw IV Ausf D was used, with a platform for the ammunition and a crane added to lift the heavy rounds. The carriers were usually moved by train and assembled near to the point of use, before being driven into position. In 1941, 13 PzKpfw IV Ausf F chassis were converted to ammunition carriers. The Karl Howitzers and Carriers were designed to smash fortifications. They were used rarely in World War II, but did see service during the siege of Sevastopol and during the Battle of Warsaw in 1944, where they were put to devastating use against the defenders.

Country of origin:	Germany
Crew:	4
Weight:	25,000kg (55,000lb)
Dimensions:	length 5.41m (17ft 9in); width 2.883m (9ft 5.5in); height not recorded
Range:	209km (130 miles)
Armour:	60mm (2.4in)
Armament:	none
Powerplant:	one Maybach HL120 TRM petrol engine developing 300hp (223.7kW)
Performance:	maximum road speed 39.9km/h (24.8mph); fording 1.0m (3ft 3in); vertical obstacle 0.6m (2ft); trench 2.20m (7ft 3in)

AMX-30 Bridge

The prototype of the AMX-30 bridgelayer was built in the mid-1960s, but delays meant that the vehicle did not enter production until the mid-1970s. Based on the AMX-30 tank chassis, with an almost identical layout, the scissors bridge was laid hydraulically over the rear of the vehicle. It took around five minutes to erect and a similar time to recover the bridge. The bridge span was 20m (65ft 7in). A nuclear, biological and chemical (NBC) defence system and night-vision capability were installed as standard. The vehicle was designed to operate in tandem with the AMX-30 tank, and has no armament of its own, relying on accompanying vehicles for protection. The major disadvantage was that the bridge is erected vertically and thus can easily be seen by enemy forces.

Country of origin:	France
Crew:	3
Weight:	42,500kg (93,500lb)
Dimensions:	length (with bridge) 11.40m (37ft 4.8in); width (with bridge) 3.95m (12ft 11.5in); height (with bridge) 4.29m (14ft 0.9in)
Range:	600km (373 miles)
Armour:	80mm (3.14in)
Armament:	none
Powerplant:	one Hispano-Suiza HS-110 12-cylinder multi-fuel diesel engine developing 700hp (522.0kW)
Performance:	maximum road speed 50km/h (31.1mph); fording 1.0m (3ft 4in); vertical obstacle 0.93m (3ft 0.6in); trench 2.9m (9ft 6.2in)

AMX-30 Tractor

The AMX-30 EBG was based on the AMX-30 main battle tank chassis and designed to carry out a number of roles, including laying mines and clearing battlefield obstacles, by means of a hydraulically operated dozer blade mounted at the front of the vehicle. In addition, the teeth of the dozer blade can be used to dig up roads, thus making them impassable to enemy wheeled vehicles. At the rear is a winch for recovering damaged vehicles. Also, the vehicle has a powerful demolition-charge launcher for destroying bunkers and other fortifications. Standard equipment includes night vision, nuclear, biological and chemical (NBC) defence system and a deep-fording kit to provide some amphibious capability. The AMX-30 tractor is integral to the movement of French armoured forces on the battlefield.

Country of origin:	France
Crew:	3
Weight:	38,000kg (83,600lb)
Dimensions:	length 7.90m (25ft 11in); width 3.50m (11ft 5.8in); height 2.94m (9ft 7.7in)
Range:	500km (311 miles)
Armour:	80mm (3.14in)
Armament:	one 7.62mm machine gun; one 142mm demolition-charge launcher
Powerplant:	one Hispano-Suiza HS 110-2 12-cylinder multi-fuel engine developing 700hp (522.0kW)
Performance:	maximum road speed 65km/h (40.4mph); fording 2.50m (8ft 2.4in); vertical obstacle 0.9m (2ft 11.4in); trench 2.9m (9ft 6.2in)

Engineer Vehicles

M728

Following the development of the M60 main battle tank, a decision was taken to create a combat engineer vehicle based on the same chassis. The M728 was finally accepted for service in 1963 as the standard combat engineer vehicle for the US Army. The two vehicles were very similar. The M60's 105mm gun was replaced by a demolition-charge launcher and a hydraulically operated dozer blade added, together with a winch, which was mounted on an A-frame. The A-Frame was laid flat over the top of the vehicle when travelling. Night-vision equipment (as well as a searchlight) and a nuclear, biological and chemical (NBC) defence system were standard. The vehicle could be equipped for deep-fording. In addition to the US Army, the vehicle saw service with Singapore and Saudi Arabia.

Country of origin:	USA
Crew:	4
Weight:	53,200kg (117,040lb)
Dimensions:	length (travelling) 8.92m (29ft 3in); width (overall) 3.71m (12ft 2in); height (travelling) 3.20m (10ft 6in)
Range:	451km (280 miles)
Armour:	classified
Armament:	one 165mm demolition gun; one 7.62mm machine gun
Powerplant:	one Teledyne Continental AVDS-1790-2A 12-cylinder diesel engine developing 750bhp (559.3kW)
Performance:	maximum road speed 48.3km/h (30mph); fording 1.22m (4ft); vertical obstacle 0.76m (2ft 6in); trench 2.51m (8ft 3in)

Leopard 1

The Leopard 1 Armoured Engineer Vehicle was designed by Krupp specifically for the requirements of the West German Army. Based on the chassis of the Leopard 1 main battle tank and almost identical to the Leopard I Armoured Recovery Vehicle, production began in 1968. The vehicle has a dozer blade fitted to the front which can be widened if necessary and is fitted with 'scarifiers' for digging up road surfaces. It can also be equipped with an auger for digging holes. The vehicle is designed to fulfil many different roles, from preparing fire positions to removing battlefield obstacles and preparing river crossings. The Leopard 1 was designed for the defence of West Germany against a Warsaw Pact attack, hence the capability for digging up road surfaces and preparing fire positions.

Country of origin:	West Germany
Crew:	4
Weight:	40,800kg (89,760lb)
Dimensions:	length 8.98m (26ft 2.2in); width 3.75m (12ft 3.6in); height 2.69m (8ft 9.9in)
Range:	850km (528 miles)
Armour:	10-70mm (0.39-2.75in)
Armament:	one 7.62mm machine gun
Powerplant:	one MTU MB 838 Ca.M500 10-cylinder diesel engine developing 830hp (618.9kW)
Performance:	maximum road speed 65km/h (40.4mph); fording 2.10m (6ft 11in); vertical obstacle 1.15m (3ft 9.3in); trench 3m (9ft 10in)

Biber

The first production vehicles were completed by Krupp in 1975, based on the chassis of the Leopard 1 main battle tank. The hull of the Biber AVLB was virtually identical to that of the tank. However, with the AVLB the turret was replaced by a two-part aluminium bridge, capable of spanning a 20m (65ft 7in) gap. A support blade was fitted to the front, to be lowered before the bridge was laid, but this was also useful for levelling surfaces on either side of the gap. One of the main advantages of the Biber was that its bridge was laid horizontally rather than vertically, which made for much better concealment. The Biber carried four electrically operated smoke dischargers to provide extra cover for its operations, but otherwise relied on other armoured vehicles for protection.

Country of origin:	West Germany
Crew:	2
Weight:	with bridge 45,300kg (99,660lb)
Dimensions:	length (with bridge) 11.82m (38ft 9.4in); width (with bridge) 4.0m (13ft 1.5in); height (with bridge) 3.57m (11ft 8.6in)
Range:	550km (342 miles)
Armour:	70mm (2.75in)
Armament:	none
Powerplant:	one MTU MB 838 Ca.M500 10-cylinder multi-fuel engine developing 830hp (618.9kW)
Performance:	maximum road speed 62km/h (38.5mph); fording 1.2m (3ft 11in); vertical obstacle 0.7m (2ft 3.6in); trench 2.5m (8ft 2.4in)

TMM Bridge

The TMM truck-mounted treadway bridge consists of four spans, launched over the rear of a 6 x 6 Kr AZ-214 or Kr AZ 255B truck chassis. Each span is extended vertically and supported by cables until it reaches its final position, at which point trestle legs are swung into place. The truck then disconnects and drives off to pick up the next span. The basic unit has a span of around 40m (131ft 3in), but more spans can be added if necessary. The bridge takes 45-60 minutes to erect. One disadvantage of the system is that it relies on legs which must be kept level – if the depth of water cannot be ascertained, problems may arise. There is nothing sophisticated about the TMM system, but it is cheap, easy to operate and can be produced in mass numbers if need be.

Country of origin:	USSR
Crew:	3
Weight:	19,500kg (42,900lb)
Dimensions:	length (with bridge) 9.30m (30ft 6.1in); width (with bridge) 3.20m (10ft 6in); height (with bridge) 3.15m (10ft 4in)
Range:	530km (329 miles)
Armour:	none
Armament:	none
Powerplant:	one YaMZ M206B six-cylinder water-cooled diesel engine developing 205hp (152.9kW)
Performance:	maximum road speed 55km/h (34.2mph); fording 1.0m (3ft 3in); vertical obstacle 0.4m (1ft 4in); trench no capability

PMP Floating Bridge

The PMP bridge entered service with the USSR in the 1960s, and was soon in use in most Warsaw Pact armies. Originally mounted on the Kr AZ-214 truck chassis, it was later transferred to the Kr AZ-255. The truck was backed up to the shore and the bridge rolled off into the water where it unfolded automatically. The full set consisted of 32 river pontoons, four shore pontoons and 12 bridging boats, the whole structure spanning some 389m (1275ft). The pontoons could also be used to form a ferry to be pushed across by boats. The PMP was exported outside of the Warsaw Pact on a significant scale, notably being used by the Egyptian Army to cross the Suez Canal during the Yom Kippur War of 1973. Note that the specifications below relate to the river pontoon bridge.

Country of origin:	USSR
Crew:	3
Weight:	6676kg (14,687lb)
Dimensions:	length (open) 6.75m (22ft 1.75in); width (open) 7.10m (23ft 3.5in); depth (open) 0.915m (3ft 0in)
Range:	–
Armour:	none
Armament:	none
Powerplant:	–
Performance:	–

IMR

The IMR was introduced into service with the Red Army in the 1970s and was essentially a T-55 tank with the standard turret replaced by a crane and an armoured cupola. A pincer device was fitted for removing trees and a front-mounted dozer blade were standard. An unditching beam was also carried, to be fitted to the tracks in order to improve traction if the vehicle became stuck (an idea pioneered by the British in World War I). Like most vehicles based on the T-55 chassis, the IMR could lay its own smoke screen. The vehicle was very limited by Western standards, carrying no demolition charge or mine-laying equipment, but the Soviets had other vehicles to perform these tasks. The IMR saw service with most Warsaw Pact countries and the former Yugoslavia.

Country of origin:	USSR
Crew:	2
Weight:	34,000kg (74,800lb)
Dimensions:	length 10.60m (34ft 9.3in); width 3.48m (11ft 5in); height 2.48m (8ft 1.6in)
Range:	400km (249 miles)
Armour:	up to 203mm (8in)
Armament:	none
Powerplant:	one Model V-55 V-12 diesel engine developing 580hp (432.5kW)
Performance:	maximum road speed 48km/h (29.8mph); fording 1.4m (4ft 7in); vertical obstacle 0.8m (2ft 7.5in); trench 2.7m (8ft 10.3in)

Centurion AVRE

In the 1960s, the Centurion Mk V Assault Vehicle Royal Engineers (AVRE) replaced the World War II-vintage Churchill AVRE as the main combat engineer vehicle of the British Army. Based on the Centurion main battle tank, the AVRE carries a heavy demolition gun for blasting enemy fortifications and a dozer blade for removing obstacles. The vehicle is also capable of laying down tracks for wheeled vehicles to help them across muddy ground, and can carry a fascine-layer to cope with anti-tank ditches. Later models were fitted with mine-clearing ploughs at the front of the hull, which were used to rip up the ground and push any anti-tank mines to one side. In addition, the tank can tow a two-wheeled trailer carrying the Giant Viper mine-clearance system. A deep-fording system was developed but not used.

Country of origin:	UK
Crew:	5
Weight:	51,809kg (113,979lb)
Dimensions:	length 8.69m (28ft 6in); width 3.96m (13ft 0in); height 3m (9ft 10in)
Range:	177km (110 miles)
Armour:	17-118mm (0.66-4.6in)
Armament:	one 165mm demolition gun; one 7.62mm co-axial machine gun; one 7.62mm anti-aircraft machine gun
Powerplant:	one Rolls-Royce Meteor Mk IVB 12-cylinder petrol engine developing 650hp (484.7kW)
Performance:	maximum road speed 34.6km/h (21.5mph); fording 1.45m (4ft 9in); vertical obstacle 0.94m (3ft 1in); trench 3.35m (11ft 0in)

Combat Engineer Tractor

The Combat Engineer Tractor (CET) was designed by the British Army to fulfil the Royal Engineers' requirement for a vehicle combining elements of an armoured vehicle and an earthmover. Between 1978 and 1981, a total of 181 vehicles were built to undertake a variety of roles such as vehicle recovery, clearing obstacles and preparing river banks for vehicle crossings. Mounted on the roof is a rocket-propelled anchor which could be fired into the earth to enable the vehicle to winch itself out if it became stuck. The CET has full amphibious capability and when afloat is powered by twin water jets. The hull is made of all-welded aluminium armour, which is supplied by Alcan. The vehicle saw extensive service during the 1982 Falklands Conflict and was exported to India.

Country of origin:	UK
Crew:	2
Weight:	18,000kg (39,600lb)
Dimensions:	length 7.54m (24ft 9in); width 2.90m (9ft 6in); height 2.67m (8ft 9in)
Range:	322km (200 miles)
Armour:	classified
Armament:	one 7.62mm machine gun
Powerplant:	one Rolls-Royce C6TFR six-cylinder inline diesel engine developing 320hp (238.6kW)
Performance:	maximum road speed 56km/h (35mph); fording 1.83m (6ft 0in); vertical obstacle 0.61m (2ft); trench 2.06m (6ft 9in)

Chieftain AVRE

The Chieftain AVRE has replaced the Centurion Mk 5 AVRE, which was used by the British Army since the 1960s. It is similar to a standard Chieftain MK 5 main battle tank in terms of its chassis and engine. The main difference is that the gun turret is removed and replaced with an armoured 'penthouse', on top of which is situated the commander's cupola. The vehicle carries three large hampers for storing equipment and a dozer blade or mine plough is fitted at the front. In addition, the vehicle carries a crane capable of lifting 3.6 tonnes (3.5 tons). At the back there is a winch capable of pulling 10.1 tonnes (10 tons). Around 50 of these vehicles are currently in service with the British Army. The illustration above shows the AVRE optimised for maxi-pipe fascines and trackway.

Country of origin:	UK
Crew:	3
Weight:	51,809kg (113,979lb)
Dimensions:	length 7.52m (24.8ft); width 3.663m (11.8ft); height 2.89m (9.4ft)
Range:	500km (300 miles)
Armour:	classified
Armament:	one 7.62mm machine gun; two x 6 smoke dischargers (front); two x 4 smoke dischargers (rear)
Powerplant:	one Leyland L60 (No.4 Mk 8) 12-cylinder diesel engine, developing 750hp (559kW)
Performance:	maximum road speed 48km/h (28.8mph); fording 1.067m (3ft 6in); vertical obstacle 0.9m (3ft); trench 3.15m (10ft 4in)

Buffalo MPV

The Buffalo Mine Protected Vehicle (MPV) was developed to clear routes of mines and improvised explosive devices. It has seen service in Afghanistan since 2003. Mines are detected with an onboard sensor suite and can be cleared using a 10m (32ft 10in) long robotic arm fitted with a claw and a camera. The arm can extend to the front or side of the vehicle. In the event that a mine is detonated, the Buffalo is protected by an armoured hull, which is V-shaped to direct blast away from the crew compartment. The vehicle can survive 13.6kg (30lb) of explosives directly underneath or 20.4kg (45lbs) under a wheel. The hull will also withstand smallarms fire and rocket-propelled grenades, plus run-flat tyres give a damaged Buffalo a chance of escape.

Country of origin:	USA
Crew:	2 + 4 additional personnel
Weight:	20,560kg (45,327lb)
Dimensions:	length 8.2m (26ft 11in); width 2.6m (8ft 6in); height 4m (13ft 1in)
Range:	480km (298 miles)
Armour:	small arms and mine protection
Armament:	mine/obstacle clearance arm
Powerplant:	335kW (450hp) Mack ASET AI-400
Performance:	105km/h (65mph)

Gepard

The Gepard self-propelled anti-aircraft gun system was designed specifically to protect armoured formations. The system uses the hull of the Leopard 1 main battle tank to carry a welded-steel turret capable of powered traverse through 360 degrees and accommodating the weapon system. The two 35mm cannon are located externally to avoid the problem of gun gas in the fighting compartment. Each of the weapons has a cyclic rate of fire of 550 rounds per minute, though it is standard procedure to fire bursts of between 20 and 40 rounds. Ammunition types include high explosive and armour-piercing. The fire-control system is based on a computer supplied with target data by two radars: the acquisition unit and the tracking unit. Other features are optical sights and a land navigation system.

Country of origin:	Germany
Crew:	4
Weight:	47,300kg (104,060lb)
Dimensions:	length 7.68m (25ft 3in); width 3.27m (10ft 9in); height 3.01m (9ft 10in)
Range:	550km (342 miles)
Armour:	40mm (1.57in)
Armament:	two 35mm cannon; eight smoke dischargers
Powerplant:	one MTU MB 838 Ca M500 10-cylinder multi-fuel engine developing 830hp (619kW)
Performance:	maximum road speed 65km/h (40.5mph); fording 2.5m (8ft 2in); vertical obstacle 1.15m (3ft 9in); trench 3m (9ft 10in)

Type 63

To meet its needs for a self-propelled anti-aircraft gun, the Chinese took the chassis of the Soviet T-34 tank (supplied to them in large numbers before relations were broken off between the two countries) and added an open-topped turret with twin anti-aircraft guns. The vehicle was severely limited in that it had no provision for radar control and had to be sighted and elevated manually, a major drawback when faced with fast, low-flying aircraft, particularly as the gun had to be loaded manually with five-round clips. The Type 63 was supplied to the Viet Cong during the Vietnam War in the 1960s, but otherwise was only used in numbers by the People's Liberation Army. Amazingly, given its mediocre qualities, it continued in use with Chinese force until the late 1980s.

Country of origin:	China
Crew:	6
Weight:	32,000kg (70,400lb)
Dimensions:	length 6.432m (21ft 1in); width 2.99m (9ft 10in); height 2.995m (9ft 10in)
Range:	300km (186 miles)
Armour:	18-45mm (0.7-1.8in)
Armament:	twin 37mm anti-aircraft cannon
Powerplant:	one V-12 water-cooled diesel engine developing 500hp (373kW)
Performance:	maximum road speed 55km/h (34mph); fording 1.32m (4ft 4in); vertical obstacle 0.73m (2ft 5in); trench 2.5m (8ft 2in)

ZSU-57-2

The ZSU-57-2 was the first Soviet self-propelled anti-aircraft gun to see service on a significant scale after World War II. The chassis was a lightened version of the T-54 main battle tank with thinner armour, the distinctive feature of the vehicle being the large, open-topped turret. This created a greater power-to-weight ratio than the T-54 and, coupled with extra fuel tanks, gave the gun good mobility and operating range. Practical firing rate was around 70 rounds per minute, with the empty cartridge cases being transported to a wire basket at the rear by a conveyor belt. The vehicle was exported widely to other Warsaw Pact countries, North Africa and the Middle East, seeing extensive action with Syrian forces during the fighting in Lebanon against the Israelis in 1982.

Country of origin:	USSR
Crew:	6
Weight:	28,100kg (61,820lb)
Dimensions:	length 8.48m (27ft 10in); width 3.27m (10ft 9in); height 2.75m (9ft)
Range:	420km (260 miles)
Armour:	15mm (0.59in)
Armament:	twin 57mm anti-aircraft cannon
Powerplant:	one Model V-54 V-12 diesel engine developing 520hp (388kW)
Performance:	maximum road speed 50km/h (31mph); fording 1.4m (4ft 7in); vertical obstacle 0.80m (2ft 7in); trench 2.70m (8ft 10in)

ZSU-23-4

The ZSU-23-4 was developed in the 1960s as the replacement for the ZSU-57-2. Although having a shorter firing range, radar fire-control and an increased firing rate made the weapon much more effective. The chassis was similar to that of the SA-6 surface-to-air missile (SAM) system and used components of the PT-76 tank. Known to the Soviets as the 'Shilka', the vehicle can create an impassable wall of anti-aircraft fire over a 180-degree arc. Widely exported, the ZSU-23-4 was particularly effective in Egyptian hands during the Yom Kippur War of 1973, bringing down Israeli aircraft who were forced to fly low by the Egyptian missile defence system. It also saw extensive combat service with the North Vietnamese during the Vietnam War, bringing down numerous American aircraft.

Country of origin:	USSR
Crew:	4
Weight:	19,000kg (41,800lb)
Dimensions:	length 6.54m (21ft 5in); width 2.95m (9ft 8in); height (without radar) 2.25m (7ft 4in)
Range:	260km (162 miles)
Armour:	10-15mm (0.39-0.6in)
Armament:	four AZP-23 23mm anti-aircraft cannon
Powerplant:	one V-6R diesel engine developing 280hp (210kW)
Performance:	maximum road speed 44km/h (27mph); fording 1.4m (4ft 7in); vertical obstacle 1.10m (3ft 7in); trench 2.80m (9ft 2in)

Anti-Aircraft Guns

M42

The M42 anti-aircraft system, commonly known as the 'Duster', was based on the M41 Bulldog tank and was one of a family of vehicles developed after the end of World War II. Between 1951 and 1956, around 3700 were built, mainly by Cadillac. The main drawback of the vehicle was its petrol engine, which restricted its operating range and its lack of a radar fire-control system, the gunner being forced to rely on optic sights. In addition, the open-topped turret afforded the crew little protection. However, it saw extensive service in Vietnam, albeit mainly in a ground-support rather than anti-aircraft role, and continued to serve with the National Guard into the 1980s. Its power-assisted twin 40mm turret was the same as that used on the M19 self-propelled anti-aircraft gun system used in World War II.

Country of origin:	USA
Crew:	6
Weight:	22,452kg (49,394lb)
Dimensions:	length 6.356m (20ft 10in); width 3.225m (10ft 7in); height 2.847m (9ft 4in)
Range:	161km (100 miles)
Armour:	12-38mm (0.47-1.5in)
Armament:	twin 40mm anti-aircraft guns; one 7.62mm machine gun
Powerplant:	one Continental AOS-895-3 six-cylinder air-cooled petrol engine developing 500hp (373kW)
Performance:	maximum road speed 72.4km/h (45mph); fording 1.3m (4ft 3in); vertical obstacle 1.711m (2ft 4in); trench 1.829m (6ft)

M163 Vulcan

In the early 1960s, Rock Island Arsenal developed a self-propelled air-defence system based on the M113 armoured personnel carrier chassis. GEC began production and the vehicle was soon being deployed to Vietnam, where it was widely used by both US and South Vietnamese troops in a ground-support role. An electrically operated turret was mounted on the M113 chassis and armed with a six-barrelled Gatling-type cannon. This had adjustable rates of fire depending on whether it was being used for ground attack or anti-aircraft defence, and was the same weapon used by F-16 fighter aircraft. In the direct-fire role the Vulcan has a rate of fire of 1180 rounds per minute. The vehicle was exported to Ecuador, Israel, Morocco, North Yemen, South Korea and Tunisia.

Country of origin:	USA
Crew:	4
Weight:	12,310kg (27,082lb)
Dimensions:	length 4.86m (15ft 11in); width 2.85m (9ft 4in); height 2.736m (9ft 11in)
Range:	83km (300 miles)
Armour:	38mm (1.5in)
Armament:	one 20mm six-barrelled M61 series cannon
Powerplant:	one Detroit 6V-53 six-cylinder diesel engine developing 215hp (160kW)
Performance:	maximum road speed 67km/h (42mph); fording amphibious; vertical obstacle 1.61m (2ft); trench 1.68m (5ft 6in)

Sergeant York

The Vulcan was noted for its short range and relative inaccuracy (though not poor rate of fire), so in 1978 the US Army issued a requirement for a self-propelled anti-aircraft gun based on the M48 main battle tank chassis to replace it. The first production M247 Sergeant York arrived in 1983, built by FAC. The vehicle has a comprehensive fire-control system including both surveillance and tracking radar. The M247 is capable of engaging both aircraft and helicopters, as well as tactical missiles (the latter capability being very important on the modern battlefield). The modified M48 chassis gives the vehicle the mobility and protection needed to operate with the M1 Abrams main battle tank and M2 Bradley infantry fighting vehicle, in turn providing viable anti-aircraft defence for both vehicles.

Country of origin:	USA
Crew:	3
Weight:	54,430kg (119,746lb)
Dimensions:	length 7.674m (25ft 2in); width 3.632m (11ft 11in); height (radar up) 4.611m (15ft 2in)
Range:	500km (311 miles)
Armour:	up to 120mm (4.72in)
Armament:	twin 40mm L/70 Bofors guns
Powerplant:	one Teledyne Continental AVDS-1790-2D diesel engine developing 750hp (559kW)
Performance:	maximum road speed 48km/h (30mph); fording 1.219m (4ft); vertical obstacle 1.914m (3ft); trench 2.591m (8ft 6in)

AMX-13 DCA

The AMX-13 DCA entered production in the late 1960s to meet French requirements for a self-propelled anti-aircraft gun. It is essentially an AMX-13 main battle tank chassis fitted with a cast-steel turret. The vehicle entered service with the French Army in 1969. A total of 60 were delivered before production ceased and up to the 1980s, the AMX-13 DCA was the only self-propelled anti-aircraft gun in use with French forces. To aid fire control, there is an Oeil Noir 1 radar scanner fitted to the back of the turret, which is retractable while on the move. The DCA turret was fitted to the improved AMX-30 chassis for export to Saudi Arabia in the late 1970s and 1980s. The AMX-13 DCA is an adequate air defence vehicle, though now rather long in the tooth.

Country of origin:	France
Crew:	3
Weight:	17,200kg (37,840lb)
Dimensions:	length 5.40m (17ft 11in); width 2.50m (8ft 2in); height (radar up) 3.80m (12ft 6in); height (radar down) 3.00m (9ft 10in)
Range:	300km (186 miles)
Armour:	25mm (0.98in)
Armament:	twin 30mm Hispano (now Oerlikon) cannon
Powerplant:	one SOFAM Model 8Gxb eight-cylinder water-cooled petrol engine developing 250hp (186kW)
Performance:	maximum road speed 60km/h (37mph); fording 0.6m (1ft 11in); vertical obstacle 0.65m (2ft 2in); trench 1.70m (5ft 7in)

Wildcat

Realising that the self-propelled gun based on the Leopard 1 chassis and the American Sergeant York M247 would be too expensive for many countries, Krauss-Maffei decided to build a new family of anti-aircraft guns for sale abroad to tap into the lucrative market for arms outside of Europe. It was decided to use the automotive components of the 6 x 6 Transportpanzer already in production for the West German Army. With a laser rangefinder, radar scanner and automatic target-tracking, the fully computerised fire-control system makes the Wildcat an effective weapon, either against aircraft or against ground targets. It is also relatively inexpensive to maintain and spares are easy to come by – two attributes which make it attractive to countries with tight defence budgets.

Country of origin:	West Germany
Crew:	3
Weight:	18,500kg (40,700lb)
Dimensions:	length 6.88m (22ft 7in); width 2.98m (9ft 9in); height (radar down) 2.74m (9ft)
Range:	600km (373 miles)
Armour:	classified
Armament:	twin 30mm Mauser Mk 30-F cannon
Powerplant:	one Mercedes-Benz turbocharged eight-cylinder diesel engine developing 320hp (239kW)
Performance:	maximum road speed 80km/h (50mph); fording amphibious; vertical obstacle 0.6m (1ft 11in); trench 1.1m (3ft 7in)

GDF-CO3

Produced by Oerlikon-Bührle, the GDF series was designed to be a highly mobile anti-aircraft defence system to protect rear-area targets such as factories and air bases. The chassis for the tracked version is derived from the M113 series of armoured vehicles; the wheeled version is based on the 4 x 4 HYKA cross-country vehicle. The GDF-CO3 has a day/night fire-control system with laser rangefinder, in addition to a Contraves search radar. The vehicle fires a range of ammunition, including armour-piercing discarding sabot-tracer rounds for use against ground targets. Its layout is unusual in that the crew compartment is at the front with the guns behind them. Nevertheless, as a mobile air-defence platform the vehicle is ideally suited to Switzerland's needs.

Country of origin:	Switzerland
Crew:	3
Weight:	18,000kg (39,600lb)
Dimensions:	length 6.70m (22ft 0in); width 2.813m (9ft 3in); height 4.00m (13ft 2in)
Range:	480km (297 miles)
Armour:	8mm (0.31in)
Armament:	twin 35mm KDF cannon
Powerplant:	one GMC 6V-53T 6-cylinder diesel engine developing 215hp (160kW)
Performance:	maximum road speed 45km/h (28mph); fording 0.6m (1ft 11in); vertical obstacle 0.609m (2ft 0in); trench 1.80m (5ft 11in)

Anti-Aircraft Guns

M53/59

In the 1950s, Czechoslovakia developed and began production of the M53/59 self-propelled anti-aircraft gun. Based on the Praga V3S 6 x 6 truck chassis with an armoured cab, the vehicle was used in place of the Soviet ZSU-57-2. Essentially a clear-weather system, the vehicle carried neither infrared night vision equipment nor a nuclear, biological and chemical (NBC) defence system. Both armour-piercing incendiary ammunition for ground targets and high-explosive incendiary for aircraft were carried. Other than its reliance on clear-weather systems, the other main drawback was its poor cross-country mobility, which prevented effective operation with tracked vehicles. In addition to the Czech Army, the M53/59 saw service with both the former Yugoslavia and Libya.

Country of origin:	Czechoslovakia
Crew:	6
Weight:	10,300kg (22,660lb)
Dimensions:	length 6.92m (22ft 8in); width 2.35m (7ft 9in); height 2.585m (8ft 6in)
Range:	500km (311 miles)
Armour:	none (vehicle as a whole)
Armament:	twin 30mm cannon
Powerplant:	one Tatra T912-2 six-cylinder diesel engine developing 110hp (82kW)
Performance:	maximum road speed 60km/h (37mph); vertical obstacle 0.46m (1ft 6in); trench 0.69m (2ft 3in)

Index